PENGUIN BOOKS

TORREGRECA

Ann Cornelisen was born in Cleveland, Ohio, and educated at Vassar College. Her books include *Women of the Shadows*, *Where It All Began*, *Strangers and Pilgrims*, and *Any Four Women Could Rob the Bank of Italy*. In 1974 she received a special award from the National Institute of Arts and Letters. She now lives in a thirteenth-century house in the Tuscan countryside.

TORREGRECA
Life, Death, Miracles

by Ann Cornelisen
*illustrated with photographs
by the author*

PENGUIN BOOKS

To

DON LUCA MONTEFALCONE

PENGUIN BOOKS
Published by the Penguin Group
Viking Penguin, a division of Penguin Books USA Inc.,
375 Hudson Street, New York, New York 10014, U.S.A.
Penguin Books Ltd, 27 Wrights Lane, London W8 5TZ, England
Penguin Books Australia Ltd, Ringwood, Victoria, Australia
Penguin Books Canada Ltd, 2801 John Street,
Markham, Ontario, Canada L3R 1B4
Penguin Books (N.Z.) Ltd, 182–190 Wairau Road,
Auckland 10, New Zealand

Penguin Books Ltd, Registered Offices:
Harmondsworth, Middlesex, England

First published in the United States of America
by Little, Brown and Company 1969
Published in Penguin Books 1991

1   3   5   7   9   10   8   6   4   2

Chapter VIII of this book appeared originally in *The Atlantic* and
is reprinted by permission.

LIBRARY OF CONGRESS CATALOGING IN PUBLICATION DATA
Cornelisen, Ann, 1926–
Torregreca: life, death, miracles/by Ann Cornelisen;
illustrated with photographs by the author.
p.   cm.
Reprint. Originally published: Boston: Little, Brown, 1969.
ISBN 0 14 01.4784 5
1. Italy, Southern — Social life and customs.   I. Title.
DG825.C6   1991
945′.77 — dc20   91–2308

Printed in the United States of America

CONTENTS

Illustrations between pages 150–151
and 246–247

AUTHOR'S NOTE

Torregreca dei Normanni cannot be found on any map, but there are dozens of Torregrecas, thousands of people like the Torresi. They all have a right to their anonymity. I spent many years with them and respect them too much to violate that right; my only wish has been to give a true picture of their lives. Isolated in its bleak beauty, Lucania is real and so are the Lucanians, who struggle today, as they have for three thousand years, to wrest an existence from the rocks and clay that make up their world.

THE SETTING

The town of Torregreca, in the region of Basilicata
in Southern Italy

BASILICATA   Region of Southern Italy, lying between
Campagna, Puglia, the Ionian Sea, Calabria and the
Tyrrhenian Sea: 9,988 square kilometers, 664,000 in-
habitants (density 66 per square kilometer). *Provinces:*
Potenza and Matera. Hilly in the east, the rest mountain-
ous (Lucanian Appenines). Principal rivers (Bradano,
Basento, Agri, Sinni) open into the Ionian Sea. *Economic
resources:* the economy is essentially agricultural, but
not highly productive; grain, olives, vegetables, vines.
Cattle: cows and goats. Limited industry. Actually in
process of development owing to discovery of natural
gas. Small-scale weaving and food-processing enterprises.
Limited communications (railroad Naples-Potenza-Ta-
ranto) complicated by the nature of the soil. *History:*
in ancient times it was commonly known as Lucania;
subjugated (272 B.C.) by the Romans; after fall of the
Empire fought over by Greeks and Longobards; it
passed then to the Normans (12th century) receiving
from them its actual name. Subsequently its lot was that
of the Kingdom of Sicily, then of Naples, and finally of
the Two Sicilies.

—Enciclopedia Garzanti (1962)

THE TORRESI

(as they appear)

Don Armando, landowner. His daughters: *Ninetta,* the pretty one; *"The Practical One"; and "The Smart One"*

Don Gaetano Fracassa, postmaster, former head of the Fascist Party

Don Domenico Matarazzo ("Rudolph Valentino"), the bank director

"Gesù Eucaristico," doorkeeper at the boys' seminary

Ferdinando Perrone, the pharmacist

Lieutenant Mazzone, commanding officer of the carabinieri for seventeen townships

Umberto Loschiavo, the Mayor

Luca Montefalcone, doctor

Sister Clemente, nun in charge of the farm complex at the Convent of San Fortunato

Anto', Sister Clemente's subnormal man of all work

Mother Superior of the Convent of San Fortunato

Sister Gioiosa, housekeeper of the Convent

Enrico, the Bishop's driver

Don Matteo Montefalcone, Luca's brother, Vicar of the Cathedral

Chichella Fascide, nickname for Domenica Andressano, the author's landlady-maid

Don Manfredo Montefalcone, Luca and Matteo's father

Donna Filomena Montefalcone (née Albanese), Luca and Matteo's mother

Titti Montefalcone, Luca and Matteo's sister

Don Girolamo Albanese, Luca's favorite uncle, his mother's brother

Don Mimmi Mangiacarne, landowner, shopkeeper, and friend of Don Manfredo

Pancrazio, Luca's boyhood friend

Don Giuseppe Fiore, veterinarian and Fascist spy

Mastro Pancrazio, town *guardia*

Mastro Antonio, town *guardia*

Don Giacomo Garibaldi Stampa, town archivist, professor of Latin

Cupid, clerk in Abruzzese township office

Marietta, Mastro Carmine's daughter, clerk of *Comune* of Torregreca

Mastro Carmine, solderer, Marietta's father

The daziere, collector of internal customs fees

Old Ida, town messenger, wife of "Gesù Eucaristico"

Nando Loschiavo, the Mayor's brother

Father Loschiavo, director of schools

Dr. Neri, medico condotto, doctor for those on the poor list

Sister Eufrasia, cook at the Convent of San Fortunato

Sister Giustizia, Novice Mistress of the Convent

The Bishop of Torregreca

Don Andrea, retired priest who lives at the Convent of San Fortunato

Tina, Chichella Fascide's sister

Vincenzo, Chichella's eldest child, seven years old at the time of
the author's arrival

Luigi, Chichella's second child, six years old at the time of the
author's arrival

Rosa, Chichella's youngest, about three years old at the time of the
author's arrival

Mamma, Carmela Andressano, Chichella's mother

Tanname (Pietro Andressano; also called Fascide), Chichella's
father

Don Pasquale Acquaviva, Tanname's padrone after World War I

Donna Teresa Acquaviva, Don Pasquale's wife

Don Peppino Acquaviva, Don Pasquale's brother and a lawyer

Concetta, Chichella's first squad boss, who later cut the telephone
wires

Giovanni, Chichella's first *fidanzato*

"The Turk," the padrone for whom Chichella worked after the war

Nunzio, the Peanut, Tina's husband, Chichella's brother-in-law

Michele the Neapolitan, Chichella's husband

Vittorio, Michele's brother, Chichella's brother-in-law

Assunta, Don Girolamo's maid

Podestà Rocco Dabbraio, Mayor of the Fascist era

"Dry Nose," a padrone, member of the *Circolo dei Civili*

Dr. Delle Monache, dean of the Torregreca medical profession

Dr. Armento, young surgeon

Drs. Di Martino and Minutillo, town doctors

Giulia, Chichella's aunt who barricades Don Gaetano in the Post Office

Nicola, one of Chichella's brothers

Soldo, a forestry guard

Signora Soldo and her daughter, Soldo's wife and daughter

The preside, the principal of a school

Professor Angerame, monument maker, teacher of design

Gianmauro, his "boy" in the shop

Sister Michelina, doorkeeper of the Convent of San Fortunato

Don Germano, old priest, forcibly retired to running pensioners' section of the Convent of San Fortunato

Don Arrigo, a priest, czar of the new schools and camps of Torregreca

Don Pasquale, a priest fighting Communism with leaflets

The New Bishop, a Calabrian of medieval mentality

Ambrico, a peasant man whose family moved into the *villaggio*

Giovanna, a five-year-old girl, daughter of the *villaggio* whore

OVERTURE

SUMMER in Basilicata — the ancient region of Lucania — ends abruptly with the first cloudburst of October. For seven months damp and chill wrap themselves around our hilltop, around Torregreca and around our lives there. The high rolling plateaus sink away under a blanket of fog, and no house or tree gives sign of life. The fields of summer, like patches of yellow velvet rubbed one way and then the other, have been ploughed into quagmires. Towns that shimmered on distant pointed hills disappear into an icy cocoon of rain and sleet. Only the mountains, their jagged peaks veined with tracings of snow, are clearer than before. The purple haze of summer that softened and rounded them has given way to a harsh cold light in which they rear up like disapproving sentinels. In the mountain valleys strings of mist feel their way over the flutings of erosion, and now that there are no growing things to irrigate, the wide, stony riverbeds fill with water.

A hundred and fifty years ago great oak forests still covered the high land and the valleys, but that was before the barons were forced to cut the wood to pay their overlords, the Kings of Naples, and Napoleon's Deputy, Murat. Through this rolling forested land the Romans hacked out the Appian Way, and drove back along it their trains of booty and captives from the East. Greek settlers had come before them; later, the Normans and soon after them the Crusaders passed this way, leaving memories in the names of towns like ours, Torregreca dei Normanni.

Winter brings damp cold and snow, landslides, and strangling smoke from wet wood to Torregreca. Freedom is gone.
The fields, the vineyards, and the pastures that were both freedom and slavery are no longer part of the world. Each town is
isolated on its pinnacle. Each person is alone in a coma that
cuts him off from every other person and almost from himself.
The body endures this chill eyrie, while the spirit is wafted off
to a warmer limbo of dreams.

The women's horizons narrow to the peephole view allowed
by their black shawls. They expect no future. Children in
ragged sweaters and boots much worn but too big for them
shuffle to school. It offers no warmth. Listless and half asleep,
they will sit for hours watching the steam patterns of their own
breath. The more industrious dig holes in their desks with their
pen points, or pick at the chilblains on their blotched, swollen
hands. Afternoons, they huddle in doorways out of the wind,
waiting until there might be a fire at home, until mother will be
too busy to nag them about their homework. And the men.
They wait out their day, standing close up against the buildings
in the Piazza, too defeated to search out a warmer roost. It
seems a dullness from which there may be no awakening. As a
change from splitting wood or watching the gradual spread of
new patches of dampness on the wall, the women gaze out on
the gray wet world. They look for no traffic to pass. None does.
But a single black figure dodging the rushing stream in the
middle of the road is worth speculating over. Where is she going? Why didn't she wait? A homeless dog crouched in a doorway brings no wave of sympathy.

A stranger wandering along the Appian Way in summer
would not sense this dour desolation, even if half-remembered
tales of brigands and peasant uprisings should come to his
mind. Rounding a curve to find Torregreca dei Normanni
perched high in front of him on the opposite hill, he would feel

he had discovered the life and being of the Middle Ages. He would not believe that this romantic amphitheater of houses, rising row upon row to its double crown of Ducal Palace and Norman tower, could be reduced to ugliness. True, there is a feeling of suspended life about the town between dawn and dusk, but it is enough to wait by the roadside. The empty shell will slowly come to life and be transformed into an Italian Casbah.

Late on a summer afternoon, there is already the whispering of a breeze, and the light has softened, changing the sky from blinding white to postcard blue. The houses and churches, at noon so flat and invisible against the sky, are toasted gold. Brown shadows now outline the baked red tiles of the roofs laid one above the other in ridges and furrows, in steep roofs or shallow pitch, climbing at all angles of the crooked streets to the towers at the top of the town. The tiles are pale apricot, new clay-red and lentil purple, some cracked or chipped, with gray and yellow lichen growing in the crevices.

Torregreca waiting, unchanged over the centuries, seems a stage set. The play is about to begin, and it would be no surprise if Frederick the Second appeared, leading his army in full panoply up the winding ramps into the town.

Instead, the peasants return from the fields, slowly, deliberately, without display or majesty. They trudge along the Appian Way, which they call the "New Road" because it has only recently been paved, until they reach the hill opposite Torregreca. There they turn off onto a steep shortcut that winds down to the bottom of a gully where a narrow bridge crosses the only sewer main. They pause for rest, and then start the slow climb straight up into town.

They come with their hoes hooked over one shoulder. On the other they carry a bundle of thorny twigs for lighting fires. Some lead donkeys draped with long, pendulous sacks of grass, topped by a load of firewood. Old women amble along, forgetful as the old are of the pair of pigs or sheep they are supposed to be driving. At the bottom of the track, while the animals mill around on the bridge blocking traffic, they will argue about which ones belong to whom. Small boys of ten leading goats on ropes stop at the edge of the road, then whoop down the hill, dragging the balking animals behind them. The old and the young alike have been "out for a stroll" with the animals, and the frivolous amusement implied by the phrase is unfair — for there was no choice. Every member of the family must do something; they were sent out to graze their miniature flocks on the road verges.

Next may come a woman with her mule's lead rope wrapped dangerously around her neck to leave her hands free for knitting as she walks. Down at the bridge a husband who wishes to appear the ruler of his destiny, at least in public, makes his wife get down from their donkey and climbs on himself. The wife, robbed of her seat for the only climb of the trip, grabs onto the donkey's tail and allows herself to be dragged the rest of the way home.

It is a slow procession. These are people apparently free from preoccupations, sure of where they are going and what they will find there. They never look at the town. They seem unaware of its battered facade, which every minute glows redder in the sunlight. That the Ducal Palace and the old Norman tower compete on high for dominance of Torregreca does not affect them. Perhaps they are right. The dukes and the Normans have gone, defeated by the passive weight of the people against their governments. The peasants have survived them; they need not be concerned with their leavings.

Tired and sullen, they "withdraw" from the day, as they say in dialect, and return to the one-room houses they share with donkeys, children, pigs, chickens, in-laws and, of course, Grandmother. The first thing they do is turn the radio on loud enough to rattle the pots and pans hanging on the walls. This one act symbolizes a return to civilization.

From the hill opposite, Torregreca seems afire with the light of the setting sun, and as though by solar infusion, alive. The town is tuning up for the evening's *divertimento*. Brayings, cries, cackling, and mothers shouting for misplaced children fuse with the wail of popular songs and the tinkle of church bells into a twilight cacophony.

Long into the night the alleys will echo with the fights and confusions of ten thousand people living piled one on top of the other in space too small for half the number. They seek the warmth of human company as horses in a pasture huddle in a corner for protection against the wind. In the past this crowding together meant protection from invaders and brigands. Today it is protection against the unknown. Neighbors are not chosen; in most cases they resent and envy one another; but their physical closeness and the unwritten law of mutual assistance, however grudging, give protection against the caprices of a vengeful God. For the terrifying unknowns of the twentieth century in Lucania are those natural calamities which are endemic and more devastating than bubonic plague or armies of Saracens. A landslide carries off or buries an entire town. A great crevasse opens up to swallow a field during an earthquake. A roof suddenly gives way in the middle of the night, killing ten people. A child who was healthy yesterday is dying today of "evil spirits in the tummy." A strong young woman after a winter cold begins wasting away with tuberculosis.

Elsewhere these natural calamities might be called fate, but in Lucania they are understood to be God's punishment for sins committed. He is a workaday pagan-Christian God who never forgets, cannot forgive, and is not above cooperating for His own ends with the magic ways of the Evil Eye or Satan's demons. There is some suspicion that He Himself is the Grand

Master of the Evil Eye. He patrols the world. He knows all, even those thoughts that scamper through unguarded minds. The Torresi wait, cringing as though awaiting death, for the moment when calamity strikes and they must pay for their failings. When it comes, they do not want to be alone on a bare hillside with only the wind and the baying of moonstruck dogs for company. They will not live on the land. They want to be in the middle of town, surrounded by neighbors who are no better off, but who can be looked to for human solace and aid.

So, in the Rabata, as the Arabs named the warren of alleys and stair-streets, cul-de-sacs and tunnels that make up all of Torregreca except the topmost layer, preparations for the evening are noisily under way. Donkeys have been unloaded, led into their quarters either at the back of the main room or under it with the pig, and left for the night with a ration of hay. Grandmother has gone to retrieve the children who have been locked out of the house since morning. Somewhere in her wanderings she finds not only the children but the family chickens, and herds them all home. With very little argument the chickens go to roost under the one bed in sight, an enormous "matrimonial bed" covered in white and supported by a headboard and footboard of intricate wrought-iron curlicues. The children are not so docile. They are tired and hot from their day of running wild in the streets, and to calm them Mother slaps each one soundly and tells him to sit down and keep quiet. Their wails and howls fill the streets.

While Mother cooks pasta on a two-ring gas burner, Father has a good scrub, using the last of the water from the large copper cauldron under the sink. He changes his shirt, slicks back his hair, and sits down at the table. It has no plates on it, but does have a collection of forks, and a large bulbous loaf of bread which he cuts. The children pull stools up to the table; Grandmother hovers between the stove and the table, undecided as to where she belongs. The donkey honks amorously, but stops at a yell from Father. Finally the pasta is ready, is fished out of the water by the dripping forkful, and dumped in one giant soup bowl. Father pours some cloudy, greenish oil over it, Mother grates goat cheese and sprinkles it on top, and they all sit down to dinner from this one plate.

As soon as Father has finished, he gets up and goes off to the wine shop, or to the only cinema in town, where once nightly a prewar Western is run off. The film changes every two weeks, but the plots and actors remain reassuringly the same. Variety is supplied by the film splitting in different places. Will it break in the big gun battle, or in the middle of the chase? It doesn't really make any difference. The audience will groan, and then sit patiently in the smoky dark until the picture, minus the rest of the vital scene, comes back on the screen. Some misogynist at the generating plant lowers the power during the final love sequence, causing Stacey and Miss Annie to darken, if not disappear, in a very avant-garde way. That famous line, "Mighty purdy hat ya got there, Miss Annie," is delivered in a voice so deep and indistinct as to give the impression that a bilious Italian walrus has been entrusted with the dubbing of the soundtrack. This is an amusement considered unfit for respectable women. The temptations are many, and the flesh — female flesh, at least — is weak, so these lurid, horsey adventures are only for the men.

The women and children stay below with the old people. If it were cold, they would go to bed, but on a warm summer night when supper has been cleared, no one wants to stay in an airless, one-room house. They drag stools into the narrow corridor street which is their drawing room, and settle in groups around the doorways. The only light comes from naked bulbs set in white enamel reflectors the size of dinner plates and hung on wires across the alley. The breeze rocks the lamps gently back and forth, showing now faces and cobblestones clear as day, now giant shadows whose heads seem to touch the roof tiles before they lurch along the walls and disappear down the street.

Women collect around the fountains with their pots of clay and copper, hoping, but usually in vain, that "those people" at the aqueduct will be merciful and turn on the water for an hour. Because they left early in the morning for the fields, they have missed what little came between noon and three. Eventually they reserve their places by lining up the pots in order of the owners' arrival, just in case water should come before dawn, when they leave again for the fields.

They return to the groups in the doorways, and sort beans or knit or nurse their babies while they gossip. The old men sit snoozing in chairs tipped back against the wall, and the children, absorbed and eager as puppies, crawl around on the cobblestones, in search of treasures which might be hidden in the day's peelings and debris.

It would be a peaceful way to spend an evening if it were not for the thunderous echoing and re-echoing of dozens of radios, all tuned to the same program. Whether this uniformity of choice is the first sign of the wane of individuality in Italy, or simply a compliment to the shrewdness of the government-controlled radio would be hard to tell. However, pop songs always win over the obscure plays or concerts of modern music offered on two of three stations. As the "wailers," those sexless men or screaming women — one is never quite sure which — are in fashion, no one can escape the plea, "Love me, love me, love me . . ." that ricochets through the streets. Next, the same voice will cry, "Come back, come back, come back . . ." or "Why, why, why . . ."

To someone unaccustomed to this background music, the medley of parrot sounds seems to bounce and boom from all directions, but the Torresi pitch their voices a shriek higher and ignore it. By the time the song ends they are screaming, and a belated echo from below joins the beginning of the commercial in a higher street. The accordion player pumping out music for a dance down the way pushes and pulls a bit harder. A woman arguing with her husband yells louder, and when he still claims he cannot understand her, she has sure proof he is drunk.

At the end of the street a carved archway with a coat of arms worked in stone opens on a courtyard where more women sit gossiping at the foot of four ladder-like stairways. Children and chickens inspect the rough tufa paving, while in the shadows cats track and pounce on each other. From the middle of the courtyard one wide stairway with elaborate stone balustrades leads to a double door much taller and wider than the others. Beyond that door lives the padrone, for this is one of the six or eight "Palaces" belonging to the large landowners who, until the advent of land reform in 1950, controlled the wealth, politics, and lives of Torregreca.

Don Armando is right now sitting brooding in the only furnished corner of his musty drawing room. He pulls his shawl closer around his shoulders, and shakes his head over the ledger he holds on his knees. He would be the last person to admit that life has been more comfortable since he was relieved of much of his land. The argument that he had never farmed or taken care of it does not, in his eyes, excuse the fact that it was "taken away" from him, stolen. Not to anyone, not even his sons who might find some legal way to claim a share, has he mentioned the high price paid by the government for his tracts of stubble and cutbank. He decided that if *that* was the way "they" were going to run things, he'd get out of farming entirely. Now he rents his land to the peasants, leaving them to worry about the weather and the harvest, and he has remodeled the Palace into a number of small shops on the ground floor, with apartments above, which bring in a not inconsiderable sum with no effort on his part. Still, with a tidy income and more room than he needs for living quarters, he is disgruntled.

Life offers no greater pleasure than his evening brood over the rent ledger, and his subsequent lament addressed to an audience he imagines sitting around him in the drawing room: *Italy was a great power when it was ruled by its rightful kings and owners. Ah yes, but that was before the rabble took over. Now even a peasant thinks he might rule one day, he has no respect for his betters, for the people who gave him bread and work. This leads to anarchy, this* . . . And so he goes on, bathing his resentment in bile.

In the kitchen, ignored by Don Armando, his three unmarried daughters sit picking their supper out of an assortment of pans. They are what is politely referred to as "no longer young," and, since their prospects of marrying are almost as limited as their charms, for the rest of their lives they will wear the musty black mourning they put on ten years ago at their mother's death. All three condescend to teach the *morning* session of the elementary school. Afternoons they must be free, like other women of genteel birth, to go to church, or stroll arm in arm along Torregreca's main street. Don Armando feels they are to blame for their single state. After all, marrying into the family brings standing to which many a man might have aspired. If only as girls their upper lips had been a bit less hairy, or even their eyes less cowlike! Their long hawk noses are signs of distinction, breeding even, and their plumpness would imply sensuality to any red-blooded man. No, somehow the fact that they did not marry is their own fault, and while he does not object to the 100,000 lire salary each dutifully hands over to him at the end of every month, he finds them poor company and even poorer housekeepers.

For their part, they seldom think of why they did not marry, but if they do it is clear to them that it is their father's fault. In Torregreca only the sons of landowners would have been considered appropriate husbands, and those who were not first cousins had plans for escaping to Naples which hinged on finding a rich wife there. In fact, their four brothers had done the same, marrying quite ugly and not terribly rich young women who had "connections." Once out of Torregreca they did not come back, and contented themselves with an invitation for their father and sisters to visit Naples each year at Easter. After his sons had extricated themselves from the family estates, Don Armando made no move to arrange marriage contracts for the girls, nor would he agree that they too leave Torregreca. There they had stayed, and if they were unmarried, there was no one to blame but their father. Ninetta, generally called "the pretty one," to distinguish her from "the practical one" and "the smart one," had once found a young man who was a trained book-keeper with prospects of a government job, but Don Armando had dismissed him as a "dirty little paper pusher." There the subject had ended. And so they live — four disappointed people forced to look out on a world that refuses to change to suit them. To the town they are rich and therefore happy.

Out in the alleys where Don Armando and his daughters no longer interest anyone, the radios will blare on until the men come back from the wine shops or the cinema, and the children fall asleep standing, with their heads in their mothers' laps. Slowly groups will break up and take their stools inside. The radios will be turned off, and even the Rabata will be quiet while everyone sleeps. In the morning the same people will awaken early and decamp silently for the fields, with only the shuffle of boots and the soft click-click of the donkey's hoofs to betray their going.

On the upper level of town where a fresh wind carries off the staleness of a long hot day, and a certain amount of big-city neon turns people and buildings alike a sickly yellow-green, the more sophisticated elements of Torregreca society are perform-ing the traditional gyrations of the evening walk. The course is

simple: up the Corso as far as the Upper Piazza; turn back
down the Corso; through the Lower Piazza and out along the
main road as far as there are houses. Exactly where the houses
end and the dark begins, all turn as though ordered by a subliminal signal and retrace their steps, which puts them automatically in the way of the same people they passed on the last
leg. There is a formula for avoiding the repetition of good evenings. At the first meeting, a full-blown salutation and conversation take place. Everything of possible interest is discussed,
including a description of exactly what everyone ate for lunch.
No matter how many times the same people meet later, a slight
bow of the head is considered adequate acknowledgment of
friendship. Failure to nod is noticed immediately and understood as a public snub in answer to some private misunder-
standing or slight. Nothing cuts so deep in Torregreca as being
ignored. And so, back and forth, back and forth they go, from
sunset to ten-thirty, eleven o'clock, or even midnight.

The Upper Piazza, known as the Bishop's Piazza, should be
the center of the town. Two sides of the square are bordered by
the massive L-shaped Diocesan Palace, which until recently
was of an undistinguished, spotted and peeling yellow ochre.
The Bishop himself ordered the repainting, and chose for the
new color one he refers to as "French gray." He felt it more
suitable for a Bishop's residence. One look was enough for the
wags of Torregreca to see that the Bishop's crest of red and
gold leaped out in brilliant contrast from the wall, and they
believe they have discovered the true reason for his choice. As
though determined to change everything, the Bishop also ordered fake stone moldings and pediments to be painted in
white around each of the forty-five windows that show on the
Piazza. These fancy trimmings, along with the "French gray,"
seem deliberate insults to the Torresi's taste, and not all the

wiles of Don Evandro, the Bishop's secretary, have been enough to convince them otherwise.

For over fifty years, the ground floor space at the two corners of the Palace has been rented to a bank and to the Post Office. Adjoining the Post Office, and making up the third side of the Piazza, behind four dusty eucalyptus trees, is the *Comune* — a square, tan, unpretentious building (with real stone moldings around its windows) where the town administration has its offices. Torregreca has an admirable record of consistency in elections. If there is a Christian Democratic mayor in office, the next mayor will be a Communist, or vice versa. No antidote for dissatisfaction with the incumbent has ever been found: neither party stays in power more than one term. The present mayor is a Communist, and like all his Communist predecessors is advocating the removal of the Town Hall from the Bishop's Piazza. Apparently the Palace exudes disapproval of all he does and infuriates him sufficiently to make a test of strength over such a minor issue worthwhile. No one, however, takes it very seriously because, in the final analysis, it is the secretary of the town council, appointed by the central government in Rome, who decides and controls everything that goes on in the *Comune*.

In back of the Town Hall, and looming high above it, is the Cathedral bell tower which time and humidity have turned a menacing black-gray.

Everyone must go to the Bishop's Piazza at least once a day for official business. Parish priests, looking haughty and extremely busy in their little Fiats, zip in and out of the carriageway of the Palace. Lines of pensioners waiting to sign their checks string out into the square from the Post Office; women by the dozens besiege the registry office for certificates; and the bank carries on a modest but important business with the merchant and landowning class. Exactly at noon each day there is a hiatus. Don Gaetano Fracassa, curved and gray from forty years as director of the Post Office, comes out to stand at the curb with his hands behind his back. He gazes around as though surveying his private domain, but manages never to look diagonally across the way where Don Domenico Matarazzo, the bank director, is performing the same ritual.

Don Domenico is young for the title "Don," but his position requires the honor. He knows he is referred to as "Rudolph Valentino" and considers it a well-earned compliment to his good looks and his amorous adventures. Don Gaetano and Don Domenico have neither spoken nor admitted the existence of the other in almost twenty years. The official version of the quarrel is that they disagreed on basic political issues but, since Don Gaetano is and always has been a Fascist and Don Domenico is and always has been a Monarchist and the difference is negligible, everyone knows there is more to it. In fact, everyone knows the whole story. Right after the war Don Domenico was a student of law at the University of Naples, though, of course, he did not attend classes there. He followed the usual method of studying at home in Torregreca and going to Naples for examination periods. He had no prospects, but when he started buzzing around Don Gaetano's daughter, it was considered an appropriate match by all. Time went on. His devotion seemed exemplary, and in due course he received his degree. Unexpectedly and quite improbably, when the bank agent was sent to a new post in Potenza, Don Domenico was appointed to the vacancy in Torregreca. In less than three months he married a girl from Matera whose father happened to be an official of the same bank, and Don Gaetano has never spoken to him since.

Also at noon, on all but the very hottest days, Don Evandro, the Bishop's secretary, comes to stand in the archway of the Palace, as though he were planning to mediate between the two warring notables. He bows first to Don Gaetano, out of deference for age, then to Don Domenico. After a leisurely checkup on the activities of the square, he strides across to Don Gaetano and has a short conversation with him in which he manages casually to express the Bishop's desires and opinions of local matters. They shake hands, bow, and smile. Then, without haste or embarrassment, Don Evandro walks across to Don Domenico and repeats the conversation, handshake, bow, and smile. He is scrupulous in his attentions to each. His deference and reserve avoid involvement in their quarrel and allow him to pass on to his third diplomatic appointment under the eucalyptus trees, where he chats at length with the town secretary.

The schedules, forms, and functions of every government office in Italy are planned in Rome and handed down as inviolable orders, to be carried out no matter what the contradictions within the system may be. Such is the genius of bureaucracy that one office of the *Comune* or the Post Office is open when everything else is closed. The *Comune* shuts its doors forever at two, unless one has a helpful friend — and almost everyone does. The six windows of the Post Office are shuttered and unshuttered on a staggered basis no more reasonable than the postmaster's digestion; however, from one until three no one will be there . . . probably. The government clerks, who resent working long hours for little money in a forgotten place like Torregreca, approach each new request with scepticism. If possible, they will intimidate the applicant long enough to make him feel in the wrong. If he still insists on his rights, they examine the details of his case with such slow, truculent accuracy that the lines of people waiting lengthen through the corridor and snake out the front door and into the Piazza. All day people mill about there, but as dusk comes on they drift away, as though there were a curfew. Shutters drop with a metallic crash; Don Gaetano locks the Post Office; Don Domenico drives away to a romantic appointment near the cemetery; and one of the town messengers scutters off toward the Corso. The Piazza is deserted. Once more it is the exclusive property of the Palace doorkeeper, who would not think of showing himself except in August, when the Bishop is away for his annual mud-bath cure. Then Palace discipline is a bit lax. Don Evandro takes the opportunity to watch television, an illicit pleasure, while the doorkeeper sits in the Palace entryway with his great friend the sacristan of the Cathedral, playing cards by the light of the carriage lamps. At night they have the Piazza entirely to themselves. Summer or winter no one lingers there, perhaps because the sharp mountain wind "chills the soul," or more probably, because of the pervading air of authority implied by the mass of the Bishop's Palace and imposed by the off-key, hourly sounding of the Cathedral bell.

The Torresi intent on their evening promenade venture to the edge of the Upper Piazza and then reverse direction, back down Corso Vittorio Veneto where the world of light and shops is more reassuring. Years of grit and tires have polished this overgrown alleyway until the stones gleam, and the street lights, the same naked bulbs with dinner plate reflectors which light the lower regions, provide an almost daylight glare. The two-story buildings of spotted white plaster on either side are exact twins each of the other, and the ground level arrangement of a door, a shop window, a shop door, a door, and a shop window, and so on down the street, does little to vary the monotony. There are twice as many doors as shop windows because, while the shopkeeper and his family live in one room in back of the store, the extra door opens on a flight of stairs to a two-room apartment above, where another family lives. The desirability of the upper flats consists in balconies that over-hang the Corso and allow the older women not up to the prom-enade to watch everything happening below.

Along the way there is a milk shop; two butcher shops; a tailor or two; five grocers who, though not related, all have the same surname; a stationery shop which also sells stoves, liquid gas, and yard goods; a hardware store; and one of the four beauty parlors in town. To protect his customers from the gazes of curious young men, the hairdresser has installed an opaque glass door with "Raymond of Bari" etched in swirling letters.

The Ducal Palace cannot be seen from the street, but it towers over the full length of the Corso along one side, in back of the two-story buildings. The half toward the Bishop's Palace houses the seminary for little boys from ten to fifteen who are studying for the priesthood. Its entrance, a wide stone archway with a carved molding of intertwined acanthus, is the most imposing on the Corso. There every evening the old doorkeeper naps in his chair with his hands fanned out on his knees and his black-visored cap pulled well down over his eyes. The cap is not only his badge of office but his most jealously guarded possession because of the tall gold letters on the band proclaiming "Gesù Eucaristico." He has almost forgotten that it was given to him instead of a raise, and he does not yet know that the town thinks "Gesù Eucaristico" is a killingly funny nickname for him.

On the opposite side of the street, dark corridor stairways lead downward between rows of one-story single-room houses and end in a tangled cascade of roof tiles and chimneys.

Even on the dankest winter evenings the shop doors are left open, probably because no one thinks to close them, and inside each, one figure, immobile as a statue, sits in the gloom waiting for trade. Should a customer stumble over the threshold, the shopkeeper will flip a switch and produce so much light that both he and his customer are momentarily blinded. Since the war, the Torresi purchase most of their shoes, clothes, farm tools and household equipment from the twice-monthly market, where traveling merchants display truckloads of goods under awnings and allow the customers to finger everything and bargain until satisfied. Only in the case of emergency are purchases made at the shops, and then preferably at night, when the shopkeeper has come back from the side job that really supports him and his family. During the day he leaves the shop to his little boy or his toothless grandmother who neither know nor care where anything is, and, if they happen to find it, refuse to sell because they do not remember the price. It would be inaccurate to say that trade in the outdated remnants of merchandise available is brisk. At best it must be assumed that the shopkeepers are catering to the old school, nonmarket types; at worst that they are waiting until stock runs out to retire from business, for hairbrushes and lipsticks are not for sale, though corset covers and straight razors are.

The pharmacist is the one exception. He does not consider himself "in trade," but rather a professional man, and dispenses with benevolent condescension the liver cures and purges that have made him rich. He is president of the Men's Catholic Action Committee, and will probably be the next Christian Democratic mayor of Torregreca. At least, it is known from a planted indiscretion of Don Evandro's that he has the Bishop's backing. No one would think of asking him why or how he can get away with selling the black rubber abortion "gimmick" which is his most profitable under-the-counter item.

Nothing very unexpected happens along the Corso. Outside a butcher shop hangs a skinned kid with the hide attached as proof of freshness. Four "hunting dogs" amuse themselves jumping and snapping at its hooves, but their approach is so languid it is clear that expectations are not great. Further along, skewered bits of kidney, liver and meat are smoldering and sizzling on a rusty charcoal burner in front of a wine shop.

Inside the shop, unshaven men in caps sit at bare, grimy tables, drinking their wine in silence. On the walls are fly-spotted posters of transatlantic ships, and out-of-date schedules and rates which give the impression that, for the Torresi at least, only third class passage exists. High above eye level are printed signs saying "Swearing Is Prohibited," "Political Discussions Are Forbidden," and "No Spitting." The "Jolly Host" sits reading a comic book in a back corner by the sink, while a baby, bare from his undershirt down, crawls around his feet. It would be romantic to think these dour-faced men are planning treason, or that Latin passion is going to devour them. Shades of Carmen! They must be scheming! But they are not. They are simply waiting for another evening to be done, static figures under the light of a naked bulb. Later, after the cinema lets out and the lures of the Piazza dim, the room will be full of men and smoke. Conversations will start up and die, start up again briefly. The nearest thing to passion will be a good-humored argument between two tables about which is richer, America or Russia. It is almost closing time. There must be a decision. One of the drunker ones, who has been peering with great concentration into his wineglass, announces to the satisfaction of all, "I tell you I know all about America. I was in Peru for twenty years. Russia is richer." They will go home quietly.

Next door an old shoemaker hunches over his bench in his shopwindow. A hooded lamp, pulled so low its bulb almost touches the bench, reflects on his smock front and spreads an eerie glow over the lower part of his face. Invisible in the shop behind him are the men who gather every night to listen while he recites Dante, for he is the local Meistersinger. He seems mesmerized, and intones the lines as a parade of fatally connected words which can have no separate existence or meaning. Still, it is obvious from his voice and slight smile that the words are magic to him and create a world where all is noble and beautiful. He will go on until no one is left to hear him.

Beyond, the Corso twists and ends suddenly in the Lower Piazza. To the left is what remains of the entrance to the Ducal Palace — a gateway and staircase of such regal proportions one can imagine the duke, mounted and too impatient to wait for his retainers, galloping up the marble steps to the second-floor courtyard. Once there was a duke, they say, the classic duke who locked his beautiful bride in the Palace tower for twenty years. Perhaps he was real, or perhaps he is an elaborate fiction invented for historical respectability by chroniclers of Torregreca. Whatever may be the real story, today there is nothing left of the staircase except a few snaggletoothed bricks, and the halls of the Palace have been cut up into a squalid maze of schoolrooms and government offices, each with a stovepipe sticking drunkenly out of a window.

The Palace walls that provide two sides of the Piazza are blank except for a row of shops on the ground floor, and a white band lettered in black that runs along level with the door tops. An effort has been made to paint out the letters, but they remain clear and legible: WE WILL CARRY EVER FORWARD THE FORCE, THE CIVILIZATION AND THE CULTURE OF ROME: BELIEVE, OBEY, FIGHT: PEACE IN LABOR, PEACE IN PEACE, DUCE, DUCE, DUCE.

Joining the L of the Palace at right angles is another line of balconied two-story buildings with shops and apartments like those of the Corso. Sticking up above them is an obelisk church tower with a big white-faced clock which keeps perfect time, though its ping-ping bell announces whatever hour comes most easily to the mechanism. The fourth side of the Piazza opens on a spur of the main road, and across the way in a square, no-period building is the local headquarters of the carabinieri. The commanding officer, Lieutenant Mazzone, is forbidden to consort socially with the locals, but must know everything that is happening or is about to happen in Torregreca. His office overlooking the Piazza has been carefully chosen, having, as it does, a view far down to the right, where the fruit and vegetable market and the public latrines are, and to the left toward the Norman tower, the Convent of San Felice, and the junction of the spur with the main road. Each evening, as the bus from the station arrives in the Piazza, Lieutenant Mazzone slowly crosses the road and joins the men for half an hour. When he has confirmed all the reports that have come to him during the day, he walks back to headquarters as slowly as he came.

The Lower Piazza is the center of town. The place to get warm. The place to cool off. The place to wait, or to see your friends and your enemies. The place to read the notices plastered up on every available inch of wall, telling who has died, what Civil Service examinations are to be held, or what provisions the *Comune* has made for unemployment. They are so thick they form a protective hide for the buildings. At any time of day a few men will be leaning against the walls talking listlessly, and tireless hungry dogs will be cruising around the marble-and-iron monument to the war dead that takes up the middle of the square. The dogs know the bus schedules, and wait for the moment when they gather like a welcoming committee at the steps and look beseechingly at each passenger. Their daily hope is a tidbit from a traveler's lunch, or a bone slung out of a butcher shop, or an ice cream cone dropped by a little girl who trips.

On summer evenings the Piazza is full to overflowing with people who are actually doing nothing, but who would participate should some novelty offer itself. Young men stand together in silence except for an occasional comment about a woman who passes. They laugh, and then are silent again. In front of each political party's headquarters knots of older men look off toward the center of the square. Behind them, sprawled out on chairs, sit the party officers, mopping their heads. The barbershops are full, and customers waiting their turn outside pull the tufts of hair above their ears, as though speculating about whether a shave will be enough or whether a haircut is necessary too. In the windowless back rooms of the four bars, men playing cards leave their games every so often to check on what is happening in the Piazza. When there is nothing new, they disappear inside again.

The Mayor, supported by two advisors, stands at the edge of the spur road ready to answer complaints. Since this is the only time he is available to everyone, a Mayor must resign himself to these nightly appearances in the Piazza.

Don Gaetano, his hands behind his back, paces up and down, following a pattern of sections and subdivisions of the square known only to himself. He speaks to no one. Don Domenico stands by the monument, gossiping with the notary and three young lawyers. Apparently his story is amusing; they all laugh. Then the notary leans forward confidentially and starts talking in a lower voice. One lawyer turns away to comment to a man passing by, but the notary, well aware that law cases are encouraged and built on casual remarks planted at the right moment, continues his story.

All this time the amblers in the promenade have been passing through the Piazza, and the men loitering there, without seeming to, have noticed every combination of people and every new dress. The wives of the doctors, lawyers, and government employees have made their first official appearance of the day, carefully arrayed in silk dresses of the latest fashion. They take care not to expose too much arm or chest, which would be considered poor taste, and they wear very high-heeled shoes which are much too small for them. Back and forth they go, teetering in the parade with groups of young girls who hope to pass groups of young men, with old women honestly out for a bit of fresh air, and with lovers who have this one chance of privacy.

This certainty of rhythm, the inevitability of daily happenings, is the lotus an outsider must resist. If not, he is lulled into believing that what has been true in Torregreca for centuries still is true and will remain so. There are a few Torresi who, to protect their own power and income, must fight doggedly against all change, or if that is not entirely successful, against its acquiring momentum. Every other Torrese yearns for change, but cannot recognize it. Nothing has improved for them. The crops are worse, prices higher, taxes heavier, graft and corruption more public, schoolrooms scarcer, and, if possible, the climate worse. This is the truth as they can see it, and revolution is the only way to reform. Salvation lies in the destruction of today's institutions and the inauguration of a new system with new administrators. They have waited for someone else to send up the battle cry, to start the revolution. Sealed in their pessimism, they have languished through twenty years of legalized upheaval since the end of the war, unaware that even Torregreca is different. For them the whole is still represented by the sum of its negative parts.

Torregreca in the 1960's is no terrestrial paradise, but, at least on a summer day, there are some positives to line up against the negatives. The land, for what it is worth, no longer belongs to a few men who hire and fire at will, but has been divided, giving a bit to those who had nothing. Gone are the days when meat was a delicacy reserved for Christmas, Easter, and the big festa. Now there are daily bus runs to Matera and Potenza, and anyone who manages to reach the station twenty-five kilometers away can take a train that has a starting point and a destination, instead of one that wanders vaguely through the hills until it tires and runs out of coal. Soon there will be water in the town all day, but in 1950 the only supply was a mile away at the Old Fountain. There is even a new, modern hospital and enough government insurance to enjoy it. All the children go through the fifth elementary class, are required to continue through the eighth — the middle school, which did not exist in Torregreca until 1960 — and can go through high school . . . so naturally there are not enough classrooms.

Graft and the weather seem to have universal immunity against all but change for the worse, so Torregreca is not unique. In other respects it may be. A letter mailed from there takes five days to travel four hundred miles; but the post is safer than a telegram, and the telephone only works one way — the Torresi can speak but not hear. The Post Office has its own peculiarities. There is never enough money to cover the money orders and pensions, and stamps are considered a monopoly of tobacco shops. Often newspapers fail to arrive because the Naples train did not make its connection with the station bus. The driver, for whom punctuality and zeal are synonymous, pulls away from the station at the proper time, no matter what, leaving newspapers, mail sacks and passengers stranded until evening.

People and machines simply do not function in Torregreca as they would function elsewhere, but there is time, lots of time before the revolution. If summer reheats optimism and makes the battle against the traditional way, "the Torregreca way," seem possible, winter will surely put it back on ice . . . change is once again a possibility which, perhaps in the future, sometime, maybe, might be reconsidered.

With the return of winter, survival is the narrow goal of each day, the preoccupation that swallows all ability to forgive or to understand. No one expects a turn for the better. The fog mizzles into rain; wind brings sleet, then comes snow, and later, landslides and floods. The Piazza is deserted except for huddled, defeated-looking men who lean against the walls in what would be the sunny corner if it were not raining. It seems as though the dogs have found homes, but they are only sleeping under parked cars. When the bus in its parking place by the monument shudders and groans in preparation for its next trip, a dozen lean mutts are flushed out from its wheel skirts. They skitter off, sit down, and look back accusingly. No one walks down the street. Whoever must be out dodges from shop to shop, remembering where broken downspouts spew cascades of water into the street. In each shop, dark and piercingly dank, women watch their own breath condensing, and wonder about ways to overcome the universal smell of mildew, while their sisters, their faces and bodies hidden in wet black shawls, plead with the shopkeeper for just a bit more pasta on credit, or bread or thread or whatever they need. Without credit, they will never make it through the winter.

No one goes to the fields, yet there seems to be no one around town either. There is no sense of life in the white cotton strands of mist that curl and twist into everything, leaving beads of dampness behind. The cobbles shine, and smoke from malfunctioning chimneys pours from open doorways. Behind the smoke maybe there are people. Day fades into night imperceptibly. The mist is a bit darker, the smoke a bit heavier, and lights go on in the houses. Low voices come from inside and occasionally a baby whimpers, but the coming of night is as unimportant as the coming of the morning had been. A dog sidles along, looking for a corner out of the wet, and finally squats two inches off the ground to avoid the cold.

These are the long nights when people talk and confide and worry out loud; when, if you do not mind your eyes streaming and your throat closing from the smoke of the little brazier at your feet, you can hear the secrets and longings of people unused to talking, or to the idea that they might be interesting to someone from "the outside" — a category which includes everyone not born in Torregreca. It was on nights like these that I listened, and they talked on and on, intrigued with their own ability to talk, and interested, in a detached way, in the events they had thought forgotten, or of no value to someone else. Fascinated with the rediscovery of themselves, they were not curious about me. It was enough that I was there, an outsider who seemed to understand their world. I was that unique person: I could not hurt them, would not judge them, no matter what they told me. I listened through the smoky gloom of three winters.

I

THE PROJECT CONCEIVED

I T seems there never was a time I did not know all this and more about Torregreca, but there was — there must have been. My discovery of it must have been as gradual as the emergence of design in petit-point embroidery, a slow filling-in here and joining-up there, until it was no longer just an outline, but a dimensional picture of the "life, death and miracles" of Torregreca. I myself talk too much for it to have been, as I remember it, a discovery through monologues that I listened to on long winter evenings. But perhaps I will only know if I begin again, as I began so many years ago.

In 1954 I had come to Italy to study archaeology. Instead, without plan and almost against my will I became interested in a private British charitable agency that worked exclusively in the villages of Southern Italy. Their representative was a young Englishwoman who apparently saw something in me worth training — maybe nothing more than my passionate curiosity — and hired me on a semi-volunteer basis. For years I roamed the mountains of the Abruzzo, Lucania and Calabria learning the practical intricacies of nursery and infant-feeding center management. Our permanent demonstrations were used by Italian agencies for training teachers and social workers. We could not be theoretical. Everything had to work every day and on the simplest possible basis. Nor could we limit the work to the centers themselves. We were consultants to town councils; we visited institutions and collaborated on community development projects. We could not hope to feed, clothe and educate all the children of Southern Italy, but using simple, easily copied methods we tried to show how children could have the best care and food for the least money. I cannot honestly say special talents were needed. It was enough to know how to wash without water, how to de-louse children or dose them for worms, how to cope with fleas and eat gracefully whatever was offered — even pig's blood pudding mixed with chocolate and raisins. In time I became a specialist, one of the few who can fix a toilet float while confuting the Montessori System or expounding on the simplicities of Bowlby's theories of child development, and too I developed that all important quality — *serietà*. In Southern Italy even the simplest project involves a crochet of relationships and has no hope of success without that intangible aura of respectability. *Serietà* is more external than a moral code. It is proclaimed by a conservative, almost dowdy way of dressing, and a manner, slightly detached, very calm, that suggests incorruptibility. I worked on my *serietà* until men lounging in piazzas no longer considered me a loose woman even though I drove a car, smoked, and enjoyed a coffee or rum punch in a public bar. Indeed I doubt they considered me a woman at all.

Our centers were in villages where poverty was as naked as the children, and nurseries, if they existed, were nothing more than infant checkrooms. Methods that worked in such communities, however, were valid throughout the South. We traveled more and more until it seemed we were a flying advice squad for an ever-spreading network of children's centers. It was on one of those trips in September 1954 that I saw Torregreca for the first time. Much of the Appian Way was still unpaved and a woman driving a car was a novelty. I stopped for gas and all the unemployed men lurking in the Piazza came over to view the car and its driver. There was a delay while someone went for the pump attendant who never came but sent word there was no gas. I was not surprised. I already knew that in Southern Italy life is reversed; the simplest thing becomes the most complex.

Many of the trips I made through Lucania included a stop in Torregreca. I came to know the Mayor, several mayors in fact, the head of the hospital, and the nuns of San Fortunato. Most important of all, I came to know Luca Montefalcone, a nomad doctor famous all over Italy as *the* man who understands the South.

Luca Montefalcone has one passion, Torregreca, his native town, and wherever he goes, for whatever purpose, he talks about it, its peculiarities and its nightmares. I do not know that I can describe him. His hypnotic power over people depends on some inner tenderness beyond the reach of words. Is he handsome? I think not. As a young man he must have been a gaunt Arab; time has only softened what was angular. Now in his late forties, neither his height nor his hawk features are so startling as his wide brown eyes that glow with the compassion and wonder of a man who has accepted his own defeat as inevitable, but has never lost his faith in others. Those luminous deep-set eyes miss nothing. More than anything he says, they encourage the timid to speak, and he listens. A silent, lugubrious man, a pessimist by birth, he can beguile the most cynical when he chooses to talk. He is respected and, I think, envied by every man in Torregreca for his wealth, his outstanding career as an epidemiologist, his beautiful wife and his powerful friends. To the Torresi he is a success; to himself he is a failure because he can neither leave Torregreca nor stay there. If he lived there, he would be forced to change it; but to enrage his own people and destroy the only security he has ever known is more than he can face. So he has gone off — to Bari — just far enough to be away and still return to Torregreca when he can no longer rationalize his sense of defeat. He cannot leave it; he cannot reform it. Defeated he flees, bound forever to his failure by his love and his hatred. A shriveled kernel of optimism still remains . . . something *can* be done with the South . . . now, maybe if . . . Then someone tries his idea. The experiment leads to a law, and the South has changed a bit without noticing it. Luca meanwhile has gone on to something else.

Before we committed ourselves to training courses or new centers or experimental sections in institutions, we discussed them with him. His advice was always good, his help often invaluable. Everyone knew him and would support any project in which he believed. In 1958 our organization went to him with the idea of a new nursery training center to be built in one of the huge agricultural towns of Lucania or Puglia.

Why not Torregreca? he had asked.

Indeed, why not? It would fit in perfectly with a housing development — the *villaggio* — being finished on the ridge across from the town. It was he who convinced the town council to cede land to us, and then urged them to go one step further, to contribute to the running expenses of the nursery in exchange for our supervision of the housing nucleus.

He charmed the provincial authorities into thinking that Torregreca was the very place they themselves would have chosen. Quietly, unofficially, he buttonholed the members of the Communist-controlled provincial council to murmur that a modern, independent nursery would stimulate change in the hundreds of nurseries run by the nuns of San Fortunato. In fact he promised miracles — miracles I knew nothing about — and then, as the final touch, he said that I would live in Torregreca, not visit the town from time to time, but live there, and supervise the building of the nursery and its running. I was to carry out three of his pet experiments: teachers' training; resident supervision of housing; and reform of the nuns. Luca's optimism was a magic carpet that wafted us from one possibility to the next. From its giddy height obstacles were blurred into mere annoying details. A lay reformer, he assured us, would charm the nuns; truculent peasants would welcome a foreigner's interference in their lives. The town had waited centuries for just such a catalyst, he argued, and the more personal problems, such as finding a house for me to live in, would be a simple matter of my preference: I had only to choose. The nesting instinct is strong in women. I forgot the problems that should have worried me, and dreamed of fixing a two-room house in the Rabata. It is all unimportant now, for nothing worked out quite the way it was supposed to. First the delivery of my new car was delayed a month, and I had to take a train from Naples with all my possessions. It was June of 1959.

In spite of its name the Naples-Taranto Express is a cross-country trolley that meanders along the river bottoms of Lucania as though it were conscious of the futility of speed. When it arrives at the end of the line, it will have to trundle back, so it lingers at deserted station huts and waits patiently while herds of sheep graze on the right of way. To the peasants who ride a few stations up or down the line it is the symbol of the twentieth century with all the advantages and none of the disadvantages of a mule. They would never complain. But I was that exception — the long-distance traveler — and five hours to go one hundred miles seemed an unnecessarily cautious approach to the Middle Ages.

All around me women swayed and groaned in an ecstasy of fear. Beads clicked; reedy voices called on Mary, Jesus and Santa Rita. Down the way a beak-nosed woman in black had veiled her face with a black-bordered handkerchief. She groped in a voluminous plastic purse until she found a bottle of rose water which she dabbed on her temples, behind her ears, and under her nose. She sighed dramatically, reappeared and folded her handkerchief neatly before returning to the school notebooks that were piled on the seat beside her. When another wave of nausea overtook her, she retired once more for the ritual exorcism. Her son, a spindly boy in very short pants and short elastic-topped socks, sat opposite her biting his nails.

Across the aisle a woman had wrapped her head in a fringed linen towel, making a burnoose from which she peered white-eyed and unseeing. Next to her a young woman spat up into a series of clean rags. Like human snails they shrank deeper into the shells of their bodies. They were waiting in cataleptic self-absorption for the dangerous journey to end.

At the front of the car men in sweaty corduroys and patched shirts hunched together in silence. Their faces sullen, their eyes wary, almost furtive under the visors of their caps, they bobbed and swayed with the train. They sought no contact with each other, even less with outsiders. They trusted no one, but preferred to brood, stringing and restringing the pearls of their discontent. A hundred years ago such men were brigands. Today they are a castrated menace; they resent, but they are afraid to act.

Except for a yellow-eyed hen who fixed me with a malevolent gaze from her perch on an overhead luggage rack, no one paid any attention to me until an irritable, red-faced man came to sit opposite me. He wore the corduroy suit of the peasant, but its very neatness and the whiteness of his shirt established his superiority. He had not bothered to take off his black fedora, but was settling down to read his newspaper when something about me roused his curiosity.

"Signora, are you a teacher?"

"No, I'm not."

"Studying to be one?"

"No, I'm not." I almost added, "I'm sorry."

"Too bad." His sigh emphasized the futility of the world. He retired behind his newspaper and several stations later got off the train without even a nod in my direction. I felt alone and inadequate.

I turned away to watch the tufts of broom, their yellow flow-

ers twinkling as they swept the summer-white sky. There was
no life on the flats of checkered slag and still less on the ridges
troughed by the fingers of some malicious giant. At last the
faintest shadow of pink rimmed the barren hills and folded
over the jagged furrows until they softened to brown plush. It
would be a desert sunset, I thought, one shot with devils'
tongues, and I would be in Torregreca.

I had arranged to stay at the Convent of San Fortunato until
I could find a house of my own, and had asked that they send
someone to meet me. They had. Stalking up and down the station platform in front of a battered jeep was a gargantuan nun
wearing a rusty black coverall and a white veil so much askew
that damp red tendrils of hair curled out around its edges. A
bent little man in ragged clothes kippered in her wake. They
were the welcoming committee; my old friend Sister Clemente
— whom I had got to know well on my earlier visits to Torregreca — and her acolyte, the half-demented Antonio who did
the chores on the Convent farm. She mopped her face in the
crook of one arm, then the other, achieving such a smear of
sweat, dirt and freckles that she looked like a disgruntled child.

"*Oyee*, you got here! Thought you must have missed the
train." Before I could say anything I was clutched to a jelly
bosom that reeked of beer and pig stalls. "Get in the jeep. We'll
take care of the bags. Anto', pick up anything you find loose.
No, you ass, not the station master's trumpet . . . *Bags! Bags!*
Over there! Go on." She watched him as he shambled away.
"Have to watch him all the time. Last month he tried to rape
me. Swear he did. Tore the clothes right off my back. We were
down at the well on the old farm and all of a sudden he jumps
me, throws me down and starts tearing at my smock. Not this
one. *This* is my second-best. Before I could get the better of
him, I was naked as a nursing mother. He's been mild as a baby
ever since. The Mother Superior says we've got to get rid of
him, but then she wants to change lots of things. New ones

always do. You'll see. Not all sweet and evasive like Mother
Giulia. This one knows what she wants. Quiet, but you can tell
you'd better do what she says and no monkey business . . . at
least she fools the others. They're running around like school-
girls trying to please her. Anto' . . . *oyee* . . . Anto', over here.
Put them in the back and sit on the tail gate . . . and hang on.
No dropping off like you did coming down!"

The engine started with a dry, asthmatic wheeze of metal on
metal. Sister Clemente braced herself against the wheel, took
her foot off the clutch pedal and sent us leaping and bouncing
toward the station hut. We came to rest in a cloud of our own
dust. When I turned, Antonio was throwing kisses to the passengers who hung out the windows of the train watching us.
The wonder of a nun who drove! "Get a donkey, Sister, get a
donkey," they yelled.

She ignored them, started the engine again and with hardly
an apology picked up her conversation where she had left off.
"Always does that the first time. Well, the Mother Superior's
pretty peeved about the jeep, but I figure Divine Providence
brought it, so we have to accept. First time you've seen it? It's a
long story. There's an old boy been making eyes at me for
years. Turns up every so often and wants to swap me something. This time he wanted a pig, but wouldn't tell me what he
had to pay. Made me drive the cart halfway to Pietrapertosa
just so he could show me . . . and there it was . . . the jeep.
Been tucked away in the scrub oak ever since the war. Always
thought he'd do something with it, I guess, but he was scared.
There aren't any papers. That was his swap for a sow and two
piglets. Of course I took it. He didn't know I had a set of tires
put by for a deal of my own; all I needed was a battery. Wait a
minute. They can't see us anymore from the station, can they?
Fine! I'll take this damned collar off. These plastic things are
just like razors; never wear one except when I'm out like this
. . . fact, I wouldn't have worn one today if the Superior

hadn't caught me. She's already mad at me. I failed my driving test last week for the third time, and she says Divine Providence or no Divine Providence, God didn't mean me to drive. *He* may not, but the highway police do. We've made a deal. They turn around and pretend not to see me and all I have to do is stay in second gear — dangerous to drive faster than that anyway. If I do, I wobble all over the place. The hills get up on their hind legs and walk right out in my way. Now don't get scared. You don't have to hang on like that. Just relax! Why don't you smoke? It's more sociable . . . get your mind off your troubles and keep you busy while I talk. I don't get much chance down there and besides I wanted to make you a proposition. If you tell the Superior I need the jeep, at least 'til we finish harvesting, maybe she'll listen. She doesn't know it, but I've offered to cut fields for people if I can have the hay. With the extra feed I can take care of two more heifers this winter . . . besides the two cows I've got now. The new man at the Co-op in Matera told me the other day he could get me a whole stall, built free, if I had four cows, but it all depends on my getting the hay, and I can't do that if I can't haul it as fast as I cut it. As a matter of fact I had another idea. If worse comes to worse, *you* have a license and you could drive the jeep. Things will be slow for you this summer while they're building the nursery — I could watch *that* for you, and you could drive the hay loads."

Sister Clemente paused, not sure she had my attention, and in a way she was right. We had twisted around and around, ever higher on the ribs of the mountain of rust-red clay so pitted and filigreed by the winter rains that not even broom clung to its banks. On the verges, lone silver thistles with gentian pompoms crackled at our passing and dipped in the blast of our exhaust. We had passed a goat balanced on a rock gazing off across the valley with aloof majesty. I have never been quite convinced that goats can look so intensely at nothing. I

believed in this one's concentration too and turned to look behind us — a prickly pear, spires of eroded clay, far, far below
the station hut and across the valley another spine of mountains veined with shade; in the distance a village glistened.
Nothing more. The goat had tricked me, and Sister Clemente
was more insistent:

"Did you hear what I said? That's only if I have more trouble
with the Superior, you understand, but it'll be easier if you cooperate. I think I've got her spooked. The other day I told her
that when I wanted to do something I'd always had to borrow
the Bishop's limousine and that I'd just have to go back to that
system if she took the jeep away from me.

"Did I ever tell you about the time I tricked the Bishop's
driver into taking me to the fair in Grassano? I said I needed
supplies and if we took the back seat out of the car, we'd be
able to get the whole load in the back. Enrico's not very bright,
you know; he agreed to it. Got the car ready with a blanket
where the seat should be — that was for Sister Gioiosa. Going
off with a man like that I had to have another nun with me, so I
bunged her in the back. Didn't make any difference to her.
She's always carsick wherever she rides. We went right after
lunch, too! Well, I looked around the fair, felt the calves' legs
and looked into mules' mouths, made all kinds of bargains for
animals I didn't want. Told Enrico I was being coy on the
prices just for the fun of dickering. He calmed down and went
back to the car to wait for me. Sister Gioiosa was still lying out
on the floor of the car moaning, so I was on my own, just the
way I'd planned it. Found a peasant from Muro I'd known
when I was a girl. He had a pretty good-looking heifer, but, of
course, he wanted too much for her. It's enough to see a
woman nosing around to make them think they can double the
price, you know.

"That's *one* thing I can't take about men. They think they
can get the better of us, and I swore when I was little I'd fix

every one of them who tried. My Dad used to say I could sure get even if I married them, but I'd be stuck, too . . . that's the other way of looking at it. To be honest there was a time I would have married anybody who wanted me. That was part of the trouble in my family. My Dad spent fifteen years in America. He was waiting for Mamma to come, but just when she was set to go . . . she'd sold everything we had, even had the bags packed . . . she went to the parish priest and he told her it was immoral, so she called the whole thing off. Dad had to come back and start all over again. By the time I was courting age he'd decided. He said the land went to my brothers and they'd have to take care of Mamma. There was enough for two of us three girls to have dowries. In other words someone had to go! The three of us had to work out which would be a nun. Let's face it — the other two were pretty. I knew more about farming, but that didn't count. My brothers didn't want to split with me, or keep me either, so I'm the one they sent to the convent — not that it's been a bad life. I do the things I like best, and I can get away from the others most of the time. Women, I don't like much, but they're all right in small doses. I sleep over the garage now — have to watch no one steals the animals, you know — and my schedule's different too, so I don't have to eat with them. I go to Mass and do my hour of Adoration at the altar, if I don't forget. The rest of the time I'm on my own. Keep beer in the Superior's icebox, eat what I want, when I want, and nobody can say a word to me.

"Now, where was I? Oh sure, about the heifer. I told this peasant from Muro I'd pay him too much on one condition . . . no matter what happened he was not to take her back. No matter what! He took the deal, and I led the heifer off. She was a beauty of a two-year-old. Had to roust Sister Gioiosa out of the back seat, and I'd just about got the heifer settled in when Enrico turned up. Oh, he yelled, and he screamed, and finally he cried a little. Said he'd lose his job. Said the car'd be

ruined. The police would arrest us for illegal hauling. I pushed
her rear in one side, and he pulled her out the other with the
halter rope. So finally I told him the truth. He'd better get the
heifer back in the car because I'd spent every lira I had.
Couldn't ship her and couldn't pay the tax on her either, if the
tax collector saw her. Even told him I'd tricked him into coming just so I could take her back in the car. No, he'd sell her. Off
he went, but the peasant from Muro wouldn't talk to him. I
made Enrico load her up again, just to get even. Then I got in
the back on my hands and knees and wrapped a cloak around
the heifer so her snout was the only thing showing. It stuck out
the window on the far side. Poor Sister Gioiosa! She was still
moaning and saying her rosary; wanted to go back on the bus,
she said. It was Enrico who stopped her; didn't want to be
alone with me. He begged her to get in the front seat. He was
so scared he was crying again. I'd stalled around until it was
dark because we had a better chance of sneaking into town
without being caught. So I sat on the floor and punched Enrico
in the shoulders with a crowbar. 'Get going!' He took me at my
word and lit out so fast the police flagged us down on the back-
side of the first curve. I told him to slow down, but for God's
sake not to stop. Then I stuck my head out, yelling, 'Make way!
Make way! The Bishop's sick. Got to get him to Torregreca!
Make way!' Old Enrico froze to the steering wheel — had to
poke him hard that time — but we charged on. Same thing happened outside Torregreca, but I just yelled, 'The Bishop's sick!
The Bishop's sick! Let us through!' Of course I was scared Enrico would slow up so much they'd want to escort us; then
they'd see that heifer drooling and mooing out the offside window. We made it, and I named her Enrichetta. Enrico didn't
think that was so funny, but one day I told the Bishop and he
about had a fit, he laughed so hard.

"Well, that story slowed the Mother Superior down a bit.
Hasn't mentioned the jeep since, but you never know with her.

That's another reason for sleeping over the garage. Don't want her to steal the jeep out from under me some dark night and she's crafty that way. She's been asking a lot of questions about you, too. Be careful. The other day when your letter came, she went to the Bishop to ask what she should do, you know, did he approve of your staying at the Convent, that sort of thing. He said he did, so that's all right, but she still wants to know more about you. She doesn't like what she calls 'worldly people' — anybody who's got free ideas. Of course she's right. She said she hoped you weren't the kind who'd go to the movies, or hang around cafés. It wouldn't do to have someone at the Convent who was loose.

"We'd better stop before we get to the main road so I can hook up my plastic squeeze-gate. Mustn't get caught without it. Superior says I give the order a bad name that way."

Geeing and hawing at the wheel, Sister Clemente maneuvered us to the lip of the road and sighed.

"This jeep's as temperamental as a mule," she said as she leaned over and looked at her own boots as though surprised to see them propped against the pedals. When, after some consideration, she was satisfied, she clonked both feet on the floor. The jeep hesitated a moment and then very slowly slipped backward down the hill.

"The brake, Sister! The brake!" screamed Antonio. There was a sudden jerk.

"Knew there was something I ought to do; just couldn't think what it was." She fumbled with the wire holding the door and finally hiked up her skirts and stepped out. She leaned into the back seat, extracted a collar, and started the same high-elbowed, neck-twisting struggle that men have with collar buttons. Antonio giggled until he cried. I choked trying to light a cigarette. Sister Clemente was not amused. Each time she had herself trussed up, one end of the collar flailed out and quivered just above her shoulder. "What's so funny?" she asked, her face red and sweaty. "If you're so smart, why don't you help me? Not *you*, Anto'. Just stay where you are or I'll belt you one. That's right, just calm down." She mopped her forehead with her sleeve and pried the collar button out of the neckband of her habit. "Maybe I need a new one. Got a packet of them right here. Wait a minute." She fished around in the bosom of her duster until she extricated her cross strung on a heavy silk ribbon. She flipped it over her shoulder and plunged deeper into the habit underneath the duster. She had to twist her hand to free it from the layers of clothing. First came a fistful of hard candies stuck to two inner tube patches, then a patented clip of minute wrenches, a billfold with a small purse mirror held between its layers by an elastic band and finally two twisted paper packets; one with basin stoppers, the other with white plastic collar buttons. Sister Clemente arranged her treasures on the seat and then looked timidly at me, much as a small boy reveals the mysteries of his pants pocket and then is afraid the grownup will not appreciate their value. I tried to be as solemn as she.

"Could I see the wrenches? I'd be very careful."

"Here, just loosen the screw and they come out of the clip. The big set is too bulky to carry. I keep it hidden, but I'll show you someday, if you really want to see them." She was glowing with pride. "Now these," she went on briskly, pointing at the stoppers, "I got these for you. They've stuck you on the top floor of the old people's wing with Don Andrea. Remember the old priest who keeps bees? Well, he collects stoppers too, so you'll have to remember to take yours with you whenever you leave your room. And there's another thing. He makes four or five trips to the toilet every night. Then he can't remember which is his room, so he tries all the doors 'til he hits the right one. Keep yours locked just to be safe. Not that he'd hurt you, but we haven't been able to break him of going to bed with his shoes on . . ." She chuckled at the idea. "Did I show you the pictures of my family? Wait a second, they're right here." She took the elastic band off the billfold and slipped the mirror into the front of her duster. "That's the fortieth anniversary. Those are my brothers and their wives and my sisters . . . and all the grandchildren. Of course, I wasn't there. And here are two pictures of me." She flashed them, then, remembering suddenly that they and the mirror were forbidden, she stuffed them back in the billfold. She sinned, keeping these pathetic shards of human life. They were of the world she had renounced. As a Bride of Christ she had no past, no possessions, no weaknesses; her only life must be in Him. And it was, but His discipline is not merciful to the lonely and the unsure. I imagined her comforting the face she saw in the mirror, sympathizing with all the tenderness that ordered compassion cannot give.

"Say, there's another thing. If you were thinking of giving the Superior gas money, or something like that, for your lift from the station, why don't you just stick it in the tin box in the glove compartment? She won't pass it along and besides I've given her the idea the jeep doesn't cost much to run." We were conspirators again; she, the shrewd horse trader and I . . . the innocent foreigner? Perhaps. But it was she who inspired my secret vice: I speculate on the pectoral inventory of nuns with ample, low-slung bosoms.

Hurtling along the Appian Way with Sister Clemente, even in second gear, can be perilous. Silent and wild-eyed with concentration, she gripped the horn and set a course that neither curves, donkeys nor peasants could alter. From the tail gate Antonio bellowed the choruses of a dirty song with witless aplomb, and I was left to my own frantic devices. So we screeched and caromed along the ridge three thousand feet above the sea until, across the way on another plateau, a damp, shaded row of houses was outlined against the sunset. It might have been just that, a row of isolated houses, if the tower had not loomed at one end, almost blocking our way as it had blocked attack for centuries. The road skirted underneath it, around the butte to the far side where houses tumbled down the steep cliff into the valley. There, below it all, the bell tower of the Convent church shone golden.

II

A NIGHT AT SAN FORTUNATO

THE Mother Superior was a dumpy, moon-faced woman with piercing brown eyes and an unpleasantly lax, full mouth. She was not the imposing figure I had imagined from Sister Clemente's description, but she had that air of Olympian perseverance that is a Superior's most lethal weapon, and she was not afraid of silence. With her hands laced across her stomach she could wait indefinitely, never betraying irritation by the slightest movement. The fierce concentration of her waiting was disconcerting. Even the innocent felt driven to self-defense; absorbed in justification, they seldom noticed that when severely tried, she worried the knuckles of one hand with the fingers of the other. I think few have run the risk of telling her less than the truth.

She received me in a small, bare room behind the kitchen, known as the Mother General's dining room. I suspect she would have preferred a more formal reception without the domestic odors of sour tomato sauce or goat cheese, or the bustle of the novices cleaning great tubs of salad greens. It was time for supper, and chains on the derricks of the huge wood-burning range clanked as cauldrons were raised and lowered. The nuns of the kitchen crew bickered peevishly. Heavenly detachment was impossible with the business of housekeeping thundering on next door. The Mother General's dining room was the inner sanctum for guests who rated more than the ferns and Victorian settees of the front parlor, and though its round, plastic-covered table and hard chairs offered little comfort, it had two very important features: a fireplace, and an old-fashioned electric icebox. A fire, kept burning most of the year, was the only luxury the nuns allowed themselves. The icebox, which was useless in so large a household, had been the first such machine in Torregreca and was an honored status symbol. As we talked, I was reassured by its grumbling counterpoint.

Coffee is a ritual in Italy as tea is in China, a preamble to real business. I had not eaten since morning and did not want the thimble of black lye that was put before me, but courtesy required that I drink it, as courtesy required that the Mother Superior make polite conversation about the weather and my trip from Naples. Once the ceremony was over and the cup removed, her questions became entirely personal. She wanted information, felt she had every right to have it, and would probe until satisfied. No matter how much I resented her questions, no matter how personal or insinuating they might be, I had to answer them. In Southern Italy the facts of life are simple: without at least the tacit approval of the Church no outsider will last more than forty-eight hours.

The Mother Superior asked about my background, both at home in America and in Italy, my tastes, my hobbies, my politics, my nursery techniques, my theories of child psychology, my knowledge of dialects, my direct experience in Southern Italy and my motivations for the work I was doing. I listened to myself in the detached way sometimes possible when speaking a language not your own and thought I sounded very young and innocent . . . certainly too idealistic to be dangerous. When there seemed nothing more she could ask, she started again from the beginning. An hour and a half lengthened into two hours. I ruffled her composure by answering her specific questions and then waiting, as she waited, forcing her to ask me something else. We were picking a cadaver that had no more meat, and we might have pecked on into the night if Luca Montefalcone had not arrived and interrupted at a crucial point.

The Mother Superior had said, "I don't see what you expect to accomplish in Torregreca by setting up this nursery. The Torresi aren't interested in change, you know. In fact they use all their energy to fight improvements."

"Maybe they suspect the motives behind the improvements," had been my blunt answer.

She waited; I said nothing. There was a knock, then a shuffling of feet outside the door. Someone giggled. Finally the door opened a crack, revealing Luca's long, solemn face.

"Ah, so there you are! May I come in, Reverend Mother? You must protect me from Sister Gioiosa. She's lost her mind."

"I told him he couldn't. I *did* tell him, but he said . . . well . . . I won't repeat what he said." A fat, red-faced nun had come in behind Luca. It was the long-suffering Sister Joyful who was always cheerful and forgetful and plagued by faulty tear ducts that made her weep even in moments of happiness.

"That will be enough, Sister Gioiosa. Don Luca is always welcome here. Why don't you get him some coffee?"

"But, Sister," he said quickly, "don't poison me this time, please."

"Well, you don't have to drink it if . . . " Then she saw his gentle, mocking smile and stopped. "Oh, you're just teasing me." Sister Gioiosa blushed and wept at the same time and then bustled out of the room.

Luca laughed. Perhaps because his brother, Don Matteo, is a priest he has an easy manner with nuns, treating them as headstrong women who need jollying, but there is always a hint of challenge in what he says to them. All nuns are unnatural black crows to him. I think he sees each one as a woman who has rejected his masculinity, and his banter seems to say I'm a man and dammit you're still a woman. They play up to him and enjoy their brief flirtations with one of the few men in their lives who can never be suspect. After all, he *is* a doctor, and his brother *is* a priest.

I had not expected Luca to come to see me at the Convent. In fact I had been quite sure he would not. Every Southerner is cautious by nature and reluctant to commit himself to anything until there is a hint of success. I wondered without bitterness if he had come out of sympathy, or curiosity — or, as was more likely, because he was already bored with the amusements the town offered. He looked every inch the English gentleman in his tweed jacket and flannels, and he took a great deal of time playing with a pipe, which was new to me. The Mother Superior and I waited in silence. She was resigned. Our game of tests and measurements had been interrupted, but it was not over.

"Welcome to Torregreca, Ann," Luca said. "Give me a couple of cigarettes, will you? If the Reverend Mother doesn't mind, I'd like to try this thing," and he waved the pipe.

The Mother Superior pursed her lips. So I had a secret vice — I smoked.

Luca shredded the cigarettes, filled his pipe, smiled at us blandly and asked for a match. When he was satisfied with the clouds of smoke, he looked up at us again and said in a puzzled voice, "You seem very serious, both of you. Has the Reverend Mother been quizzing you?" He nodded to her and smiled. Then, to me, "You must remember, Ann, anyone who comes to Torregreca is a curiosity. Everyone wants to escape — only a lunatic would choose this exile for himself. You'll spend a lot of time explaining yourself to people who suspect your neat explanations. You see, truth is black and white to you. To us, it's something we construct from the things people don't say. We're used to the devious compliment and the well-decorated lie and to respect we don't deserve. You Anglo-Saxons won't play the game. You're such controlled people . . . so cold . . . you just look at us with those bright blue eyes and smile. Oh yes, that's the way it is, Ann. We don't understand silence, and we don't understand directness. You've learned to talk when you have nothing to say — to be patient when you want to say, 'Get on with it,' but your composure gives us a feeling you may be laughing at us. We're afraid of being mocked, of appearing to be fools, aren't we, Reverend Mother? That, in a way, is why I've come down tonight. Matteo has been looking for a house for you, but the answer is always the same. 'She's a woman. What's she coming here for? We don't know anything about her . . . we don't want her. We won't rent to her.' He hasn't found anything, except one woman, a widow named Chichella Fascide. She's a peasant with three children, lots of debts and no work. She *might* rent her apartment in the *case popolari, if* you kept her on to do the cleaning and shopping. She'd rather rent just one room because she hasn't anywhere to take the children." He lifted his shoulders. "It isn't what I had expected for you, either. I came to ask the Reverend Mother if she could help us. People will get over their diffidence in time, but you need a place to live."

I only half-listened while they discussed me as though I were a piece of luggage to be stored in a locker until needed. With raised eyebrows and hunched shoulders they vetoed each other's suggestions. I mused on the devious Southern mind and kept my Anglo-Saxon thoughts to myself. They need not have worried about a place for me to live. I knew better than they that the Torresi were suspicious of a woman alone. It was the old question of *serietà*. Their women of good family seldom walk down the Corso alone, never travel alone. Only a wanton runs free. Luca and the Mother Superior were busy convincing each other that rumors of depravity could be silenced by respectable company. Between them they would find a noble but impoverished lady of the local Catholic Action and appeal to her sense of moral duty until she agreed to let me share a bedroom with her daughters. I knew about those kitchen-centered lives. We would eat in the kitchen; the only fire and the toilet in its waterless cubicle would be there; and it would be there, too, that I would be allowed my one wash of the week — on Saturday evenings, in the sink, with a saucepan of water heated on the stove. No, they need not have worried. I would see this Chichella Fascide as soon as I could. With care I would find out from her everything there was to know about renting a house in town. If not, my years in the South had been wasted. I was busy with my own plans when the Mother Superior stood up.

"I'm sorry, but I'll have to leave you. It's time for our evening prayers, but stay if you like, Don Luca. Sister Gioiosa will be in the kitchen; she'll show you out when you want to leave." Turning to me she said, kindly enough, "You'll need rest after your trip. Tomorrow is soon enough to worry over problems. I'll see to your housing, then in the afternoon we can chat."

She moved without seeming to move, gliding along as though propelled by a small electric motor. I felt she had already dismissed us from her mind and was organizing the important facts of her next job. Later, in a moment of tranquility, she would consider us again. No detail would be overlooked. She made no point of it, but she left the door into the kitchen open. Luca sat down again, lighted another of my cigarettes, and cocked an eyebrow toward the door.

"No man can be trusted . . . not even Don Matteo's brother!"

"Oh no," I objected, "I'm the one who's dangerous. You don't understand the way a woman's mind works."

"Never say that to an Italian! He understands everything he needs to about women." He was only pretending to be offended. "Besides, the Mother Superior isn't a woman, she's a nun."

"Watch out, you're proving what I said. Men always underestimate. She's woman enough to suspect a man's excuses for another woman. Why did you do it? She's even more on guard now."

"That can wait," he said, motioning toward the kitchen.

Then, after a minute, "I'm never down here now, you know, unless they hear I'm in town and want me to visit a sick nun. But whenever I do come, it reminds me of playing here as a boy . . . of the night I saw the souls of the dead. Yes, I *saw* them."

He began to talk quietly, rambling through his own memories, at times laughing at himself, at others hurt by the loneliness a little boy is never allowed to admit. He was not telling me a story; he was remembering, backtracking and jumping ahead, finding connections where perhaps none had existed. Rooms were again cavernous, and men he would now dismiss as petty were again as important as they had claimed to be.

Could he have told me so much as I remember in that one night? I doubt it. But I shall always remember it as the tale of a summer's night, interrupted now and then by bells that jangled in the high, irritable way of Southern bells. The little fire hissed and died out to a smudge at our feet, and still he talked.

Luca's story had more to do with a lonely little boy than with spirits — not that he dwelled on his loneliness. Loneliness was a simple fact of life, like birth, boarding school, or the war; one of the bones on which the flesh of his life had been hung. He had told the story of the souls of the dead so often he could no longer distinguish between truth and embellishment. The first time he told it he had been whispering to a group of boys clustered around his bed in the dormitory of his Naples boarding school, San Gennaro in Perilis. It must have been his second or third year there, because he still thought of himself as a "leadhead," as the sophisticated city boys called the provincials. It was this very story that had catapulted him into the group of "experienced, worldly" young men who tyrannized the school.

He had never minded being a "lead-head." There was a certain solidness about the other country boys that he understood. The mincing city boys were bloodless and without imagination. They were smug. They recognized no power but their own, no life better than their own. More than ever, Luca saw the world as divided into two kinds of people: those smooth, frail, self-confident people who had never noticed there was a battle to fight; and the others — the Torresi — to whom God's malice was as real as the dirt they plowed. Still he liked school and even the other boys, but he resented never being alone.

It was at San Gennaro in Perilis that for the first time in his life he had been physically uncomfortable. He was always cold in spite of the heavy, scratchy blankets that mashed him down into the mattress. He went to bed depressed and woke up depressed in the stark white dormitory he shared with forty boys and a priest who snored. He had never forgotten that room with its windows closed against the night air and its stench of disinfectant and dirty feet. He queued to wash his face in the morning, and he queued twice a week for a shower he did not want. The torture queue was for toilet cubicles: There was never enough time. And he queued for discouraging meals of bread, pasta, potatoes and beans. Twice a day he went to Mass and dreamed of spinach and figs and wide fields where no one could disturb him by rattling the door. His mouth watered to the imagined sweetness of the carob pods that had been his candy in Torregreca. Then it was time to queue again.

Luca had worked hard. There was nothing else to do. He was considered bright, a "lead-head slog," though he never did well in religious education or Italian. He thought religion women's stuff, and the persnickety little priest who taught it had done nothing to change his mind. He had tried, even to the point of carrying the book in his pocket and studying in queues, but had given up when the priests began to treat him with a private, almost caressing gentleness and hinted that he might feel a vocation. With Italian, the problem was entirely different. At home, even in school, he had always spoken the dialect of Torregreca. He thought in dialect, was himself in dialect. In dialect he could say exactly what he meant. Now, suddenly, he had to carry on his life in Italian, a written language almost as academic to him as Latin. The simplest phrase was a stilted translation. Sometimes, bewildered by a word or a construction, he lost the point of classroom discussions. When asked a question, he suffered as a stutterer suffers; he knew what he wanted to say but could not get it out. Grammar was beyond him. He tried to remember rules by finding the equivalent in dialect, but of course there never was one. From those first years of struggling came a private system of diagrams, one simple image that would explain what was complex. So the Unification of Italy was a gnarled olive tree whose trunk was a twisting together of three sinews — the Piemontesi, the Church and the Kingdom of Naples — each branch was a person or a place. Musicians have a shorthand of notes; Luca had diagrams.

Sunday lunch at his aunt's house was his only escape from the barbed wire of Italian, and even that had its drawbacks. His aunt's husband was an official of the tax office, a pompous little man who sneered at and had taught his children to sneer at "those cavedwellers in Lucania." Sometimes after lunch, when the others were asleep, his aunt took up her mending. Then Luca could tell her his troubles in dialect. She was a kind woman who listened sympathetically and tried to comfort him, but when Monday morning came, she was too busy with her own five children to give Luca much thought. She never knew it, but this preoccupation with her own family led to some of Luca's happiest days. Once she forgot to tell his school that the family would be away on Sunday. Luca arrived and found no one at home. Rather than go back to school, he had wandered the streets of Naples. That was his first free Sunday. He said nothing to his friends, but when he grew restless, he would tell his aunt he had to stay at school the following Sunday. The priests, ignorant of any change in plans, released him on the Sunday morning; by the simplest trick he had the whole day to himself. He saw the elegant places his uncle boasted of — Via Roma, the Royal Palace, the Galleria. He haunted fruit and vegetable markets, eating persimmons straight off the carts and buying broad beans that he could hoard in his pockets until he felt the urge to nibble at them. He smiled to himself when he thought of the money that bought these luxuries.

At the end of the previous summer he had made a formal call on his father. It was a duty expected of him twice each summer, so once in June, once in September, he waited his turn outside his father's storeroom-office, in line with the peasants who farmed the family land. Father and son had little to say to each other. Luca could expect a lecture on the necessity of using the Fascist salute and little else, but this particular time he had something he wished to discuss with his father. His mother had sent him an embroidered bodice and he felt that, at his age, he should be saved the indignity of such surprises. He proposed to choose for himself the suit, boots, four shirts and two sets of underwear allowed him each year. He had come to ask for an order letter to his father's tailor in Naples. Don Manfredo had been so startled by this aggressiveness that he had looked up from his ledger and taken the time to inspect his son rather carefully. Luca blushed. It was the first time in years that he had really had his father's full attention and he was not sure he had been wise to disturb him. Don Manfredo seemed to be taking inventory of the boy's person, but agreed to write the letter and added:

"I see you're growing up. Here's fifty lire. Before you go back to school, stop off at a good house in Naples and find out what the world's about — but pick a good one, a clean one."

Luca had nodded. No point in telling his father he already

"knew." He would just keep the money for something more interesting, like broad beans and persimmons and oranges from carts — and as it turned out, for tram rides. Trams went to fascinating places. At the end of one line he had found Pompeii and the ruins, and an old, crippled guard who sat in the shade eating bread and salami that he washed down with long swigs from a bottle labeled "turpentine." Luca had been happy and a little tipsy on the ride back to school. Another tram had taken him to Pozzuoli where he spent the day watching the fishermen. For weeks after, he dreamed of going to sea, of nets and traps and oilskins and loads of fish, until finally he gave in and went back on the tram. It was clear and sparkling, the kind of deceptive winter day that hints of spring before noon and pierces the gizzard with cold by nightfall. He found a boat about to go out and begged to be taken along. They had made fun of him and his Sunday suit, but in the end had told him to hop aboard, one more hand would be useful. Outside the port, wind chopped at the water, making shivery patterns; then waves rolled toward the boat, lifting it and sluing it down, sideways into a trough of gray oil. And once, and twice and — one of the men was telling him how to lay nets — and three times. He was dizzy, then he was sick. The rest of the day he spent between the railing and a pile of tarpaulins that stank of fish. He wanted to die. He gave up the idea of going to sea, but he never gave up his free day, even if he did nothing more exciting than sit on the seawall and plan what he would do next summer in Torregreca.

For all his anticipation, summers were disappointing, or at least not as he remembered them. Before he had been sent away to school, they had meant long months of freedom with Uncle Girolamo, his favorite uncle, who was one of his mother's brothers — the only one she was not proud of. Some said Girolamo was a traitor to his class, others that he was "different," which was even more incriminating. He irritated them

by paying no attention. He was known as "The General" because he had served in the army rather than hire a substitute
as was the custom among the young bucks of the landed gentry.
He had felt it his duty, and as a daily reminder to the others
still wore a topee, khaki bush jacket, breeches and puttees. To
anyone who asked why, he explained blandly that he found it
the most comfortable outfit for the long days he spent in the
fields supervising his land — another duty that his fellow landowners neglected. He went about his business with the easy,
high-headed dignity of a very tall man. Each morning at dawn,
without a glance to right or left, Don Girolamo stalked across
the Piazza and out to his land. More often than not Luca was
right behind him. On those long walks he told Luca about
Lucania, all about it from the time of its pre-Roman settlements right through the Kings of Naples. He dreamed of refor-
estation; pointed out where dams could and should be built;
taught Luca how to spot birds and where they built their nests
and how to hunt them. He made a slingshot for the boy, then
later taught him to handle a shotgun, but always he returned to
the glory of Lucania, to the dignity of man and the right each
had to an equal share in the world's wealth. Luca did not always understand what he said, but he listened and asked questions and watched. He watched particularly when Uncle Girolamo talked to the peasants. They seemed to find hope for the
future in what he said. In the human anthill that surrounded
the Piazza and the palaces of the *civili* it was whispered that he
was the peasants' champion. They came to the fields to listen to
him; they stopped him on the road to ask advice; and they
trusted what he told them. They even tolerated his brief but
violent affairs with their wives and daughters, and named the
children of his sudden passion "Little Generals."

Over the years Don Girolamo had become Luca's everyday
father, the man who knew where to find snakes or buried treas-
ure and could show him how to clean a bird. The boy could ask

for advice or comfort from him and be sure there would be a
full measure. Meanwhile Don Manfredo became more and
more a dignified figurehead to his son. Tall and silent with a
dramatic widow's peak and the hawkish nose he had passed on
to Luca, Don Manfredo filled old Palazzo Montefalcone with a
Mosaic righteousness, but took little part in its life. He spent
his mornings hunting, or in happy consultation with his friend
Don Mimmi Mangiacarne in the back room of Don Mimmi's
shop. They were shaved by the same postman; then, pink-faced
and smelling of orris root, they wrapped themselves in their big
black capes and settled down to a hand or two of cards. Sometimes they studied hardware catalogues and worked out elaborate cost estimates for Don Manfredo's secret dream. Ever
since the notary had managed to impress on him the exact proportions of his wife Donna Filomena's dowry, he had planned
— without ever telling his wife — to remodel Palazzo Montefalcone. With figures reeling around in his head he came home
for that dinner that had always been the dread of his son's existence, the one thing Luca had never managed to escape. He
and his father sat in silence while Donna Filomena and Luca's
sister Titti tuned up for their mealtime duet. Their themes
were very different, but their constancy created a certain harmony. Donna Filomena rippled back and forth over the distinc-
tions of her ancestors while Titti whined her complaints about
all the children in town. It seemed marvelous to Luca that the
two women did not have to listen to sympathize with each
other. Sitting there in the big blue-and-white tiled kitchen, he
knew without thinking everything that would happen: at what
moment the peasant woman Maria would bang the plates in
the stone sink and when she would make silly, pacifying noises
at baby Matteo who gurgled for attention from his cradle in the
corner. This was a rhythm Donna Filomena had established,
and she expected the others to keep step. Always, as she cut
herself a wedge of cheese, she told Titti not to interrupt her

elders. This was the moment when she turned to her husband and said, "And what did you do this morning," hinting by her slight overtone of scorn. "How did you waste your time today?" Titti imitated the manner with Luca. Being a year older, she was very superior and never lost a chance to tattle on him. Luca's revenge was to have his friends play vicious jokes on her while he watched at a discreet distance. She was the perfect butt, never suspecting dirty work until it was too late, so the animosity between them spiraled gently into loathing.

To Luca his mother and his sister were as much alike as two women of different generations could be. Donna Filomena was tall and spare with squinting brown eyes and a jaw too heavy for her angular face. It was her nose, however, that was her most distinguished feature. Only generations of breeding could produce one so long, so thin, so high-bridged that the bone shone white and insistent almost to the very tip. Titti had the same nose and jaw, softened now by puppy fat, and further-more Luca had caught her with a mirror practising the toss of the head the Torresi so admired in their mother.

Locally Donna Filomena was considered the ultimate in re-finement, partly because of her exalted family, partly because she had prophetic dreams. The poor flocked to her for advice which she gave with electric accuracy. In recompense her in-structions were to be followed to the letter, and if she discov-ered she had been disobeyed the offender was barred from her presence forever. Between her oracular activities and her man-agement of the family lands, she spent much of each day hold-ing audiences. The few remaining hours were taken up with accounts, the inventory of the huge cheese and wine stores in the Palace cellar, and her favorite pastime, the study of land survey charts. She had a sixth sense about land — what to buy, what to sell and when — and enjoyed a real-life Monopoly game at which she never lost. Her acumen, she said, was a gift inherited from her father, the fifth Barone Albanese di Castel-

squadro. No one dared correct her, but she was confusing him
with her grandfather who had bought vast tracts of expropri-
ated Church property at the government auctions. Her father
had been an affable man, more of a hunter than an entrepreneur, and always delighted to have responsibility taken from
him. He had even allowed his Filomena to choose her own husband. The choice had suited everyone. Don Manfredo was
handsome, of an old landed family now a bit impoverished,
and was thought to have very sound ideas, though he never
aired them. He had agreed with Filomena's plan to divide life
into his and her compartments. Marriage would not disrupt
his life. She would handle the land, the peasants and the
houses. He could hunt, talk to friends and even be political if
he liked. The children, of course, were hers, but Don Manfredo
did occasionally interfere in Luca's upbringing. He wanted his
son to be a man. He predicated cold baths . . . very masculine
. . . very strengthening . . . hadn't the Duce said so himself? Physical fitness was most important. Donna Filomena had
granted politics as a male prerogative, but she would not overlook the suggestion that what was good for the Duce was good
for her son, and the fights that resulted sent Luca scampering
off to his retreat in a dusty back salon of the Palace.

In fact, if he managed to escape unnoticed in the after-dinner
confusion, he went there every winter afternoon. It was his secret place, the place where he could do the things that interested him. There in peace he could pull a high-backed chair
over to the window, open the shutter a crack and read with his
back to the dangling wall-paper and the piles of apples and
potatoes that his mother stored there. In the dusty quiet he got
on with his projects, a play about the crusades (he thought the
Saracens had been neglected), an illustrated history of Torregreca, and taxidermy. He was still embarrassed about his
friend Pancrazio's dog. The book had made it sound so simple
— pine oil — that he had comforted Pancrazio by promising to

preserve the dog forever. He had planned to supervise the work, not do it himself, but when the scruffy ginger body had been presented to him in a book bag, he could not refuse to take it. He had gone to the Cathedral to think it over and in the dim privacy had taken another look at the dog. He decided to go to a mule skinner. The hide that was given back to him had been discouragingly limp, but he had gone home, found a needle, thread, the pine oil and a braid of vegetable fiber used for stuffing pillows and had retired to his "office." Hours later he was able to show Pancrazio a satisfactory, if lumpy, reincarnation of his dog. They visited it daily, but after a week they had to admit there was a pungent odor that did not come from musky apples. They buried Pancrazio's dog and then started serious experiments in taxidermy. Pancrazio's father was a shepherd and could supply them with dead, or near-dead animals. Luca could not bear the idea of killing them in cold blood. If they were brought to him alive, he cared for them. To his dismay some lived quite a while and feeding them became a problem. At one time he had two baby goats, a rabbit and a kitten alive in that back room, but there was little danger that anyone would catch him. Once a month Don Manfredo wandered from room to room checking his calculations for the remodeling. He muttered to himself. "Maybe another bath here, instead of . . ." Bathrooms would be very important. He was convinced that Italy would flourish under Fascism and that Torregreca would have sewers and piped water supply. He visualized the rooms elegant with the kind of chrome-and-leather furniture he had seen in Rome the time he had been a member of the Lucanian delegation that called on the Duce. Hadn't the Duce told them, "Let every Italian be a man of the future. It is up to Italy to shape the future of the world as it has always shaped the taste of the world." He was right; and Don Manfredo despised the weaklings who objected to the Duce's laws. After all, government rules people as a father rules his children. It disciplines, it teaches what is right: values and ideas. Without the Duce there would be anarchy. Everything depends on order . . . yes, that's the important thing. Now, let me see, those iron brackets must go. There were some glass-and-metal fixtures in Rome . . . Suddenly, Don Manfredo would sense he was not alone. "Who's that? Who's there?"

"It's just me, Father," Luca answered from the depths of his chair. "I'm doing my homework."

"Oh, oh yes, good idea. Must keep up with your studies," and he would drift off, never wondering why Luca studied in that dark back room.

Luca stayed in his winter retreat until he thought he could intercept Uncle Girolamo as he came out of the *Circolo dei Civili*. At least he would go and wait for him in the Piazza. When he did come it was not the same. Don Girolamo's personality was seasonal. With the first chill, misty dawns, he gave up walking and went to his fields in a horse-drawn buggy. He wrapped himself in a long black cartwheel cape of beaver cloth with silver clasps and a chain at the neck. The puttees and topee were replaced too, by the shiniest black boots and a black fedora. Overnight he became a padrone; he even played cards with the others at the club, the *Circolo dei Civili*. Each winter Luca puzzled over his uncle's treachery. He was too young to feel the living death of winter or to need a way to defraud time, to frustrate its erosion of morale. When his uncle came, he was preoccupied and irritated by the nonsense discussions of his friends. The last year Luca was in school in Torre-greca his uncle talked of nothing but a man named Matteotti. The injustice of it! A government of murderers is what we have! Don't these idiots see this is the end of free expression! It made no sense to Luca, but still he felt at peace as he walked along beside his uncle. Something interesting would happen. There was always the next summer to look forward to.

But summers were not the same after he went to Naples,

after his mother's illness. During vacations in Torregreca, he no longer stayed in Palazzo Montefalcone, but with two aunts who lived in a doll's house all trim and decorous in the very middle of the Casbah. It was a female haven with starched, crocheted doilies and photographs that glimmered in the light of votive candles. The aunts were both deaf, and a bit spavined about the knees, but the thought that they might be of use had rejuvenated them. When Luca was sent to Naples, Titti had been moved into the aunts' spare room. Two maiden ladies became three who lived in perfect, fussy harmony. Luca was a summer intruder who made a nuisance of himself by refusing to sleep with his aunts and forcing them to dismantle a small room kept as a shrine to their dead brother. They tolerated him; he left them alone.

Don Girolamo was a disappointment too. He was either silent or absorbed in dire prophesies that exasperated Luca. "Remember," he would say, "hypocrites don't have to be strangers. My friends are all hypocrites. They'd follow cannibals if it would save their privileges. Remember, Fascist truth isn't the truth the rest of the world knows. They embroider on history, next it'll be science and your textbooks. You won't know what happened in the world, you'll only know what they want you to *think* happened. Don't fall for it. There's nothing sacred about the printed word. You can doubt without falling into mortal sin . . . and the priests are no better than the padroni. They'll make a deal with the Fascists. They need each other. Black shirts, black tunics, rule by police, rule by priests . . . it's all the same breed. You'll see, even if I'm gone."

Luca called it Uncle G's purge; later he saw it as prophecy . . . years later. When he lost patience with his uncle he went off poaching with old Blackbelly or cadged rides from bus drivers. He went wherever the bus went, and in the three or four hours before the return trip he explored the towns at the end of the line. He made friends with the new veterinarian,

Fiore, who was unpopular because he started every conversation, "Well, if that sainted man, our Bishop, is willing to sacrifice his life in this mission land, I must follow his example, but . . ." Fiore was known to be a police spy, and he gave himself medical airs that offended the members of the true profession, but he was kind to Luca who was, by then, interested in anything sick. The veterinarian took him on his rounds explaining about spontaneous abortion in cows, and undulant fever and cancerous eyes. Luca had been impressed by the personal quirks that later made Fiore a comic figure — his shaved head, his monocle, the crop he carried, and his boots that shone like patent leather. Innocently Luca called him Don Giuseppe, though no one else in town would honor him with the title. Uncle Girolamo objected to the friendship, but Luca insisted cows and goats were not interested in politics. "They are, if Fiore takes care of them," was his uncle's grumpy answer.

The peasants still talked about his uncle, but in a different way. They understood and forgave his silence. He was protecting them, for no one would touch him if he protested the castor oil and billy club treatments the police handed out to stubborn peasants. No, he would never be hurt; his peasants would get a double beating instead. Uncle Girolamo avoided everyone, talked to no one, and when Luca asked if he was afraid of something, he winced. His answer was cryptic. "Afraid? Yes, like all Southerners I'm afraid of defeat . . . not for myself. These people are better with no leader than with one who leads them to final defeat. This time it'll be final."

No, after that night that Luca would tell the boys about years later, summers had never been the same. Nothing had. It had been late in August, the year he "finished" the Torregreca school — fifth grade — and he still had another three weeks of freedom before he went to Naples and San Gennaro in Perilis. It had been a summer of dog days. The stones were scorched and brittle and the stubble in the fields smoldered. Everything, even people, seemed to be crumbling to dust. The ancients who spent their days in pursuit of shade talked of the end of the world: hell's fire was upon them. For months only a dribble had come from the Old Fountain. A five-liter barrel of drinking water cost double the usual price, and the women who hauled it from the fountain threatened to raise the price still higher to compensate for the hours they wasted in waiting. The annual typhoid epidemic struck like an avalanche, carrying off the strongest first. Some said it was the pox, not typhoid at all. Each morning the bells tolled, in the only honor done those abandoned, infected dead who could not be buried in consecrated ground. Then, in the cool twilight, a grim procession of stretchers bearing the feverish living passed through the Lower Piazza and slowly on until it came to the Convent of San Fortunato. A priest with a ragged acolyte led the way, chanting prayers. The priest never took his eyes from his book except to make sure his acolyte had not melted away into the crowd. Carabinieri, beside him and at the end of the line, protected him from possible assault by the frenzied relatives; still he did not want to meet their eyes. The precaution was unnecessary. The people who had come to watch stood well back against the buildings for fear they too would be contaminated. It was enough that each victim had by his side one relative who would stay with him and nurse him . . . and face almost certain death.

There was no hospital, only the abandoned Convent. Sixty years before, patrician ladies with their dowries, hangings, furniture and servants still renounced the world for its elegant asylum. Their gentle amusements had been undisturbed by the teeming village that baked on the ridge above them. The Unification of Italy had broken into this timeless isolation. Even the Republican sentiments of the Mother Superior of the day had not been enough to save them. She had rebelled against her spiritual leader, the Pope, and had flown the first Republican flag in Lucania from the campanile of San Fortunato. The Bishop died of an apoplectic seizure, but still the Convent lands had been confiscated and the order disbanded. The buildings remained virtually deserted until 1936.

Over the years San Fortunato fell into ruins. The roofs caved in; its walls sagged until it offered meager shelter to the homeless who squatted in its protected corners. Shepherds took refuge from the wind with their cheese kettles and their dogs. Sometimes they used the Convent for lambing and then moved on. The townspeople never went there except in time of plague. The church, no less squalid than the rest of the building, still had a roof. Without water or light or toilets, it served for quarantine. An armed police squad rounded up the street cleaners, forced them to sweep the floor and lay new straw, and then marched the poor devils back to town to double as stretcher-bearers. They would be kept under armed guard until the emergency were over. There was no escape. Each morning the great door of the church was unlocked and the stretcher-bearers sent in to haul out the corpses of those who had died in the night. No doctor was brave enough to visit the living. The door was bolted tight again until dark. The evening procession was a roundup of the dying, those whom the doctors had ordered taken to the Convent. Each went with a relative willing to nurse him. And so it went until the epidemic subsided or, as it seemed that summer Luca remembered so well, until all the Torresi were dead.

Youth is callous. To Luca a procession meant the excitement of a festa, and now every day was festa. Mumbling as the others mumbled, his eyes fixed on the ground, he would follow the last of the carabinieri across the Piazza, down the road and into the valley. Once they reached the bridge, the procession was over for him. To go on would have shattered his illusion of festa. He had already seen the shrieking, clawing struggle be-

tween the stretcher-bearers and the sick and their relatives.
There could be only one end: the sick were too weak to walk,
the carabinieri held guns on the stretcher-bearers. They had to
win.

Toward the end of the second week of the epidemic Luca
changed his mind. He had heard the wife of one of the Montefalcone peasants talking to Donna Filomena about what happened in the Convent at night when the oil lamps at either end
of the church guttered out. It was then that the spirits of the
dead came to whisper to the living, to warn them there was no
rest in death if you could not be buried. She said they swooped
through the church into the rafters, around the altar, everywhere, moaning. She knew; she had been there closed in for
seventeen days with her little boy, and now he was dead too —
but his soul could rest. She had seen to that, she said slyly.
Luca remembered the boy, red-haired, not more than five.
Donna Filomena was excited. "Well, tell me. What did you do?
Tell me!" Silence. "I order you to tell me!" Luca sensed there
was something not right about his mother. "Tell me . . ." She
was yelling; her face was congested, her eyes did not focus.

"If you never breathe a word, Signora . . . I tried everything, Signora, I swear I did. It was a curse. Nothing would
break it. Oh, I had a special potion, but it did no good. Nino
was worse every day. The nights were long, sitting there listening to those restless souls of the dead who had gone before him.
I had time to make a plan, to think it through. One morning he
was on fire . . . he couldn't last much longer. He cried a little,
then toward noon . . . he turned cold. Signora, I knew what I
had to do. I prayed 'til the sun was low and then I talked to
the other women. They listened and agreed. When the stretchers came that night I told the policeman I had been chosen to
wash for everyone, that we had to wash those rags of blankets
and towels. We had to or we'd all die. 'Eh,' says he, 'you'll die
anyway — but go on, get the stuff ready. You can leave with us.

I'll tell the guard to let you in when you come back.' Asses they are! No woman would wash at twilight! It was too dark inside for them to see what I was doing. I wrapped my poor Nino in those blankets and towels — God forgive me — then I picked up the bundle, stuck it on my head and marched out of there. He's buried now — his soul's at rest, not wailing in the rafters at San Fortunato. Next morning when his straw pad was empty, all the women would say was, 'You're too late this time. You can't get *him*. Maybe he walked, maybe he was carried, but he can rest now and the souls of our dead are happier.' And you know they couldn't do anything about it."

The story had had a strange effect on Luca's mother. She alternated between feverish chattering and long heavy periods of silence. His father explained she was going to have a baby, which made her very emotional, and he had added in a confidential man-to-man voice, "We better make sure nothing else upsets her." Luca did not want to upset her, but after he heard the story he was determined to *see* the soul of a dead man, and there seemed no way except to follow the procession on across the bridge and up to the church door.

Each night, at the first turn of the great rusty key, the prisoners inside moaned softly. They were consoled. Charon had made another crossing. Behind Luca the nurse-relatives howled in desperation or fainted, but he would not be distracted. As the heavy door swung open he peered inside, hoping to surprise a soul before it could hide. The woman had said when the lamps guttered out — in the dark, she meant — and he reasoned one might be deceived by the blackness of the church. Day after day he saw nothing. Later he couldn't explain, even to himself, why it became so important for him. He just knew he had to prove that the souls of the dead existed by seeing for himself; otherwise he could never believe.

He wondered where they went by day. No one had a satisfactory answer. So he decided he must wait for them at night

— outside the church since he could not get in — and he would have to sneak out of Palazzo Montefalcone without telling anyone his plan. His father would never allow him to go, particularly now that his mother was so "sensitive." He chose his night and waited until he could hear no one moving around. The lights were out. Carrying a pair of soft, felt shoes for later, he tiptoed along the corridor away from the bedrooms, down a stairway, and out into an inside courtyard. From there on it was easy Out through a stall that had a second door leading to the street. He slipped the bar in place, stuck the key in his pocket and then ran down the street without bothering about his shoes. At the edge of town he stopped to catch his breath. He was surprised by the chill in the air and the strands of mist that warned of fall. They glistened silver in the moonlight filtering through a marbled sky. Long before midnight he was wedged in the fork of a tree across from San Fortunato. He was cold and, as time went on, sleepy and cramped. He would stay just ten more minutes, then he would go home. The leaves crackled around him, but no branch obstructed his view. He could see the campanile and its long, black shadow very clearly, and beyond it the slanted expanse of the church roof, squared at its apex for the insertion of four mullioned windows. The tiles in shadow rippled and zigzagged away from him in a dizzying pattern. As Luca put his hands up to rub his eyes, a bloodcurdling howl came — from the campanile, or so he thought later — a howl he had heard one other time, in the winter when wolves starved by three weeks of deep snow had come down to bay on the ridge opposite town. Luca almost tumbled to the ground. Before he could haul himself around on the branch that had broken his fall, the wail had tapered off to a moan of agony; then abruptly it came again. It pierced Luca's ears and left them buzzing. He looked; there was no one in sight. One bell in the tower pinged. Luca stared at it and could make out a figure, wispy, soft and loose-jointed, that coiled around the bell, then slipped under its lip. There was another ping, and another, before the shadow curled back into sight and drifted off to, and then through, a mullioned window. Luca could just see the tip of his gown, he thought, then he came back out with another, smaller, shadowy figure. They went to the bell, both curled under its lip; ping, ping, ping, ping. They were flipping the clapper back and forth, playing. Playful souls — it hardly seemed right. Out they came, moaning, moaning louder until they set up a rhythmic wail that they accented with the heavy clong of a larger bell. One on either side of the bell, they were taking turns leaning on it, rocking it and moaning. Soon they were joined by a third and then a fourth almost transparent figure. They moaned and rocked together. When the third howl split through the night, Luca dropped out of the tree and hit the ground running.

Down to the bridge, across the valley he sprinted, and up into town by the steepest goat path on his hands and knees. Thump, bump, he heard behind him, but he had no more energy for running or for fear. He had to stop. Thump, bump, on down the hill went the stones he had loosened in his frantic climb. He laughed. Stones! Then the souls had not followed him. Why should they? They wanted to warn the sick. But he had seen them. He knew they existed. They were there ducking around the bells, batting the clapper, wailing. He could never doubt again. Still he was glad to slip the key in the stall lock and tiptoe in felt shoes back along the dank corridor to his room.

Luca did not tell the boys clustered around his dormitory bed that he had been scared that night. He just told them, rather grandly, that if anyone ever doubted that the souls of the dead were about by night they could state that their friend, Barone Luca Montefalcone, had seen them with his own eyes. Small wonder that his stock went up with them.

That was not quite the end of the story, but it was the end of

what he had told the boys at San Gennaro's, because it took
him a long time to understand what happened later that night
when he was safe in the Palazzo. He had thought it was a
nightmare. He heard his mother crying. He could still remember how she had sounded, as though she were hysterical or mad
with fear. "Manfredo, you won't. Promise you won't send me to
San Fortunato! Manfredo, by all the saints in heaven, save me.
Don't send me to the Convent. I don't want to die. I don't." His
father's voice had rumbled on and on until Luca stopped
dreaming and fell into a deep sleep. Early the next morning his
father had awakened him and told him to pack his things — he
was to leave immediately for Naples. A solemn Uncle Girolamo
had driven him to the station in his gig.

It was 1945 and the war had ended before Luca spent another night in Palazzo Montefalcone. True, he came for summer vacations and stayed with the aunts, but, as he said, after
that it was never the same. Had she been anyone else, Luca's
mother would have been sent to San Fortunato with the other
victims of the plague, but Don Manfredo had given her his
word and he kept it. He never allowed a doctor to see her but
tended her himself, said in fact that she was away while he
hid her in one of those forgotten back apartments of the old
house. He nursed her back to physical health, but she would
never be quite herself again. After the birth of the little girl she
had been carrying at the time of her illness, she became vaguer
and in many ways kinder. Afternoons, she received those who
lined up outside her door, though often she could not remember who they were. Even Luca, who also called on her twice a
summer, was greeted with blank but regal courtesy. Don Manfredo was almost too busy to see his son now. He had given up
his leisurely habits, everything including the dream of remodeling Palazzo Montefalcone. Money was suddenly too tight for
such caprices. Each morning he went to a ground-floor store-

room where a desk had been set up for him in the aisle between two long rows of wine barrels. He left only to sleep and eat. The rest of the time he checked and rechecked his peasants' reports, for he knew, as any wily padrone did, that they were not to be trusted. For their part the peasants missed the loud, friendly arguments with Donna Filomena, and soon caught on that Don Manfredo was so busy carping about details that he missed real dishonesty. The peasants were careful to give him the Fascist salute, and they counted out every grain of wheat, but they stole as many lambs and piglets as they liked. It was an unhappy household centered on the minute lives of those living within the four walls of Palazzo Montefalcone. There was no room for Luca there, and he soon understood he would have to find his own way alone.

". . . I only meant to tell you about that strange night at the Convent," he said. "In my mind it has always been the end of one world and the beginning of another . . . and instead I've told you the story of my childhood. I suppose every man feels his own life is unique and every change is a spastic detour. We couldn't get through the road we were on, so we have a ready-made excuse for changing destination. Have you ever seen those toy cars with electric motors? If they run into an obstruction they veer off and race along until they are blocked again . . . that's the way human beings want to think they act. Fate changed their course as suddenly as lightning can destroy a tree. Fate shunts them from one decision to the next. But, you see, I don't think we make big decisions. I think we're born in one place with one set of limitations and the decisions we make, or those made for us, are small and always based on the prejudices of that immediate little world. The big decisions are preordained by that myriad of little ones . . . there is no escape. Human life is a repetition, with infinite variations, of all those little decisions. Look at it this way. If there were only big decisions we would be on the attack all the time . . . we would climb the landslide in our way or make a detour and march on. Instead we're on the defensive, warding off one small disaster with a sidestep, slipping away from another, backtracking to avoid yet another, and in the end we explain it very solemnly as fate. Maybe the spirits of the dead did haunt the church that night, maybe they didn't, but I almost believe they wander the earth seeking peace. I'm a grown man and a doctor, but you can't belittle childhood realities out of existence. Those spirits were real to me then, and they're still real. It's easier to believe in spirits here, you know, than in any other part of the world. We need them to share our misery. We're not Anglo-Saxon. We nourish our superstitions and we worship our dead. We trust them because we trust their mistakes. We can't trust atomic energy or synthetic meat . . . they have nothing to do with our world. Now I'm too far afield and it's past time for me to go. Sister Gioiosa will be locking the gates on me, won't you, Sister?" He had not raised his voice, but there was a giggle from the kitchen.

"I'd never do that to *you*, but the Superior'll be along soon accusing me of falling asleep . . . maybe we'd better close up."

We helped her turn out the lights and lock up. It was a slow process. Somewhere on her ring was a key for each door we went through, but she seldom chose the right one the first time. Finally we reached the arcaded cloister where the moon shone so bright we could see the shadow of the well's yoke on the rough stone paving.

"Have you ever noticed the frescoes here?" Luca asked. "Dampness has ruined whole sections, but come some morning and look at them. They're the record of a thousand years of diocesan history — by a mediocre painter — one of the gorier sections shows the priests of the Chapter murdering their Bishop. You see, Torregreca is unusual in every way. I hope you can be happy here. Good night, Ann, I'll see you tomorrow. Good night, crazy Sister Gioiosa."

And he was gone.

III

MATRIX OF DAYS

Early the next morning, dressed in a prim, long-sleeved cotton dress that would not shock the flesh-shy Torresi, I headed for town, a fifteen-minute walk. It was sultry and the musk of sunbaked chaff and manure was in the air. The peasants had trailed to the fields hours before, leaving the town silent: abandoned cardboard scenery for a crusader epic. The Lower Piazza was forlorn with its patched-up buildings and its mongrels lying tail to nose in the needle shadow of the war monument. Miniature twisters of yellow clay dust cavorted about and already the paving stones were hot enough to shimmer. Off in one corner, almost hidden by a lank oleander bush, was the office of the town *guardia*, one of the eight varieties of police who keep order. Two men, one very tall and thin, the other entirely round, were lounging in the doorway. They straightened up, bowed formally and beckoned me over. Their uniforms might have come from a military jumble sale, but loyal to a vague esprit de corps both men wore frayed white shirts and black ties. The tall one introduced himself as Mastro Pancrazio and added:

"I'm easy to remember. I'm the only man in town who's been painted by Carlo Levi." He had a thin, dour face and sad blue eyes and was much too absorbed by his own problems to waste energy on his work. He was accurate and nothing more. Most of every day he stood in the office doorway watching the Piazza without seeing it, driving trouble off with a sneer which had more to do with keeping his false teeth in place than it did with anything he saw. "Told everybody you'd be along this morning

— not before. Let me see, got a list somewhere. Yeh, here it is. Told the Mayor you'd meet him here at noon. Told the others who wanted to see you to come too."

The round policeman, Mastro Antonio, stood by, wigwagging his eyebrows in appreciation. He had no portrait to boast of, but was famous on his own as a man who never forgot anything he heard — particularly dirty stories. Too nervous to sit still, he trotted all day long and was the perfect foil to Mastro Pancrazio. His eyes were always bloodshot, his voice hoarse from long evenings in wine shops, but he never missed a day of duty. He made it his business to know exactly what every Torresi over five was up to and the biographical elements and admixtures of the citizenry were so cross-filed in his mind that a half-remembered name or address was enough to produce a family history. Fortunately he was neither a gossip nor a blackmailer. He collected tidbits and related them to other tidbits for his own pleasure as another man might work a jigsaw puzzle.

"Knew Don Luca went down to the Convent last night, so seemed safe to say you wouldn't be along then. Must have been late when he came back. Hadn't come before I went home," he said, lifting his eyebrows interrogatively. I decided he could just stay curious. And he was prepared to stay so, because he had something important he wanted to tell me: his daughter would be a perfect assistant in the nursery, and he had taken the liberty of telling her to meet me in the Piazza at noon. This reminded Mastro Pancrazio that he had promised two cousins that I would see to it they were given houses in the *villaggio* near the nursery.

My mornings in Torregreca were to be peppered with similar conversations. I would be trapped by people who wanted favors: a house, a job, a pension, war damages, places for children in camps or institutions, or cures in hospitals. Some asked with straightforward courtesy, others demanded, and a few tried blackmail and threats. "*Se volete, potete,*" was the cry. If you want to, you can. They assumed I was omnipotent. I tried to help anyone who needed information, but I had no jobs, no open sesame to hospitals and institutions, and I would neither accept nor write recommendations. Housing was assigned by a committee of town council members and provincial authorities. I controlled the places in our nursery — nothing more. I learned to say "no" firmly, but kindly. I started that first morning. In a town where work and food are scarce, everyone needs something. I could not help Mastro Pancrazio's cousins, and it would have been illogical to take Mastro Antonio's daughter as an assistant when her father had one of the town's few permanent jobs. I told them the truth as tactfully as I could. Years later Mastro Pancrazio told me he had not believed me, but as time went on and I refused to give preference to anyone, he decided to help me and he did. He was the best social secretary anyone could have!

My business that morning was to apply for my residence permit at the *Comune,* so I went on to the Upper Piazza where the palaces of authority contrived to make the human being seem insignificant.

Recently the Bishop had given Don Mimmi Mangiacarne, Don Manfredo's crony, an unused storeroom next to the Post Office for his shop. It was nothing more than a windowless closet, but there was plenty of room for the disordered collection of dusty boxes, bins, rusted picks and rolls of wire that made up Don Mimmi's inventory. The shop was not so much a commercial venture as it was an excuse for Don Mimmi to have an office in congenial surroundings. He did not want customers, but friends to come by to chat and let him talk about his six sons, who somehow had infiltrated the national and provincial ranks of authority. Each morning he was there before eight, sitting outside if the weather was fine, inside if not, waiting patiently for something to happen. Although other shops closed

from one until four, or even five, his did not. His lunch was sent
from home, the plates wrapped in a large white towel which,
spread on the counter, doubled as a tablecloth. This special
catering allowed him to witness the closing of the *Comune* at
two and the reopening of the Post Office at three. He could nap
in the intervening hour. Three mornings a week the barber,
who was also a postman, came to shave him and tend his boils.
It was a ceremony, a sort of royal levee, that Don Mimmi enjoyed most when he could sit outside. He was not in the least
self-conscious about the towel draped around his neck, nor the
lather, nor the felt hat pulled well down to protect his eyes
from the sun. He was attended by the barber and usually by
Don Evandro, an emaciated young priest with feathery black
hair that fanned out in a halo behind his high-domed forehead.
He was the Bishop's secretary, his temporal and religious ma-
jordomo. The diocese was Don Evandro's business and no detail of its life escaped him. Every application to the Bishop had
to be approved by him. He suspected the motives behind each,
but if his reasoning was devious, his conclusions were accurate.
His loyalty was beyond question. As the puniest of five boys in
a peasant family, he had been contributed to the service of the
Church by his father, who made it clear that his seminary tui-
tion was the last help the family would give him. Without special talents or a powerful backer, he had been relegated to an
abandoned parish in the bowels of Torregreca where the people referred to themselves as "Christians" (to distinguish them
from soulless animals) but felt no obligation to attend church.
On good days four or five old women wrapped in black shawls
dozed through the services and left only when they were
shaken awake. Don Evandro would have stayed there forever,
notable only for his refusal to starve to death, if the Bishop had
not been looking for a secretary who was versed in local machi-
nations but not a member of any faction. The young priest had
served the Bishop well, knowing when silence was tactful and

intervention necessary. In return he had power. Important decisions, public or personal, could not be made without first consulting him. His judgment and support were so respected that no town secretary dared act on his own initiative. Torregreca was ruled by divine edict of the government in Rome — and Don Evandro. There were rumours that he had his vices, but whatever they might be, they were too subtle for the gossips, who had found nothing more to support their claims than a mild gluttony for sausage and a predilection for gossamer-fine undershirts. Had they known, these morning sessions with Don Mimmi might have come under the general heading of sin, for Don Evandro reveled in the golden tales of luxury which had been so much a part of the old man's life, but never of his own.

Blinded by the glare of the Upper Piazza, I stumbled into the middle of the shaving tableau: Don Mimmi, his face lathered, his walrus moustache doves' wings of suds; the barber sharpening his razor on a strop; and Don Evandro standing by with a water jug in one hand. The priest recovered first, welcomed me to Torregreca, hoped I was comfortable with the nuns and demanded, tactfully, when I would make my formal call on the Bishop who, though ill, acknowledged no one's right to act without first consulting him. "We must be patient," he said smoothly. "Someday we too will be old." Don Evandro was too astute for guarded threats about the Bishop's power or local custom. "Come, you must meet one of the most important men in town. Don Mimmi."

The old gentleman struggled to his feet, tugging at his towel with one hand and tipping his hat with the other. Pure reflex made me stick out my hand, which meant that to free his own he had to drop his towel. We were in a terrible tangle, but to make up for it he bowed very low leaving a smear of sticky lather on my sleeve. Then, his deep voice quavering, he launched into a courtly speech.

"Welcome to Torregreca! May your stay here be rewarding and in every way to your satisfaction. We are a humble people, perhaps even ill-mannered, but in our souls there is only charity for our neighbors. This civilization flourished a thousand years before Christ, our Savior. Our ways are rooted in the past and you, who come from a new world, may find some of them strange. You cannot have known the glories of the Kingdom of the Two Sicilies as we have. You cannot be expected to yearn for the riches and fame of those centuries, but accept my word for it — this is a glorious people engaged in a death struggle with the forces of evil. We shall win, we *shall*, I say! We shall return to the days of sanity, order and Christianity. We shall!" His voice cracked with emotion and he had to stop. He cleared his throat. "I don't know that I've explained myself too well. I want to welcome you to Torregreca and to offer my assistance for whatever you might need, at any time. We are truly honored to have you join the army of the faithful."

Exhausted, he flopped back on his chair and panted. The barber gently took the hat from his hand and put it back on his head. Don Evandro retrieved the towel while I thanked Don Mimmi in my most subjunctive, baroque Italian. It was not clear into which army I was being drafted, but it seemed entirely safe to be against evil. I was, at length — until he was sighing, "Ah, that's good," "Yes, that's good." Reassured, he wandered off on general statements about my work, and how few women would consider being seen at such an early hour, and who in the town might be useful to me. I excused myself, mentioning my errand at the *Comune,* my residence permit.

"You don't need one here, I assure you. We know from looking at your face and from the good you have already done for the less fortunate souls among us that you are a kind and righteous person. You need no official paper with us. It is enough that we know your spirit. I respect your desire to comply with our regulations, but I tell you it is not necessary. If you wish to make a little call on Marietta . . . ummm . . . what's her name? . . . Mastro Carmine's girl, who sits up there all splattered with ink . . . why, call on her, but it is not necessary. I'm sure His Excellency the Bishop, and the Mayor would agree."

Town halls vary only in size, not in decor or atmosphere. A rancid bouquet of sweat, wet wool, manure and cheap cigarettes permeates the very walls. In the entrance, posted where no light bulb would ever illuminate them, were the notices of marriages, tax defaults, land sales, draft lists and examinations for state jobs. At the back of the hall, lighted by a ray of light from an open door on the floor above, were very steep stairs without a handrail. I knew before I went up that I would find that Latin demon, the usher, at a battered table in a room with an infinity of doors, but no windows. I did. He was sitting under a large white plastic crucifix laboriously marking his coupon for the weekly football pool. He stopped, with the tip of the pen resting on his tongue, and stared at me. Before I could say anything, he scuttered across the room and disappeared through a doorway. I waited, convinced he thought I would go away if he did not come back. Ten minutes later he peeked at me from the door of his exile. "Right this way, please." He stood aside and I found myself alone in a small room with four desks, four towering bookcases and a tile stove which might, once, have been Pompeian red, but was now frosted with white as though hundreds of pots of milk had been allowed to boil over and dribble their contents down its tiers. Papers were everywhere; on the floor, on chairs, desks and in bookcases. Full ashtrays, used as paperweights on leaning piles of documents, had spewed their butts and ashes. I removed a tray of yesterday's coffee cups from a chair and settled down.

Waiting to file requests for permits seemed to be my fate. For years in the Abruzzo I had fought a losing battle with a clerk named Cupid, who was not only a devout Fascist but a hater of all foreigners. When he could think of no other form of insult, he left me waiting half an hour, even an hour, without a chair. There I had been rescued by a moustachioed old gentleman who sat in the next office muffled in a fur-collared overcoat, a felt hat and the kind of flowing cravat associated with the old-fashioned, intellectual socialists. He was very gallant, lending me his chair in exchange for a cigarette and a talk. He always introduced himself, in one all-together phrase, as Don-Giacomo–Garibaldi–Stampa–Professor–of–Latin–and–Town–Archivist. We came to know each other well. The Fascists had accused him of subversion and had kept him in prison for twenty years. His wife died of shame, he said, and two of his sons had been killed in Africa. Still he felt no rancor; he dismissed Fascists as childish bullies. The end of the war had brought disappointment too, for the authorities considered his knowledge of Latin too outdated to allow him to teach. The appointment as archivist had been a democratic bribe, and he imagined himself back in prison if he refused, though actually sorting out twenty years of confusion suited and amused him. If he had it to do over again, he would not be a socialist — he would be a revolutionary! Still he was careful to retire with his chair before Cupid returned. Each time he urged me to insist on my right to a permit, no matter what Cupid said, and then left me as suddenly as he had come, with a bow and a prayer that I would understand why he felt it wise to leave. "No doubt we'll see each other again," was his fateful prophecy.

Treatment in Torregreca was to be very different. The door opened slowly and a bald head popped around at me, stared deep into my eyes and said "Not here?" The door closed. There was no sound of footsteps, but in a few minutes the same thing happened again except that the man had bristly black hair and said *"Scusi,"* before he vanished. In all, five gentlemen slipped their heads around the door to stare; I was on view. My sixth vis-

itor was the first to have a body. She sidled through the crack
in the door and leaned against the jamb, fixing me with the
patient eyes of a cow. Her rake-handle figure was not disguised
by the pleats and lamb-chop sleeves of her dress and her pos-
ing, copied from some long forgotten vamp, only emphasized
rag-doll awkwardness. Poor Marietta! With her delicate features and shiny brown hair she could have been pretty, but that
was not enough. She longed to be seductive. Her efforts only
made her vapid and boneless. She never did things abruptly.
She slipped and glided, edged and back-stepped with a tentativeness meant to be winsome. Whenever a man, married or
unmarried, came into sight she simpered witlessly, apparently
expecting to arouse manly passion. She lurked in the Piazza on
summer evenings trying to strike up conversations, and when
that failed she headed for home along the ill-lighted main
street, waylaying young men she knew, hoping for an invitation to coffee or a stray compliment. They understood her and
were kind enough, but instinct warned them not to be too gentle. She was the only child of Mastro Carmine, a tinsmith who
developed airs and graces when the Aqueduct Authority hired
him as maintenance man for the town water lines. Of course he
was hired for his soldering ability, but his was also the hand
that controlled the valves. He decided when ten thousand people would have water. *He* was now a member of the ruling
class, one of those who command — a State Official.

Mastro Carmine's whole personality changed with his new
job. Although he never gave up his square Hitler moustache or
his peasant conviction that a black suit and a black fedora
mean elegance, he was too cosmopolitan to be seen in work
clothes. Instead he wore a *vestito spezzato* — a split suit — the
coat and vest of a brown suit with the trousers of a gray one, or
vice versa. At least it was clear that he had two suits. He became active in the Church party, talked a lot about "political
conscience," referred to his half-acre vineyard as "my lands,"

and aspired to the title Don Carmine, though everyone called him Mastro Carmine as they always had.

He moved from a two-room house without windows to a new four-room apartment which was one of the fringe benefits of his position, in lieu of a decent cash salary. He splurged on new furniture — tiger-grained suites and red plush upholstery for everything, even the cover of the enormous new sewing machine that dominated the entrance hall. He had bought it all on time. His debts frightened him and he yearned for the good old days of narrow streets and plain neighbors. Every evening he took a chair outside his front door and sat in the drafty gloom of the landing waiting for someone to pass, for something to happen. There seemed to be little joy in power. He had taught Marietta that she no longer knew the people with whom she had grown up. He did not understand when almost the same snubbing technique was used on her. The sons of the ruling class needed no prompting: they did not know her.

If the Mayor had not been kind enough to walk her home several evenings, she might have remained marooned in the domestic limbo of the apartment. She was flattered that he had bought her a coffee: it might lead to something. When it did not, her father took the situation in hand and made an appointment to see the Mayor about a "private matter." Stripped of moral double-talk, Carmine's proposition was clear — either the Mayor could appoint Marietta to a clerkship in the *Comune*, or he would be accused, publicly, of sexual immorality, lewd proposals to a virgin lady, and lustful behavior. The Mayor would never have been able to prove his innocence. Marietta was enchanted with the job and presided over the ledgers for births and deaths, marriages and police relations in a manner worthy of Burke's Peerage.

This morning she said nothing, but eased in behind a desk without taking her eyes off me. She simply stared — impersonally — nor did she seem about to say anything. We were in danger of slipping into a trance.

"I came to apply for my residence permit. I'm sorry to bother you, but I know it should be done as soon as possible."

"Residence permit," she murmured, as though she had never heard of such a thing. "Oh, yes, residence permit. Then you speak Italian? Say something else!"

"I've spoken Italian for a good many years now. Almost no one speaks English down here, you know." She was still watching me. I might have been a performing snake. "I studied in Florence. It was frustrating. I understood everything that was said to me, but I was too timid to answer. When it was starve or talk, I learned soon enough." I stopped and waited.

"You sound Italian. . . but then your family must be Italian."

"No, I just had to learn."

"I suppose you're rich," she said in a vague, disembodied voice. "All Americans are. How old are you?" She would find out soon enough if we ever filled out the permit, but I told her. "Oh, really. You look younger," was her answer. "I suppose most blonde women do look younger," she went on, "that is, until they get wrinkled and shriveled. But where are my manners? Wouldn't you like a coffee?" She called for the usher who arrived too promptly. He must have been at the keyhole. Eventually a dirty little boy brought a tray with wet cups, spoons in a glass of water and a battered jug with coffee sweetened until it was syrup. He leaned against a desk and settled down to listen to the rest of the story of my life. The usher and two clerks lounged in the doorway. From the expressions of wonder on their faces it was almost as exciting as a new film, but it did come to an end. I asked again if I might file a request and Marietta began to riffle piles of papers saying, "There must be the right form here somewhere. Maybe this one . . . no, that's the character reference the Mayor signs for immigrants. I wonder. Maybe that would do."

I could hear cars out in the Piazza and voices. The commercial day was beginning, just before ten o'clock. Nice leisurely pace, I thought, noticing that even the flies were making adventurous sorties on the old coffee cups.

"This must be it. Now let me see. What do the instructions say . . . ?" She typed the application, listing properly my name, address, date of birth, place of birth, profession, religion and marital status. Then in round, childish script she filled in the form, which was printed on a fine grade of yellowing blotter paper.

It had taken over an hour and, though I was sure she must have something more important to do, she insisted on leading me downstairs and into the Piazza. "Because," she whispered, "I have something to say to you where no one will hear us." Outside the sun was so hot it stung my face.

"Don't worry about your permit. The Mayor will sign it today and the approval of the *Questura* in Matera is a matter of form." She spoke so softly I could hardly hear her. I glanced around, but there was no one near us. "I was honored by your visit and feel we've made friends today. This is the beginning of much closeness and love — and to prove my friendship I must warn you. The Torresi are treacherous, two-faced people. Watch out! I know what I'm talking about and I know you will need friends. Count me as one of the most loyal. Good-bye, and remember what I've said." Once more she fixed me with those wide, dull eyes. They seemed to implore me to understand her, to take warning.

Don Mimmi had retreated to the musty darkness of his store, Don Evandro to his official duties. But both the Post Office and the bank were open and attracting business. Across the way on the curb I saw Luca talking to Don Gaetano, the postmaster, who seemed to be inspecting the Piazza stone by stone. After forty years' tenure, three more than the Bishop, the Upper Piazza was his private realm. He spent much of each day there on guard, with his black smock thrown open and his hands stuck deep in the pockets of his baggy trousers that were hiked up so high they cut across his tie just below the knot. His body was permanently curved in the bureaucrat's hunch which pushed his head forward like a turtle's and forced him to look up at whoever talked to him. He was nodding at Luca, who waved to me and shook hands with Don Gaetano.

I had started down the Corso when Luca caught up with me. "I've saved you an hour and a horrible cup of coffee!" he announced, slightly out of breath but pleased with himself. "Don Gaetano wants to keep your mail in the Post Office. He says it'll be faster if you come for it and then not even the postman will know what's in it. There's no point in hiring a box . . . they're overpriced. He'll just stick you in with the *Comune*."

"That's nice of him, but I'll have to drink the coffee when I go to thank him, won't I?"

"Um, hadn't thought of that." Luca sounded disappointed, but I could not see his face. He was staring at the tips of his shoes. Then he jerked his head up. "I wouldn't thank him too much, if I were you. It's just come to me that by keeping your mail in the Post Office he has more time to look it over himself. Gave it away with that crack about 'even the postman won't know.' Who'd think of something like that? Obvious. Someone who *does* want to know. That's old Gaetano for you. Never got over Fascism. Everything used to be reported to the police, but they wouldn't be interested anymore. Now who would be? I know — the Bishop. Of course, the Bishop." He squinted in concentration. "Come on, let's sit in the sacristy for a minute while I figure this out."

We were opposite the back door of the Cathedral, but I could see little reason for going inside.

"Luca, I can't use the sacristy as a public waiting room; besides why should we go 'in' anywhere?"

"I'll tell you. If we stand here another thirty seconds, everybody in town will be wondering what we're talking about. You keep on the move if you want to avoid gossip here; besides, I think better sitting down. Now come on. If you're with *me*, you can do anything you want in the sacristy. There's nothing sinful about sitting in the cool." He pulled the door open and motioned me through into a dark side corridor formed by the back of the choir stalls on one side and the sacristy wall on the other. In the gloom his voice seemed deeper than it had in the street. "See over there, Ann. There's a frieze set in the dado. They found it when they dug out the crypt for the Bishop's tomb. Matteo said it would disappear if he didn't do something in a hurry, so he had it stuck in the wall there. Take a look at it. Seems to be Daphne turning into a laurel. Of course Apollo looks more like a satyr, but that just amuses Matteo. They say it's unusual to have the laurel worked with acanthus." Down in a corner of the narrow hall near the door was an oblong of pink-white marble, more of a plaque than a frieze since it was bordered on all sides and almost indistinguishable from the trompe l'oeil painted marble panels of the dado. I had to strike a match to see clearly. The rough chisel marks were still visible in the unpolished background, but the patina of the figures in relief gleamed in the flame. The border was marble lace.

"Does Don Matteo know how it got into the crypt?" I asked.

"No, and he doesn't dare ask anyone for fear the Arts Commission will take it away. Or worse, the Bishop will hear about it and object to it as inappropriate. It's not exactly Christian." Luca was feeling his way along the wall looking for the door. I lighted another match. In one corner of the plaque, close to the lower border, was an animal — a wolf, or from its bulk more probably a bear. Apollo was Diana's brother; the bear was her symbol and she was the goddess of childbirth. I wondered, but

Luca was impatient. "Come on, I'm holding the door. You go in the sacristy and I'll hook up the secret wires so we can have some light."

Once in the room I understood. From a small rose window, high above what might be an altar, frail shafts of sunlight were clouded by a fog of dust particles that danced in the air. The lower two-thirds of the room were obscured by a cottony darkness. Three walls were lined with wooden stalls, each with griffin armrests and black oak panels that reached upward to the ceiling. I could just make out a cabinet, taller than I, running the length of the fourth wall and above it ecclesiastical gentlemen, Bishops of Torregreca I imagined, had been spotted about on random nails which must originally have been set for a different collection. This was the Chapter Hall, surely, not the sacristy. The lights flickered and then stayed lit. About halfway to the ceiling above each stall hung a swan-necked fixture with a glass custard-cup shade. Only a few actually had bulbs. The door opened and I turned, expecting Luca. Instead a very old, bent priest shuffled in. When he saw me, he stopped and teetered for balance.

"I'm terribly sorry," I began. "You see . . ."

"Not at all, not at all. I didn't mean to intrude. I'll only be a minute. Just came to pick up something in the next room." And he disappeared through a door I had not even seen at the end of the high cabinet. Luca came back, muttering about the wiring as the priest reappeared from the back room. He wished us good morning and left without a backward glance.

"Now that should cause more gossip than standing in the street."

"Oh that's just Don Alfonso. He's nearsighted and forgetful. He won't even be sure who he saw," was Luca's answer. "Now leave me alone for a minute while I think. Look at the wood carving over there, the thing that looks like an altar. It's local work, Torregreca in the sixteenth century, and those winged cretins in the sky are the town protectors — saints every one."

Luca chose a corner stall and sat with his head back against the paneling and his legs stretched full length in front of him. He might have been taking a nap. The wood carving that was supposed to hold my attention had a primitive, dusty charm. I blew on it, but the details were still outlined in gray fur; there was a tower, a child's tower, tall and crooked with crooked toy houses around it, and above in the sky, dragging their very large feet across the rooftops, were the protectors of Torregreca struggling to maintain their lighter-than-air status. One seemed to be Saint Rocco holding his hand in front of him as a perch for a wooden Staffordshire poodle sort of a dog. The others I could not identify.

"Yes, I think I've got it. Old Gaetano has had a bad morning, or he'd never have given himself away. He'll watch your mail and report anything interesting to the Bishop. They never saw eye to eye until after the war. Gaetano believes in authority, absolute authority, and once Mussolini fell, the Bishop was all that was left." He paused; but sensing that I was not to interrupt, I started to dust the carving with a handkerchief. "He got a chewing-out this morning from the regional director for opening the windows in the Post Office. Seems the clerks complained to their union in Rome — the drafts were giving them colds. Swine! Haven't the nerve to face old Gaetano . . . ask him not to open the windows. Oh no, not them. Then the old man steps out in the Piazza and finds some boys trying to tear the lids off the mail slots. He drove them away, but the carabinieri wouldn't come. He wanted to arrest the kids . . . cited the law and the paragraph number. He carries the civil code in his jacket pocket, you know, so he can 'enforce the law,' he says. It's his bible. He must have been flustered, or he would never have given himself away. Anyway, watch out. Keep an eye on your mail and let me know if it has been opened."

"But, Luca, I won't get anything worth that much trouble, and most of it will be in English."

"Worse! More apt to be plots in code," he laughed. "And what were you up to at the *Comune?*"

"Now who wants to know everything?" I waited, but he made no excuses. He just shrugged. "Nothing very important. I went to apply for my permit . . . gave everyone a bit of a thrill. They came to gape, and then Marietta couldn't find the right form."

"Humm, Marietta's an interesting case. She's suddenly a devout church mouse. Matteo says she has her eye on an engineer who's doing some work for the Bishop's Palace. But you shouldn't have gone, Ann. It was a mistake to *apply*. Never let them treat you like one of the rest. You must always present yourself as special . . . different . . . superior. Be arrogant, ignore them! Never be one of the herd. The only way they'll respect you is the old '*Lei non sa chi sono io!*' You don't know who *I* am. Everything is privilege and bluff here. The more supercilious you are, the more important you must be. It's the only way to deal with authorities."

"Now wait a minute," I said. "I have to have my permit, and the way to get it is to apply for it. If I make a few friends in the process, so much the better. Let's go back to the Corso. I have better things to do than start the gossips up my first day in town."

"Ah, such innocence!" He might have gone on, but he was interrupted by a deep voice from the door.

"Donna Anna's got more sense than you, Luca. She's no innocent. Four different people have told me you were in here. The last was Don Alfonso. Come on, the party's over!" It was Don Matteo, smiling and not so irritated as he tried to sound. I made a face at him and he laughed. There was no way to keep him from using the title "Donna" with me. I had objected often that neither my age nor my accomplishments warranted it; his reply was always the same: "If I have to call every twirp in town 'Don,' then I can surely use 'Donna' with you." And that was that. Matteo, though younger than Luca, was balding and plump enough so that his cassock was more of a slipcover than a flowing robe. His full, very red mouth and twinkling brown eyes offset the long, hooked Montefalcone nose. He was merry, blushed easily and laughed often. Matteo was the domestic brother, the one who should have married, who loved and took care of a house and needed company. Instead he had hobbies. He restored pictures and followed the excavations of the Magna Grecia. He had a habit of lifting his eyebrows in an emphatic *circonflexe* which gave him such a look of plaintive desolation that the old ladies of his parish called him "The Sainted Don Matteo."

"What are you two plotting in here? If you want to scheme, do it right out in public — in the middle of the Piazza."

"Why not in the middle of the Corso?" I asked.

"Heavens no! That's for walking. The Piazza's for standing. Don't you know Don Evandro snoops and gives orders right under the gossips' noses, and they never catch him? They think he's just chatting in the Piazza. It's the national pastime. Now come on, out!" He took Luca by the arm and held the sacristy door for me, then the street door. "Now where are we going?" he asked when we were out in the sunlight. "Oh, that reminds me, did Luca tell you, Donna Anna, that the *daziere* wants to see you? We'll walk that far with you. It's just down the way here."

"Are you sure you want to see him today?" Luca's voice suggested that I was in enough trouble for one day without seeing the tax collector.

"I'll try the hard ones today; then tomorrow . . . "

"Then tomorrow you can start jumping the hurdles they put in your way," commented Matteo. "At this pace you'll tire in a hurry." I had never heard him make a more bitter remark about the Torresi who were, at that very moment, murmuring about us inside all the doorways of the Corso. Ancient buildings bleached flat by the sun made a corridor of the street. There were hundreds of people within the sound of our voices, but there was no one in sight. A bony hound peered at us from the wedge of shade he had found between a store shutter and the wall. Flies whined loud and the air was heavy with the miasma of stagnant sewers which only Mastro Carmine's generosity, or the evening breeze, could carry off.

"Don't let Matteo discourage you, Ann. This tax collector has been here six months and still hasn't brought his family from Sicily. No one would rent to him. He couldn't find a house, until the other day when a cousin of ours agreed to lease him a four-room house in the Rabata if he put up a two million lire deposit. He doesn't know it, but he'll never see that money again. Everyone in town's laughing. It's fun skinning a Sicilian; but you can get some comfort from the fact that they'd never be able to take *you* that way." Luca's good humor had returned and we had reached the tax collector's office. Neither he nor Matteo had any intention of joining me, but I guessed they would pace back and forth from Piazza to Piazza until I came out. They nodded and strolled off down the Corso.

Fifty years ago Norman Douglas wrote, "We hear much of the great artists and speculative philosophers of old Italy. The artists of modern Italy are her bureaucrats who design and elaborate the taxes; her philosophers, the peasants who pay them."* It is even truer today, and there is no better example than the *dazio,* a consumer tax, and its administrator, the *daziere.* As originally conceived, the *dazio* was a logical system of customs between the city states of Italy, but today, one hundred years after the Unification of Italy, it is fiscal idiocy that

---

* Norman Douglas, *Old Calabria,* London, 1915.

every morsel of food brought from Bari to Torregreca, every fig from a tree outside the town limits, every plastic comb from Milan and toilet bowl from Naples should be taxed as a foreign import once it comes to rest in Torregreca. Nevertheless the *dazio* exists and the *daziere* is the official snooper who makes peasants unload carts, and truckers stop to have their papers checked before they deliver their goods. Too often the men who relish such careers are bullies. At best they are easy to dislike. I found a rotund little man with a moustache, lying back in his chair, his tummy sticking up in the air.

"Oh, no, no! You mustn't come in until I have my coat on. Just a minute. Psst . . . Mario, bring up a chair, then take half an hour." A bald, rheumy-eyed man stepped past me. Immediately behind him was the *daziere*, a figure of bizarre splendor in a loud tattersall suit with a tight, belted jacket and flowing plus fours. It was his *sportivo* business suit, his idea of what every gentleman should wear in the wilderness. He was not interested in clean shirts or shaving, but was meticulous about his accessories: his pearl stick-pin, his swagger stick, his Alpine hat with a brush and his highly polished black boots. Cold weather produced the same costume in furry tweeds and herringbones. To his irritation the Torresi ignored him. I never bothered to find out his name.

"Forgive me, forgive me. Disgrace to be caught like that . . . this weather . . . do come in. Sit here, or is there a draft? Can't be too careful. Weather's treacherous here — whole damned town is for that matter. That's why I particularly wanted to see you." His voice softened to a whisper, his manner became more unctuous. "I wanted to warn you, to protect you so that you will not suffer as I have suffered. You know we have a bond, you and I." He paused, and leaned over the desk, breathing garlic and fresh brandy at me. "A bond of blood, you might say. I was born in Siracusa." He sat back in triumph and leered at me. I could not take my eyes off the curving, tortoise-shell fangs that were his little fingernails. He used them as scoops to clean under the other nails in an unconscious, perpetual motion that was both hypnotic and revolting.

"Siracusa?" I murmured.

"Yes, Siracusa. We're co-nationals, you see. You know in Sicily members of the brotherhood help each other. *We* must help each other in the same way . . . a brotherhood of Americans!"

"Syracuse, New York? You were born there, not in Sicily?" I must have sounded incredulous. He insisted on showing me his identity card; his birthplace was, indeed, Syracuse, New York. He might have been cooing to a favorite kitten as he stroked its back.

"Let's drink a glass of whiskey — in the American way — to us, to our brotherhood. Don't move. I'll just pull the shutter down so we can . . . "

"Just a minute! *Was* there something you wanted to discuss with me? If so, we'll do it with the shutter up. If not . . . I have a great many things to do. For your information, I do *not* drink whiskey in the morning, and I do *not* feel a blood kinship to all two hundred million Americans; still less to those who just happen to be born there. I would appreciate it if you said whatever it was you wanted to say quickly."

The *daziere* had been insulted and he knew it. He pounded on the table and spat at me that I was behind in my tax payments for the construction materials for the nursery. He would file a complaint of fraud. Then we would see how high and mighty I was! I suggested he check his files for my exemption permit before he embarrassed himself publicly.

"You will bow to the authority of the *daziere*," he shouted. "I can fine you for failing to sign the manifests — and I will." No manifests had ever been presented to me, but I refused to sign the copies he produced until I had checked the specific quantities with the foreman. It was yet another insult; I questioned his word. We were now clearly enemies and we remained such throughout his tenure. I never again went to his office. Once a year, undoubtedly when he was in trouble for lax administration, he sent his clerk to the nursery to beg me to sign the receipts. I did, if I had the duplicate and could be sure I had received the goods. Two years later the *daziere* was removed for "irregularities in accounts."

I sailed out of the *daziere's* office straight into the arms of an old crone wearing a long skirt and a wool shawl draped over her head and shoulders. She hugged and kissed me and crooned in dialect, "Where you going, dear? Out shopping? Can I do anything to help you?" No day in Torregreca was complete without this ritual encounter with Old Ida. She was the slightly addled, toothless and almost blind errand boy of the town. The joys of her life were limited to the loving conversations she had with the people she considered "important." She had decided I was to be one of them. "If there's nothing I can do for you, I'll be moving along, dear. I'm too frail for this work, but my husband's old and no good. Got to keep body and soul together." And off she went, cackling to herself. Her husband was "Gesù Eucaristico," the porter at the boys' seminary.

There were more people about and a general air of bustle. The hour before closing might bring some trade. Shopkeepers came out and stood in their doorways playing with the metal chain curtains hung to keep out flies. Like high priests, butchers sharpened their knives behind raised altars of gray, veined marble and smiled confidently toward the street though they offered nothing more enticing than hoofs fringed with dried, jagged skin. One grocer, two merchants and one butcher stopped me to explain quite frankly that they had supported the idea of the nursery. Two said they were members of the town council. They assumed I would not forget them when ordering supplies. One favor deserved another.

Even with the delays I arrived in the Piazza at noon, just as the Mayor stepped out of a barber shop to meet me. This kind of precision had already earned him the nickname "The German." A month later we were both known as "The Germans." We followed each other's progress carefully, for this Piazza sport of dubbing people was an accurate barometer of standing. The wags moved me on from "The German" to *La Brigadiera,* a female brigadier, partly because I was considered very tall and commanding, partly because I walked as much as I could — always at a good clip in hopes no one would stop me. Undoubtedly there were many nicknames I never heard, but one that still follows me like a shadow is *La Guappa,* a Neapolitan word often used about the ferocious papier-mâché monsters of Carnival and Piedigrotta. The implication is that I snarl and bark, but I do not bite. Nicknames are not meant to please, but I came off somewhat better than the Mayor. Before his term expired he had to be away from Torregreca most of every week and could return only on weekends. He became *Il Musichiere,* who comes on every Saturday night, after the ebullient master of ceremonies of a popular Saturday night variety-quiz show on television. Umberto Loschiavo deserved better. He was a tall, thin young man whose looks were not remarkable except for his curly, carrot-red hair. No matter what the season he wore a gray suit and very large sunglasses which were silvered in such a way that they mirrored everything the Mayor saw while masking his face so effectively that it seemed at best expressionless, and sometimes hostile and critical. Everywhere he went, he went in tandem with his brother, Nando, who might have been his twin, even to the suits and sunglasses, had he not been a full head shorter. Because of an extreme stutter, Nando listened but never spoke, which prompted the crack that the

Mayor had four eyes, four ears and one forked tongue for defense. Both men were lawyers, marking time until a local cabinet minister could "arrange" suitable appointments in the civil
service. A key factor in their election had been their availability, as well as their contact with the minister and their youth,
which exonerated them from any embarrassing political past.
The "right-thinkers" had all been pillars of Fascism. They
were now the holy pillars of "Christ's Party," the *Democrazia
Cristiana*, but they were smart enough to know they needed a
bit of camouflage — a dab of democratic paint and recon-
struction starch — if they were to defeat the Communists. Fair,
energetic Umberto had seemed just the man. But the very traits
that had appealed to the party committee now made him unpopular, for he refused to go along with deals even for them.
Elsewhere he would have been considered politically naive; in
Torregreca he was branded a traitor. For himself, he was not
worried, but it saddened him that his father, who for thirty
years had been director of schools in Torregreca, would be left
to weather the force of the Torresi's displeasure. It would be a
social censure, not a professional one, and it would only happen after his two hard-nosed sons had disappeared to their
ministerial sinecures in Rome. If no transfer could be arranged
for father, the petty jabs and vendettas of his erstwhile friends
would poison his last years like daily doses of arsenic.

But that morning the Mayor was gay and happy. He ordered
tables and chairs set out in the shade of the dusty oleander
bush by the *guardia*'s office and then called for aperitifs for
everyone, even Mastro Pancrazio and Mastro Antonio. Passersby stopped, shaded their eyes from the white glare, and
peered at us. The crowd grew until those in the back could not
see what they had stopped to see; those in front, listless and
open-mouthed, gawked as though transfixed by some emana-
tion visible only to them. Mastro Antonio tried to widen the

circle, but children wriggled to the front again and were soon at the rim of the tables. Our party changed. Don Matteo came, teasing us for sitting in the noon sun. I did not ask about Luca. I could see him standing under an awning watching us, ready for flight if there were any sign he might be involved. The Mayor's father came, threatening to whip the children if they would not leave us in peace, but they laughed at him — he was known for his kindliness. Lieutenant Mazzone of the carabinieri rated more respect. The crowd pulled back and was absolutely silent for the first time as he marched up all pressed and polished and shining pink from a new shave. He saluted briskly, then bowed over my hand and kissed it with such easy grace that I thought, indeed, we were at court.

Southerners are diffident with any member of the National Police, but the commanding officer is the embodiment of a power so absolute, so ruthless that he must accustom himself to a vacuum of fear that precedes him and freezes men into attitudes of self-conscious innocence. This young man had great poise. He seemed able to combine efficiency with wisdom. Nothing escaped him, but he could control seventeen townships without interfering in their normal life. As the two outsiders in town, we became great friends. Many an evening in the Piazza we amused ourselves talking about the vicious appetites of the local fleas or the discomforts of being without water. We laughed merrily at each other's tales of woe and convinced everyone we had nothing else on our minds, when, in truth, we were both stalling until the people we wanted to see came by in the *passeggiata*. We had a mutual assistance pact. For weeks that stretched into months I had no license for my car; Lieutenant Mazzone sent me the day's posting of the highway patrol each morning, that I might avoid them. When I had to get to Rome during the floods, he sent two of his men with me to dig me out of the mud slides. In turn I found special supplies for his men who had worked night and day rescuing people, and wrote glowing letters of praise to his commanding officer. And I helped with the hobby that consumed all of his off-duty time: applying for a transfer. He tried for special training courses, dangerous commands, anything that would get him out of Torregreca. It took four years, but he was eventually promoted, transferred, and decorated for the effectiveness of his administration.

It is hard for a young, moon-faced man to be dignified without being pompous, but sitting at ease in the Piazza that morning, sending boys off to find the *pretore* (our local judge), the *medico condotto,* the presidents of the political parties, and the local health officer, Lieutenant Mazzone managed to be important and informal at the same time.

The first to come was the *medico condotto,* a doctor who may have his own practice, but is paid by the government to care for anyone on the town poor list. Dr. Neri was a mild-mannered little man who reminded me of a myopic rabbit. He was painstaking in his work and kept very much to himself. That day, in June 1959, he offered to examine the nursery children three times a year and recommend any special medicines or treatment they might need. He is still (in 1967) faithful to that promise and has never been willing to accept a lira in return, though each visit throws him into a state of near apoplexy. He is terrified of driving, but it would be beneath his dignity to walk, so he overcomes panic by fortifying himself with cognac. The gossips say he leaves the nursery and goes straight home to bed.

The health officer proved to be quite another matter from Dr. Neri. It was his *duty* to certify the health of each child at the beginning of the school year, but he could neither be forced nor wheedled into doing his work. He slept on the balcony of his apartment in full view of his neighbors while his wife signed any certificates that were brought to the door. The system had worked for twenty-five years and it showed no signs of collapsing yet. When he appeared in public he was unshaven and seedy in food-spotted clothes. As the Mayor whispered to me, "He won't help you, but he could cause trouble."

That morning, Lieutenant Mazzone and the Mayor manipulated our court session into an official game of musical chairs. The losers, those without chairs that is, had to go off. So it was that I met the town council, though not a single member ever sat down. The health officer had his aperitif, but was a loser in the next wave of arrivals. The head of the Communist Party and the head of the Demo-Christian Party were allowed equal time, but were ruthlessly unseated by Don Matteo and the pharmacist. Don Evandro competed with the *pretore*, another round-faced young man with no inhibitions, in telling silly jokes, and Don Gaetano nodded to us as he passed on his way home for lunch. He would not join us because, of course, he was mad at Lieutenant Mazzone.

The crowd stood immobile, probably appreciating the niceties of the situation far more than I did. Dogs sniffed at our feet, but jumped away at the slightest wiggle of a toe. Once they were driven back by two carabinieri who stood guard behind us. The island of shade had widened to the edge of the crowd when Lieutenant Mazzone signaled one of his men and had a brief conversation with him. In a matter of minutes a police car was working its way toward the tables. "Whenever you feel you must go to the Convent, the car will take you. I will not allow you to walk in this heat." He sounded very firm, but he was smiling. When I whispered I had not known how I was to make my exit, he nodded. He had known. I think we became conspirators then. There was no excuse to manufacture. I thanked everyone, had my hand kissed a dozen times and was ushered to the car by the lieutenant and the Mayor.

People crowded around and dogs began to settle in the shade of the radiator. The driver drove them away with a blast of the horn. The plenary session was adjourned.

That first day was much like any other day in Torregreca. I saw the same people, repeated the same conversations, had the same promises and the same warnings made to me each day. I was never as much an object of curiosity to them again, but they would always stare at me. They would always ask me intensely private questions as though they had some right to know the answers, and demand favors that I had no way of granting. They were kind and welcoming, most of them, in a way that is seldom found in busier parts of the world. I must be honest: they fascinated me. Luca was right. The truth was to be found in what they did *not* say . . . and they seemed to say so much. But the open friendliness of that first morning was important for another reason. These were the *pezzi grossi* of the town, the ten per cent who controlled the other ninety per cent, and forty-eight hours later only three of them — the Mayor, and Luca and Matteo Montefalcone — would speak to me when they came face to face with me in the street. On my permit application I had given my religion as Protestant. Marietta had been quick to sound the alarm; the witch-hunt was on.

IV

TRIAL BY ORDEAL

$\mathcal{S}$UNDAY evening, as I went through the cloister of the Convent toward the back stairs that led to my room, the Mother Superior appeared in the doorway of her office.

"Signora, I would like a word with you." It was a courteous order with no suggestion of choice. She closed the double doors carefully and walked behind her desk without looking at me. When she turned, she held her crucifix well in front of her body — like a shield, I remember thinking.

"Today I've been informed of a very grave fact . . . if fact it is . . . and, of course, I have denied the truth of it for your sake and for ours. You *are* staying with us, after all; the implication is clear. However, you will understand why I must ask you to deny what has been said." She paused, clearly expecting me to reject her facts, but not knowing what they were, I remained silent. "I see," she said slowly, raising her chin and stiffening her mouth until her next words came from rigid lips. "You choose not to understand. Very well. Four different people have come to warn me today — among them Mastro Carmine's daughter, Marietta. They felt it their duty to tell me. You are a Protestant?" I nodded.

Collected for a battle that had already evaporated, the Mother Superior stared at me, trying to find some explanation in my face. She was not angry; she had not met the devil, but she was surprised at my easy, almost casual confirmation of her fears. I must have been the first non-Communist Protestant she had ever seen. Even then she accepted that excommunication, which had driven so many Italian Catholics into maverick Protestant sects, had had no part in my life. That an intelligent person could reject the True Church was the wonder to her.

"You will wait for me in the Mother General's dining room." Strange how easily mothers and Mother Superiors demote adults to children. I went off meekly, wondering why I had not announced that the Italian Constitution guaranteed religious freedom, or, even more to the point, that the application form I had filled out was a leftover from the Fascist era and peppered with illegal questions, among them the question of my religion. Thirty minutes can be a long time in a room with nothing in it more amusing to look at than dishes — time enough to wonder what the treatment of a modern day heretic might be. Hot irons, a dungeon? Savonarola was a heretic, after all, but not a Protestant; was that better or worse? The grunt of the icebox interrupted my thoughts. I peeked inside. A dish of strawberries probably intended for my dinner looked tempting. I decided it was appropriate for the condemned to smoke; a note of gentle defiance. It was while wandering back and forth with my cigarette that I first noticed, almost hidden by a cupboard, a vividly colored print of Christ on the Cross framed in a deep shadow box. The next time I passed it had become Christ, bearded and severe, pointing to His own glowing red heart. I was too deep in my own thoughts to be surprised. I had the explanation now for the strange things that had happened during the day. Why Don Gaetano had been absorbed in a minute inspection of cobblestones when I passed. Why Don Mimmi seemed not to recognize me, and why Lieutenant Mazzone had saluted, but had not stopped to introduce me to the elaborately coiffed lady who hung on his arm. Once out on the road, away from the Piazza, the remote glow of the street lights had kept me from knowing who did not speak, but I had felt I was being avoided. Now I understood. They had learned that I was a

Protestant; it would be safer to let me await my fate alone, not to be too closely associated with me. Suddenly I focussed: the picture was a crucifix again. Closer examination showed it to be a print of the crucifixion with vertical baffles. If the viewer moved a few feet to either side, it became the Sacred Heart. Religion and optical magic! I unhooked it to take it over to the table where the light was better.

The door was flung open and in stalked Sister Clemente.

"Put that down," she ordered in the same harsh, arrogant voice she used with her subnormal farm laborers. She snatched the picture away from me and passed it back over her shoulder without looking. A hand took it. Unseen, Sister Eufrasia, who presided over the kitchen cauldrons, had come in behind Sister Clemente. Had she not been short and fat, she would have been the classic Halloween witch with her beaked nose, bushy black eyebrows and aluminum teeth. Her disposition matched her figure. Her good humor, buoyed by a steady stream of complaints, spurred her to produce thousands of tons of spaghetti a year. Her extravagant appreciation of any joke, no matter how feeble, was well known. In fact anyone who found her giggling to herself while she stirred her pots assumed her glee was a delayed reaction to some mild, ecclesiastical fun. After eating her sour brews I am not so sure; it might have been the joy of revenge that made her so happy. She was about to celebrate what she called her "Twenty-fifth Wedding Anniversary" as a Bride of Christ.

"All Protestants are thieves . . . and murderers," muttered Sister Eufrasia. "Murderers, I say! And to think I killed a rabbit for your lunch tomorrow." This was to be her leitmotif throughout the informal inquisition. "For murderers and thieves — one of my rabbits — *ma* . . ."

The two nuns lined up four chairs on one side of the table and motioned me to one opposite. We sat in silence, waiting,

looking at each other uncertainly until the door opened again
and the Mother Superior came in followed by the Novice Mistress. In any convent where novices are trained the Novice Mistress is an Olympian personage, a severe paragon of religious
virtues and comportment. Sister Giustizia lived up to her calling. She was so slender nothing obstructed the knife folds of
her habit. Her veil was always straight. She drifted through the
Convent at incredible speed, her skirts swinging gracefully but
never enough to expose even the tips of her shoes. She was all-
seeing, all-knowing and, as the novices soon found out, relent-
less. What was not right, was wrong. She admitted no middle
ground. She never softened. Everything she saw was, at best, a
disappointment. Though she saved her reproofs for the girls
under her care, the other nuns stood in awe of her, sensing her
unspoken disapproval in the way she pursed her lips and tilted
her head inquiringly to one side. You could believe she had
been born full-grown in a nun's habit — without physical
weakness and certainly without little brothers and sisters who
suffered with measles or wet their beds. It was almost a comfort to me when, years later, I found out she was human; she
was tortured by an earthly, feminine plague — varicose veins.

Now they were four lined up opposite me like black crows
on a fence. There would be no sham of fair play.

"I'm sure you'll understand why in such circumstances a
Mother Superior must not act alone. She must have the advice
of other members of the religious community." As the Mother
Superior talked, her face relaxed. Her mouth no longer seemed
rigid, clamped to her teeth as it had been earlier in her office.
The absolute propriety of what she was saying brought serenity. "As you know, various talents divide nuns into two groups;
those who perform administrative or directional chores, what
we call *lavori di concetto,* and those who are more fitted for
manual work. Before God we are equal, of course, but it is
proper that both sides of our community be represented in con-

sidering your problem. Now . . . state please, in their hearing, what you have already confirmed to me."

I raised my eyebrows in question, but did not answer.

"You know exactly what I want you to say." Her voice, normally so soft and calm, had an edge. I waited. She would not state I was Protestant. My silence might force her to the embarrassing admission that she listened to gossip. Finally exasperated, she said, "Very well. Have it your own way. It has been brought to my attention — if you prefer, there have been rumors — that you are a Protestant. Are you?"

"Really, rumors are quite undependable." The Novice Mistress pinched her lips together in distaste. Then she went on. "There is a certain lack of dignity . . ."

"Are you a Protestant?" broke in the Superior.

"Yes."

"You realize you cannot stay in Torregreca." In the face of my silence, she continued. "The Bishop will never allow it."

"He knows all about me, Reverend Mother, but if he didn't and objected to my staying, could he actually *force* me to leave?"

"Liar!" Sister Eufrasia had deserted her rabbit for the moment and was leaning across the table, waggling her finger at me. "The Bishop never knew about you. All Protestants are liars."

"Sister Eufrasia, I will *not* be called a liar. Don't forget, if I had given my religion as Catholic on the application, no one would ever have known the difference."

My rage had brought her bolt upright in her chair. "I didn't mean *you.* I meant Protestants . . . Oh, I'm getting muddled. No offense meant." She could not quite forget all the years she had known me. "You're not a liar."

"That will be enough, Sister Eufrasia," the Mother Superior announced firmly. "Now, to your question. I'll make my answer very simple. Without a residence permit you cannot stay in

Torregreca. The Prefect of Matera would not go against the wishes of the Bishop. Instead of your permit you would be given three days to leave the country."

We sat in silence until the Novice Mistress asked permission to question me.

"Signora, I have heard there are many different sects. To which do you belong?"

I was in trouble. My knowledge of ecclesiastical terminology in Italian was so limited that I dreaded the thought of a theoretical discussion. My first compromise was to identify the Episcopal Church with the Church of England.

"I belong to the Anglican Communion, which is the national religion of England as Catholicism is the national religion of Italy. England is a Protestant country but Catholics are not excluded. Why should Protestants be excluded from Italy?"

"Because they always have been," was Sister Giustizia's dry answer. Logic was her daily trade. "And what are your connections with the sect now active in Torregreca?"

"I didn't know there was one."

"In front of four witnesses you would pretend that you have no part in the Protestant conspiracy? *Vergogna* [Shame]!"

"I don't 'pretend,' as you say, at all. I state flatly that I know nothing about any such conspiracy." It all sounded so melodramatic.

"Ah, you know nothing about it . . . Indeed . . . Then you deny having contacts with the Communists as well? You are not active in the Communist-Protestant scheme in Torregreca? You should know, before you answer, that the excommunication of Communists has been very effective. The party hold has been weakened . . ."

"*Superiora*, did you hear they had a pastor come from Matera yesterday to bury an old man?" Sister Clemente could stand it no longer, she was fairly bursting with news. "And this morn-

ing there was a wedding. What do you think of that?" She gave
a gleeful cackle.

"Immoral," sniffed the Novice Mistress.

"I say they're all murderers!" Sister Eufrasia.

". . . You haven't heard the best yet! Last night he played
the guitar and read the Bible at the bride's house. People were
dancing and singing in the street outside — they didn't go in,
of course, but they whooped it up. They say this pastor doesn't
know much about the Bible, but he sure can play the guitar."
Clearly, Sister Clemente was sorry she had been left out of a
good party.

"That will *do,* Sister Clemente. We are discussing something
quite different." Sister Clemente blushed at the Mother Superior's rebuke. "However, tomorrow morning I'll remind Lieutenant Mazzone of his duty. He is becoming lax, I fear. Laws
must be enforced. Fortunately we are well protected against
such disgraceful exhibitions. Now, as to the sect, Sister Giustizia, I believe they call themselves Evangelists. Quite different
from the Anglican Communion. As I'm sure you know." Her
voice was frosty. She turned back to me and without changing
her tone asked, "Would you explain why you are Protestant
and what the beliefs of your church are?"

And so here it was, what I had hoped to avoid. The real
difference between the two churches is one of approach; the
believer's approach to God, the church's approach to the believer. I had two barriers to face, one of language, the other of
concept. Once I tangled with dogma, no matter how I tried,
my religion would sound a mediocre substitute for theirs.

"My Church is much like yours. It would have to be. It was
formed by men who rebelled against a few of the extreme
Catholic practices of their day. We use, virtually, the same
Bible and the same prayer book . . . but not in Latin. They
must always be in the language of the country so that they are

understood by everyone. Our God is your God. Christ was His son, born of the Virgin Mary for the redemption of our souls. He is our emissary with God. In every basic way our Churches agree. There are only two formal differences between us. My Church does not accept the virgin birth of Mary or the infallibility of the Pope. Surely the important thing is belief in Christ and the Eternal Father, in the Christian concept of the world and Christian love . . ."

"I beg your pardon," Sister Giustizia cut in. "What you call 'differences' are, and will remain, heresies in the view of the True Church."

The Mother Superior was kinder, but no less firm. "You allow yourself to be excluded from Divine Grace for these 'differences' you consider unimportant. It seems a high price to pay."

Then they all talked at once. Sister Eufrasia objected to heathens touching the Bible. Sister Clemente wanted to know if we denied all saints, as she had heard. It was unthinkable to Sister Giustizia that we did not accept the infallibility of the Pope. I tried to answer them, always avoiding any definition of God, for theirs was a wrathful God to be appeased, mine a forgiving God who asks repentance. My prayers to God appeared arrogant to them. Their saints as intermediaries suggested official channels to me. My minister was less divine to me than their priest to them. I wanted to avoid any argument about the Pope, if possible. In twenty centuries of Christianity, I doubt there has been a more lovable Pope than John XXIII, and it would be difficult to keep the argument to the office and away from the person. This was before the Ecumenical Council and its concern for "separated brethren." In the Torregrecas of the Catholic world, to be a Protestant was to be a pagan. Television and the Council have begun to color that absolute view. In theory, Protestants are Christian now, even in Torregreca. In practice there have been few changes made, except those specifically *ordered* and then with regret. In the summer of

1959 he who was not Catholic was godless. In a sense I had won a victory. We were discussing the differences between two Christian religions, not those of a pagan cult and The Christian Religion. We argued for two hours, not about dogma, but the Bible. Sister Giustizia and Sister Eufrasia objected to the availability of the Bible, for reasons so entirely consistent with their personalities that another time I might have been amused. Sister Eufrasia spluttered because It might fall into the hands of the Infidel . . . and convert him, I commented. Sister Giustizia was a bedrock case. Diffusion of the Gospels, properly edited, was one thing; the entire text another. People vary in intelligence and training. Their interpretations might vary — dangerously. Free to read the Bible, they were free to misunderstand. She was immovable. There should be no reading of the Bible without the supervision of a priest. Its sale should be controlled as the sale of drugs, the written permission of a parish priest taking the place of a prescription. How could I justify equal access? she demanded. I switched to more pertinent material. How did they explain that American Catholics and American Protestants lived side by side without persecution? How could they explain the same relationship in England? Why was the Catholic Bishop of London on the board of my organization which was totally nonsectarian? If Protestants were, by nature, so insidious, why had I signed a statement that I would voice no opinions or interfere in any way with Italian politics or the national religion? Politics and religion are private concerns in which a foreigner has no voice. I have none in Italy; a foreigner should have none in my country.

"Well," snorted Sister Clemente. "That's more than *we'd* do if we were sent to work in England or America."

"Sister Clemente!"

"We have a duty to convert pagans — even murderers and liars." Sister Eufrasia was on surer ground now. "I suppose you have a duty, too — to convert, I mean. Oh, n-o-w, don't try it on me." And she pointed her index and little fingers toward the ground in the traditional sign against the evil eye.

"Sister Eufrasia, how much do you know about the Reformation? About Protestantism?" I could not resist asking. "The words give it away. What were people protesting against? What needed reforming?"

"Sister Eufrasia will have learned quite as much as she needs to know from my predecessor," interrupted the Novice Mistress.

"I've forgotten. Didn't it have something to do with a king of England who wanted to get rid of his wife?"

"It's getting very late. I believe this subject can be saved for another time." The Mother Superior was quite right, but I sensed she objected less to the time than to the direction of the discussion. "Let's go back to the main issue. What do you intend to do now, Signora?"

"Exactly what I came to do — run a nursery. I'm not interested in converting children, I'm interested in helping them." I turned to Sister Eufrasia. "If the king of England wanted to get rid of his wife, who was protesting? Where did the name Protestant come from?"

She looked baffled. "*Signo'*, you got my brain tied up in knots. Talk to them about it. What I want to know is this . . ." her metallic teeth glistened at me. "Do you still want that rabbit tomorrow? I can do you a nice sauce . . . umph, never thought I'd feed one of my rabbits to a Protestant . . . makes you think!"

"Now look, I've got an idea." Sister Clemente was too fast for anyone to stop her. "That king of England had a daughter, Bloody Elizabeth. I bet they were protesting against her."

"She was Protestant herself; besides, it's her Catholic sister Mary who's called 'bloody' everywhere else. Bloody Mary killed everyone who objected to Catholic practices —"

"Please don't confuse Sister Clemente and Sister Eufrasia

any more," ordered the Mother Superior. "I think the best thing
to do is refer the matter to the Bishop. His decision will be
final. If he agrees that you may stay, we'll consider the matter
closed. If not, well . . . anyway, I'll discuss it with him in the
morning. Don't you agree that's the best solution?"

"Yes, in principle. I have an appointment to see him in the
morning. We could go together . . . no, no, don't misunderstand. I'll wait in the Piazza. If he confirms that he has known
for months that I'm Protestant and that he has no objections, I
will keep my appointment. If not, well, if not, I think it will be
a sad mistake. You lose a nursery for your own poor, but worse,
you admit that one Protestant, a woman at that, is so dangerous
that all the priests and nuns of Torregreca could not counteract
her influence. You'll make me more important than I am — and
you will look frightened at the same time. I don't envy you. To
answer your question, I'll accept the Bishop's decision."

"*Superiora*, don't you think she should have some tea? She
hasn't had any dinner." Sister Eufrasia was back to her usual
interest in essentials.

"Certainly. Fix it, fix it." Then to me, "Meet me in my office
at nine, please. We'll go to the Bishop together. Now we'll
leave you to think on the True God and seek forgiveness for
yous sins. Good night." The Mother Superior stood up to lead
the way. Sister Giustizia barely inclined her head. Sister Clemente said nothing until the others had disappeared, then she
gave me a broad wink and signaled she would be back.

I saw no one for ten minutes, but the whispers and clinkings
of pans that came from the kitchen reassured me about the tea.
Then the door opened and Sister Clemente announced, "*Arriva
il tè*." With mock dignity she bowed out of sight revealing Sister
Eufrasia with tea and biscuits on a tray. "Hurry up, you fat old
thing! Get in there, she's starving." As an afterthought Sister
Clemente asked, "You don't mind if we join you?"

"If you think you can risk it, come ahead."

"Ah, you're not so bad. The Mother Superior told you . . . we don't know about ideas. They do. We know about work — and people — that's more important."

She went to the icebox, looked startled by something she saw inside, and brought out a bottle.

"Nothing I like better than a beer before bedtime. Want some?" she asked Sister Eufrasia who giggled like a teenager.

"Well, if it's all in the family, I guess I'll have some brandied cherries."

When we were settled, each with her own tipple, Sister Clemente said, "Now, tell us more about this history business."

It was a long, still night interrupted only by Don Andrea's hourly trips to the lavatory and his bumbling with the doorknobs on his return. There was nothing to distract my thoughts from the next morning. I had met the Bishop once a number of years before. His only knowledge of me would have come through Don Matteo, if Don Matteo had remembered to speak to him. Surely he must have. It had been his idea: "I think it would be wise to tell the Bishop about you," he had said. "A young woman coming to live alone is an unsettling thought to any Southerner. The flesh is weak. It wouldn't do to create the climate of sin." He was daring me to take him seriously, but we both knew there was too much truth in the idea to ignore it. "Let me see what I can find in your past!" He found nothing scandalous until he said, "Are you a practicing Catholic, or one of those modern ones?"

"Oh, but Don Matteo, I'm not even Catholic. Didn't you know? I'm a Protestant."

"Presbyterian, I hope." I shook my head: Episcopalian.

"Umm, that's the story of my life. If I want vanilla, there's nothing but chocolate ice cream. I want to know more about Presbyterians, and the only live Protestant I've ever met is another flavor." His eyes had danced. "I know about your

Church. You're just fallen Catholics with a dash of puritanism thrown in. Not interesting. Presbyterians, now, they really are stubborn. But that's all right, the Bishop is an understanding man. It's better, though, that he knows before you come."

And that had been the end of our conversation. He *must* have talked to the Bishop, I told myself, lying there in the dark. Sleep would not come. I went over and over the words, new words, that I had heard that night, trying to memorize them. If I were familiar with them I might talk more easily. When I remembered that hesitancy sometimes rouses sympathy, I gave up, to wonder about my duties as a Protestant. Were the nuns right that I had an obligation to proselytize? No, I would not be muddled into judging myself by their standards. The Inquisition must have been a nightmare, at least for the innocent who could not prove what they were not. Each explanation must have made them seem more devious.

When I fell asleep it was already light, and minutes later Sister Gioiosa woke me with another thimbleful of black coffee. It was eight o'clock. As soon as she left I poured the inky brew down the basin and looked for Sister Clemente's stopper. It had disappeared, so I turned on the tap. No water! The day was off to a good start. The Mother Superior and Sister Clemente were waiting for me by the jeep which, for this special ride, had a backseat throne of straw covered with a burlap sack. I hoisted myself in and set my feet. It was useless. Nothing kept me from slipping and slithering around until I was a pincushion of straw spikes. Once in the Upper Piazza the Mother Superior and Sister Clemente left me to pick myself clean in the stinging heat of the canvas-topped jeep. Half an hour later I was plucking away, absorbed in this idiot work, when I was startled by a voice at the window.

"Si-gno-rra —" It was Don Evandro, scolding me with that one, drawn-out word. "What in the name of paradise are you doing out here in the sun? You must come in. His Excellency would want you to wait upstairs. The Mother Superior will be finished soon. Here, let me help you out of that pigsty."

He handed me down and started slapping at my clothes. "Permit me. You mustn't be seen this way." When he thought I would do, he led me into the dank blackness of the Palace entry which, on first impression, seemed a perfect place for raising bats. Once I became accustomed to the dark, I saw there was an archway opposite us that led into a large, sunny courtyard. With the two sets of arch doors closed, this was a room; with them open, it was a driveway through the body of the Palace into the courtyard. To our right a vast baronial staircase with a shoulder-high stone railing and giant stone urns for balusters led up to a landing, then curved back on itself and disappeared into the upper regions. No light suggested that it ever arrived at a floor. Far above us in the murk I could see tapestries flapping like limp flags against the wall. We started up the low, broad risers. On the second landing I came level with the tapestries and realized that what had looked small and thin from below was actually a hanging the size of a ballroom. The draft became icier with each step. Two more landings brought us finally to windows overlooking the Piazza. To our right, along the front of the Palace, were the diocesan offices. Don Evandro turned to the left and went a few steps down a corridor of one wing. He stopped at a highly polished double door and rang a bell. There was sibilant whispering on the other side and some scuffling before the door was opened by a prim nun with downcast eyes and hands folded in front of her as in prayer. She appeared too reticent to speak, answering Don Evandro's suggestion that I be shown into the *salone* with only a nod. She motioned me to follow her down the hall, opened a door and stood aside for me to go into a completely dark room.

"If you'll wait here, His Excellency will be along shortly."

"Thank you. But, Sister," — she turned back to me — "before

you go, could you open a blind? It's very dark in here." She said nothing and for a moment it seemed she might just close the door and leave me there. She shook her head impatiently, but started for the windows. Light, apparently, would not break any rule she could think of, though she had the reluctant air that I remember in the maids of my youth of someone who has been imposed on. She was methodical, pushing aside curtains, opening windows, folding back the outside shutters, reclosing the windows and rearranging the curtains. If one shutter was to be opened, they all must be opened. The flood of light revealed a drawing room for Goliath. Two stories high, it had six windows, three on each of the long sides, that went from the ceiling to within two feet of the floor. At each, lace and batiste curtains were flanked by deep red plush draperies. The narrower walls, those without windows, were covered by gigantic mirrors framed in massive curlicues of carved, gilded wood. I have never understood how they were lifted to the second floor, or once there, how they could be securely hung. Tilted slightly downward they reflected the white of the marble floor and the diocesan crest of Torregreca which was intricately worked in multicolored pieces of marble. My first impression that it was a stand-up room proved wrong, for between the windows there were stiff little groups of gold-framed loveseats and side chairs covered in red damask. I tried them all; they were uniformly uncomfortable. Like steel mushrooms they forced me to balance my body on a hard dome while my feet dangled several inches above the floor. My shoes were leaving telltale sandy tracks on the gleaming floor, so I settled for a straight chair facing the door.

In less than ten minutes my prim nun opened both sides of the double doors and the Bishop waddled in, smiling, waving at me to stay seated though he would have been offended if I had. Anyone who judged him by his walk was apt to make a mistake, for there was nothing of the fuddler in this short, tubby little man. His head, which was large for his body and square, was that of an aged, blue-eyed mastiff. Deliberate, his attention concentrated for the moment on the person before him, he radiated a private joy which he seemed to want to share. Even formal clichés of greeting were revived by his slow, deep voice to something like their original grace. But for all his gentleness and compassion he was not a man to be pushed and, lest you forget and try, he had a way of widening his eyes, lifting the folds of skin that hooded them, in a silent warning of displeasure. Thirty-seven years before, he had come to Torregreca as a young Bishop, bringing his sister to be his housekeeper. They were of a landed Neapolitan family unaccustomed to life in what he considered *terra di missione*, but they had come willingly, never thinking it was a commitment for life. Often I have heard him chuckle, a visceral grumbling of joy, and say "I have been fortunate. Each life should have one great love. In mine there have been two: God and my Lucanians." And he understood his Lucanians. Their sullen, unexpressed resentments, their reptilian attacks against wrongs they had tolerated for generations, their loyalty, their superstitious fear of God, Zeus, Ceres or the evil eye, whichever force seemed to be leading the race at the moment, all were explainable to him; for all there were remedies. Much had changed in Torregreca, and Communists and Catholics alike gave him full credit. His door was never closed and everyone in the diocese knew it. His children had drained him of energy, demanded his patience and his influence, and repaid him with personal devotion though they could not love his God or his Church. Still he was not bemused by human vanity. He would offer God's love and his own understanding as long as there was breath in his body without illusions about those who would soak up all he offered and ask for more.

"Ah, welcome to Torregreca. We have been looking forward to your arrival." He extended his right hand, not flat for

me to kiss, but vertical. He smiled very gently, encouragingly.
We were to shake hands. "I hope the nuns have been kind to
you. If not, I have a *bit* of influence with them . . ." He
chortled and glanced behind him where the Mother Superior
stood smiling uncertainly.

"They've been very kind and patient, but I'm afraid I'm causing them trouble."

"Oh, I think not. From what I hear, Sister Clemente is more
enthusiastic about you than she's ever been about a new heifer."
He paused. "But let me get you some coffee. Perhaps . . ." The
Mother Superior had already slipped out. "Now sit down and
tell me about your plans. I apologize for the chairs. The Communists say we live in such luxury, but they've never tried these
chairs. Dear me, they get harder each year. Now, what are your
plans?"

"My plans? Well, of course, primarily the nursery. There's
still a lot to be done. Right now I'm a building supervisor. The
foreman's been very careful, but we don't always agree. Yesterday it was the gradient from the gathering basins to the cesspool. He says it's not important: I say unless the gradient is
steep enough to force the flow into the cesspool, we'll have the
usual back-up and stench . . ."

"Ah, drains! Very important things, drains, and too often
overlooked — until it's too late," he chuckled. "Has the structure
been approved by the provincial medical officer in Matera?"

"The plans were, but now that the building is almost finished
I have to request the official permits and lure the medical officer to Torregreca so that we can go over the entire plant together. The same thing with the provincial director of schools,
and the local director as well. Then I have to negotiate the food
contracts too. You know, probably, that the government is sup-
plying much of the nonperishable food, which means a big load
off our budget."

"Now about the food. If there's any question, I mean with

the local men in Matera, refer them to me. Sometimes they listen to me." His voice was not as benign as his words. He knew the slightest pressure from him would bring a flurry of results, apologies and excuses. "And the equipment? Is it to be made here in town?"

"Some, yes. I must order that, have the building cleaned out, and then start on curtains and dolls' houses and toys. It won't be easy. I'll have to be away some of the time, training the teachers."

"Away? Surely they're to be local." There was a note of disapproval in his voice.

"Our policy is rather like that of the carabinieri. We never leave a teacher in her own town. That way she has no ties, no old debts to pay off. Now, while they're working in other nurseries, I want to brief them, as it were, on the problems of Torregreca; emphasize manual work with children, for instance. I don't know whether you agree, but it seems to me that many of the children here are behind in manual coordination."

"And verbal expression," he added quickly.

"Of course, I can't open the nursery until there are people actually living in the houses."

"Didn't I understand you were to be on the evaluation committee?"

"Only semi-officially, I believe."

"No, no, not at all. I told the Mayor you must be on the committee. I don't know how well you know the South. Don Matteo has told me . . ." he hesitated for a brief second, hinting that he might have been told a number of things. "He told me that you are well aware of the problems. Take my word for it, you must be an active member of that committee. Particularly now we dare not have any question of its honesty. Without going into my reasons, it's enough to say that politics govern much of what we do these days. Each member of the committee has private obligations and ties, and only an honest neutral like yourself can embarrass them into doing their duty. They must act as responsible adults and give out those houses honestly."

"I'll do my best, but that may not be enough. At least I can assure you I have no obligations that would influence me."

He nodded, but his eyes twinkled and for the first time I realized he was amused by the generalities we were packing into this very specific conversation. The Mother Superior came back carrying a tray with two cups and a small silver pot, as he was saying, "Yes, that's what we're counting on, your honesty. Now, tell me. I've been talking to the Mother Superior about your living arrangements. I realize that the independent young women of today are not attracted by communal living, but it would give us great pleasure if you chose to remain at the Convent. You will always be welcome there, but where would you like to live? In the nursery?"

There was no longer any question, apparently. I was to stay in Torregreca. Understanding that I was expected to follow his conversation, not lead it, I answered as though there had never been any doubt. "Only the teachers will have quarters there. I've heard of an apartment in the old *case popolari*, belongs to a widow who might rent it."

"A widow?" he murmured, more to himself than to me. "A widow, in the old *case popolari*. A widow. Hmm. Could only be Michele the Neapolitan's widow. Call her Fascide, don't they? I've known her mother-in-law, Carmela, ever since I was a boy. She's dead, too, may God rest her soul, but I went to grade school with her brother. Fascide ought to be all right."

"If that works out, I might be able to move in a couple of weeks. Until then . . . if the nuns could stand me that long . . ."

"As long as you like." He motioned for the coffee to be poured. "I have an extra job for you. And I'm quite serious. Wake these people up. Show them there is no shame in physi-

cal activity. I hear you like to walk. Keep on doing it. When
your car comes, drive it — show them it's not immoral for a
woman to drive. Don't give in to the system when it means giving up honor. Speak up and defend your ideas, but you'll have
to do it in a way they understand. The other day you argued
with the *daziere*. Oh, yes, I know about that too. I know about
most things that happen in Torregreca, you know. You were
right, of course. He thought he'd play on your inexperience.
Now he's found out and so have the others. Don't ever be
afraid to do what is right. I told the Mother Superior this morning about my experiences in America with Protestants. American Catholics are narrow, one could almost say puritan, but not
you Protestants. You have energy. Use it! Use it on the nuns as
well. They can change. Make Sister Clemente get rid of those
long-legged beasts she keeps down there. They're bags of
bones. Convert her to Iolchsheerays. Produce twice as much.
Don't you agree?"

I was mystified.

"She doesn't feed them properly. Why, I've seen them in
England. Scientific, balanced diet's what they need. They'll
never grow on slops. I don't care if that's what the peasants
have always fed them. Don't you agree?"

I nodded. This was no time to tip the boat, but what were
we talking about?

"Better hams, too!"

Iolchsheerays? Iolchsheerays? Light at last — Yorkshires. I
laughed. "I'll do my best, Your Excellency, but I won't be able
to change very much."

"My child, however long you stay, you'll change something,
but never much. I've been here almost forty years. There's been
change, but never enough. The hope that tomorrow another infinitesimal canker may be healed is what keeps me alive. Now
forgive me, I must go. There is a waiting room full of people to

be seen." He stood up. "But I will see you to Sister Clemente's elegant carriage."

"No, please, you mustn't lose more time this morning. You've been most . . ."

The folds around his eyes lifted and he seemed to refocus.

"Young woman, you know your business . . . and I know mine. This happens to be mine. Our meeting is not entirely private. The cordiality of it and our mutual understanding must become public property. Now, come along."

As we went down the wide staircase he talked of the weather and the dampness of old palaces with a determination that vetoed interruption from me. I was never able to thank him. He did not want me to. Don Evandro appeared at the foot of the stairs and watched as we went out to the door. The Bishop took my hand and held it.

"You must come to see me whenever you want. I will always see you no matter what the circumstances, no matter what may have upset you. Just come. One thing more. I have charged the Mother Superior to treat you as any child away from home — with love and understanding."

He turned back into the blackness of the entry, leaving the Mother Superior and me to face some thirty people who stood immobile, their chores in the Piazza forgotten. We smiled and they smiled back. This news would travel fast, too.

V

CHICHELLA

THAT afternoon I went to the old *case popolari* — the first of the postwar public housing — on the Appian Way, just where the houses of the town end, where each night the promenaders turn to start their course back to the Piazza. I always thought of it as the beginning of the dark.

My knock at the Widow Fascide's door was answered by the high eerie wails of formal mourning that swelled and shrilled ever faster to a crescendo of howls. I understood I was to wait. This was one of the conventions of Southern grief, which is not so much a personal torture as a public marathon.

(Every act, every gesture, every word is prescribed, and any deviation will rouse comment. The actual moment of death electrifies the mourners. They fling open the windows to let the dead man's spirit out and open the doors to invite people in; then settle down for the harrowing hours of the watch when the women chant, one singing the virtues of the dead man, the others wailing the chorus. They tear their hair, claw their faces, and weep until it seems they can mourn no more — but they do, through a long day and an even longer night. They will only stop when the body is in its coffin and borne away to the church on the shoulders of friends. So they wail on. They change off, and a new voice takes up the litany of virtues; the chant continues. But practical concerns are not forgotten for mummery. Arrangements are discreet. Hidden by the comings and goings of neighbors, clothes are sent out to be dyed, a coffin is ordered, a priest hired, bell ringers paid, and a Confraternity is found to walk in the procession. When it is all over, the death of the living begins. A widow may have no fire in her house for two months. She depends on neighbors for food. She may not play her radio for two years. She must always wear black, of course, but she must wear a black scarf over her head, even in her own house for six months, and outside for two years. She must never be seen. If she must shop, she does it before dawn or after dark. She may not go to the Piazza. She cannot go to a festa, a wedding, a christening or even a funeral. As Chichella Fascide told me once, "It's all set out like a bus schedule. The one who's underground is lucky. The one left behind dies slowly with everyone watching, checking, making sure you do it the right way — the Torregreca way." Slowly the restrictions dwindle away. In five years gold earrings may be substituted for black loops. A festa, even a wedding, is permitted. At the end of twelve years, or fifteen, a widow might put off her weeds if, by some chance, another close relative has not died, but she is old by then, set in her habits, cramped in her pocketbook and loath to give any ground for comment.)

Chichella Fascide was a fresh widow of four months. She was expected to spend her days wailing and could not open the door before she vocalized enough to satisfy her neighbors who appeared on their landings, craning their necks upward to inspect her visitor.

"Who are you?" "What do you want?" "What's she done?" they called at me like crows. Young women with high cheekbones and beak noses, they might have been Italian Indians. Their voices were shrill and at the same time flat, and sounded, as I found they always did even when asking the time, as though they were in the midst of a violent argument.

"I just want to talk to Fascide for a minute. I'm a friend of Don Luca Montefalcone's." In one voice they yowled, *"Oyee,* Chichella. Open up. There's a lady to see you. *Oyee,* Chichella . . ."* but she already had. Black, peppercorn eyes were peering at me through a crack in the door. They showed no sign of tears. She opened the door further and inspected me as I inspected her. She was somewhere in her thirties, I guessed, and very solid, though she later insisted she had been terribly wasted by mourning. A delicate face accented by heavy eyebrows and a large but well-balanced mouth seemed mismated to a short, stocky body. Stubby fingers fumbled trying to knot her head scarf under her chin. She must not show her shiny black hair that was pulled into a bun at the back of her head.

"Well, you don't expect me to wear it *all* the time, do you?" She laughed, showing small, very white teeth. I remember being surprised at her broad, childlike fingernails and at her breasts, not that they were large, but they seemed very much in the way of her short arms. Her eyes twinkled at her own joke. *"Trase, trase . . ."* and a Niagara of words without meanings. Diphthongs tripped over diphthongs in what sounded like the spewings of an irate woman with a head cold. My first, full-dress encounter with the lingua franca of the peasants left me stunned. Dialects change from district to district and from town to town, and also, as I found out, in Torregreca from neighborhood to neighborhood. Chichella spoke pure "Tarnese," as she called it. She understood Italian, but even with intense concentration could not utter more than a sentence or two in what was supposed to be her native language. I grabbed at words: husband, *povertà, miseria,* and *piccinin,* her children. She never took her shrewd eyes off my face. The instant I opened my mouth she burst into tears and rocked her breasts back and forth, cradling them as though they were a baby. She moaned on the verge of wailing, but still she watched me, in no way hypnotized by her own expression of trauma. I could feel her determination. This was not just begging self-pity; she had a specific purpose and I wanted to know what it could be. I turned to go.

"Don't you want to see the apartment?" Grief could wait. I thanked her, but explained I had only come to ask if she knew of anyone else who might want to rent an apartment, or better yet a small house in town. Her eyes narrowed; this was not going as she had planned. As I was saying that I understood her desire to stay in her own home, I was grabbed and dragged into a small bare room lined with wooden chairs. It had the air of a third class waiting room in a railroad station and was surprisingly dark, although there was a French door that led to a balcony where I could see a jumble of stovewood, derelict boxes and broken pots. Beyond, framed by two more eggcrate buildings of the *case popolari*, was the Norman tower, one-dimensional in the glare of afternoon light that could not penetrate the gloom of this dreary parlor. In the middle of the room was a table with a crocheted doily so starched it provided a frill for the plaster dog that nested in its center. Off in a corner on a stool was the radio, put to bed like a parrot, with a black sateen cover, and over it all loomed a dish cupboard which like the rest of the furniture had been painted with ochre shellac and then grained by the dexterous use of a comb. Creating this "pretend walnut" is an essential art in the Torregrecas where almost no one can afford the real thing, but to the uninitiated, the swirls and color bring on an attack of bilious vertigo.

"See how neat it is?" It was. It had the impersonal order of any room that is never used. I had finally understood what made the room so dark; the walls were cocoa brown and furry from smoke. "Come, now you must see the bedrooms." Obviously the doors had been kept shut for the walls were less stained. Instead they were covered with a fluffy meringue of whitewash that had been lifted away from the plaster by humidity. Near the ceiling there were speckles of black mold. In one bedroom were a chest of drawers and a huge "matrimonial bed" of tin "pretend walnut," covered with an immaculate, white cotton jacquard spread. In the other, which was much smaller, there was a pathetic array of sleeping equipment: a trunk with a lumpy sack of ticking arranged on the top, a deck chair stretched to the maximum, and a chromium-framed, extendable love seat. In both rooms; faded pictures of relatives, the men mustachioed and uncomfortable looking in ties, the women very prim with religious medals strung around their necks, glimmered at me. Each was lighted by a minute electric bulb poised at the end of a gooseneck of thin metal piping. A plaque of Saint Anthony lighted from behind beamed a saccharine blessing over the "matrimonial bed." Speechless, I went on to the bathroom which was narrow and basic: a half-tub filled with water, a toilet without a seat, and a basin both of whose faucets were lying, detached, in the depression made for soap. It was all very clean. It went through my head that anyone who settled down there would be in full view of the traffic passing on the Appian Way. The kitchen was almost bare except for a sink and a miniature wood range which was the only form of heat and was also the source of the oily brownness covering the walls. A low cupboard with a two-ring gas burner set on top and some bowlegged chairs were the only furniture. There was another balcony with a morass of wild roses growing out of tin cans. Depression blanked out my mind.

"You see, it's clean. The mattress is new. You won't find anything better." She stopped. "I need the money. I'm a widow with four children . . ." and she began to moan.

A lightning resignation paralyzed my will for the first time. It was to become a chronic affliction of my life in Torregreca; after all, if I looked further, wouldn't I find the same kind of genteel squalor, probably dirtier, more dejected? "But you just want to rent a room. I need the whole thing."

She shook her head violently.

"You're willing to move out? How much do you want for it?"

So, standing there in the kitchen, we started the wrangle that is the crux of any deal. This was something she understood. Her eyes snapped at me as she explained how she had arrived at her price. I objected. She cried. I made a counter-offer; she protested. It was a play to her and she was Bernhardt. It took us probably thirty minutes to split the difference between her idea of the rent and mine. I promised a daily amount for the work she did for me. We agreed it would never take more than two hours, and I advanced part of the first month's rent to have the place completely whitewashed. Unless she were willing to have that done, I would not take it.

The neighbors had waited for news as long as they could and then wandered in to stand with blank faces as though they were waiting for a bus. Chichella was used to communal living, but I was not. I asked them to leave us to our discussion, and when they did not move, I led them by the hand to the door. A few minutes later others came in and we repeated the scene. Two crones, almost blind judging from the opaque look of their eyes, came in, walked up under my nose and asked, "Who are you?" Chichella had to scream a full explanation at them. Then I showed them out. The only person I was unable to depose was Chichella's sister, Tina, who had been alerted by the neighbors. She was younger than Chichella, tall and proudly erect with flashing blue eyes, tawny hair and perfectly modeled small features. She was the classic peasant beauty of romantic imagination, but she was also a shrew with a viper's tongue and a mulish will. My reaction was chemical, not logical; I disliked her on sight and I never had any reason to change my mind in the years that followed. That day she would not budge, though she was so busy fawning over me that she really caused little trouble. When I left it had been agreed everything would be ready for me in ten days. As casually as that I committed myself to Chichella's care, but it was probably inevitable because, as she told me months later, she had had a dream. She had seen the Madonna at the top of a long, long flight of stairs. She clambered up, but no matter how she tried she could never reach the top. Finally she stood still and heard the Madonna say, "When a stranger comes, do what he tells you and he will lead you to safety." Dreams are very important. Properly interpreted they can lead you to the right combination on the numbers wheel, tell you whom to marry, and what land to buy. I suspect they are more useful after the fact as a confirmation than as a guide, and I do not for one minute believe she dreamed of the Madonna. Had she known anything about the flight of birds, pagan augury would have done as well. She had made up her mind that I was the solution to her problems.

One afternoon ten days later I *did* move in with my trunks and the supplies I had sent from my organization's stores: towels, washclothes, blankets and cotton yardage from which to make curtains. I was shocked to see that the chalky whitewash had brought out a feature of the apartment I had failed to notice; the doors and windows were a violent, sickening pea green. Chichella dithered around pulling out drawers to show me they were empty and lined with "clean" newspaper. She was careful to teach me how I could hang my clothes on great crosstie nails that stuck out from the walls where one least expected them. The trick was to do it without rubbing whitewash off on the shoulders of dresses and coats. Eventually, when we were muddling around in the dark, I flipped a light switch and was greeted with the distant twinkle of a ten-watt bulb. In the whole apartment there were three ten-watters and in the kitchen one seventy-five-watt bulb which, after I assured her I would pay the light bill, I was allowed to move from room to room. At that, it was not a very convenient arrangement and I soon put off unpacking until the morning and sent her home, which I realized meant a basement storeroom without light or water where she and three of her four children were camping like refugees. Left to myself there seemed little I could do. I made a cup of tea and then started circling around looking for a place to sit as a dog twists and turns and backs before he settles down. Finally I gave up and had my tea standing at the kitchen window. I think I had a wistful hope that a car or truck might go by, but nothing broke the stillness of the night except my neighbors' radios.

The light fixture in the bathroom was too high for me to change the bulb and I did not want to put on a tantalizing show for the neighbors anyway, so I settled for a sponge bath in the penumbra. It would have been possible in a familiar bathroom, but not there. I found a pot in a small pantry-closet off the kitchen. I was glad later that I had not been able to see the true condition of either the pot or the pantry. I heated some water, but it turned out there was no stopper for the basin. After bailing hot water into pitchers and buckets and mixing in cold I did get cleaned up. Remembering to leave the tub faucet open in case water came in the middle of the night, I went to bed. The new mattress which had been so stressed in our negotiations was in a sense new. It had been stuffed with fresh corn husks! They crackled and crunched and tickled me if I shifted my weight. From the bathroom came greedy sucking and burping noises. The ancestors glowing in their demonic lights seemed perched around the edges of the bed just waiting for me to close my eyes. I must have fallen asleep. The last thing I remember was the Voice of Moscow on my little transistor radio crooning the latest sins of the capitalist villains of my faraway country. I might as well have been on the moon.

I was not at all sure just where I was when a bus trumpeted under my window like an enraged elephant at two o'clock. It was the warning signal for passengers. At four, with the first streaks of light and the clip-clip of donkeys on their way to the fields I was up, planning the campaign which somehow must make this into a place to live.

For several days Chichella was very patient with me. She made me watch her washing dishes with detergent so that I

The town in the landscape

The town; in the foreground, the Convent of San Fortunato

▲ *Returning from the fields*

▼ *Procession, from the Gate of the World*

▲ Men

▼ Women

▲ *Chichella and her children, 1959*

▼ *Nuns*

would be convinced she had given up her method of wood
ashes and sand. She made me smell the laundry for proof there
was no bleach. In shopping she was less successful. There was
no meat for sale, no *parmigiano* and no milk that was safe to
drink. The butter was rancid from being too long in transit
from the North. I refused to accept murky, raw olive oil, or
pears of poured concrete. There was *pecorino* but it tasted of
old cellars and bad drains. It seemed I would have to live on
figs, spaghetti and eggs which cost the handsome price of ten
cents each because they were "out of season." Absorbed with
bending heavy wire for curtain rods and setting wooden plugs
in the wall to hold the drapery irons, I still had mind enough to
notice Chichella's ingenuity. She went around telling people
that I planned to lay in a large stock of wine. Sample bottles
began arriving and no matter how I insisted, there was no way
for me to pay for them. When we were unable to attach the
new toilet seat, she called a plumber who seemed determined
to discuss the remodeling of the bath with me. Only when she
started making signs behind his back did I understand; let him
make the estimate and he would not only attach the seat, but
the faucets as well. "He would never have come just to do our
chores," was her lucid reasoning. If he did what suited him, we
would do what suited us. After a lot of dickering and arguing
with a carpenter who wanted to make me a "masterpiece of
inlay" for a clothes cupboard, I ordered a monument of plywood that I planned to paint white and put in the bedroom.
Until it came I lived from suitcases and Chichella had no
chance to inventory my clothes, but when the final coat of
paint was dry she was careful to be there "to help."

For a while she watched in silence. When she could stand it
no longer, she said, "*Ma, Signo'*, are you going to open a store?
And all those shoes! Nobody alive can wear more than a pair at
a time. Why, I'd be rich if I had two pairs: one wet and one
dry."

I did not try to explain. It is true I had fur-lined boots, mountain boots, heavy rubber-soled shoes, loafers, tennis shoes, high-heeled black, low-heeled black, brown, blue and I no longer remember what else, but she would never have understood that I used them all at various times and in various places. "Too bad," she muttered. "They're the right length, but they're too narrow." I turned to find her jamming her square feet into the only pair of Ferragamos I owned. Not long after, I realized that my slippers seemed, somehow, to be getting larger and larger. When I questioned her she pulled a very serious face. "But you wouldn't want me to track mud around the floor I've just mopped, would you?" I declared those slippers hers. She smiled innocently. We had started another variety of graft.

I had found an innerspring mattress at an exorbitant price in Torregreca. Rush-bottom chairs were being sent to me, but for a simple armchair and a reading lamp I had to go to Matera. When I had finished making the curtains and bedspreads, had scoured out all the cupboards, reorganized the kitchen and rigged up temporary bookshelves, I tackled the slow business of painting all the windows and doors. I had not thought to mention it to Chichella. It was not a question of having painters in; there are none in Torregreca. Painting is done by carpenters and they cannot conceive of working without boiled linseed oil that has a suspicious odor of fish and never, never allows the paint it has diluted to dry. It was just another chore for me to do before the curtains were hung and I could call the place more or less finished. At the same time I planned to re-paint the border at the base of the walls that protects white-wash from the splashing tongue of the mop. In an effort to save money Chichella had done it herself — freehand — so that it looked like a profile of the Dolomites. With the first piece of furniture I moved I discovered she had also skipped those parts of the wall she expected to be covered. *Eh, be', pazienza!* I was resigned to the system. She had probably saved a dollar or two.

A first coat was on the windows and I had started the doors when she stormed in, red in the face, her eyes snapping. My ear had improved, but it would have taken a native to understand her avalanche of Tarnese. One thing was clear: she wanted things left as they were. She eyed the curtains laid out on the bed and spewed again. There was no way to interrupt her, so I made a pot of coffee and suggested we sit down over it and discuss the situation.

"I've never had a cup of coffee in my life and I don't intend to start now!" was her answer. While she stood, and I sat drinking coffee I did not want with what I hoped was epic appreciation, I told her that the apartment would be as I wanted it for as long as I had it, but that I guaranteed I would leave money for replacing everything I had changed. She turned, stalked out and slammed the door. Knowing that the worst thing I could do was to show any doubt or lack of determination, I went back to painting. Late in the afternoon I hung white glass curtains and side curtains of the only material I had in quantity — a startling Kelly green cotton. I had finished in the sitting room and the bedroom when the front door opened.

"They say it's all right. It looks nice," Chichella panted.

"Who says?"

She led me to the window. Below in the courtyard were at least fifty neighbor women with their babies and their chickens milling around their feet. "*Complimenti, complimenti!*" one of them yelled. "*Stanno bene, stanno!*" screeched another.

"See what *my* signora can do?" Chichella shouted back. "She's clever, you'll see."

I felt like a disheveled Queen Elizabeth waving to the crowd. They waved back. Our problem was no more, the neighbors approved.

Chichella may have thought she could ride the crest of that wave, but she was soon enough in a deep trough of her own. She had found temporary work washing, by hand, all the hospital linen, whereupon those neighbors dubbed her "The Merry Widow" — she was not sticking to the rules.

Her days went something like this: at dawn she started splitting wood for the laundry boiler; from eight to two, after loading the wood up four flights of stairs to the loft, she shunted the mountains of bloody sheets and bindings from tub to tub, to boiler to rinse tub, and then to dry. At two she raced back to me, did my cleaning, collected my shopping list which she had to have someone read to her, and went off to the wife of a local official to wash the lunch dishes and sit with the baby for two hours. She did my shopping, and then tried to round up her own children and feed them.

During the two months she worked at the hospital, she was supposed to be paid $15 a month, though she never saw a penny of it until I complained to the director six months after she did the work. Her normal income was clear-cut and meager. I paid her $20 a month for the apartment and $12.50 for the chores she did. The woman whose dishes she washed seldom gave her more than 15 cents a day; half the time she paid her nothing. The family resources, then, were limited to $32.50 a month and an uncertain bit. A year later a government pension of $10 a month was added. According to her peers she should not even have had the $32.50, though she was expected to live somehow and pay her husband's debts — $1,000 of debts. Except for pasta, food in Torregreca was as expensive as in America. She had herself and three children to feed (the fourth lived with a sister-in-law) and clothe; school books to buy for the two boys who were in school and her rent on the apartment she rented to me was $5.

Now she was "The Merry Widow" and the few women who had called on her to sit gossiping in the evenings no longer came. Children threw stones at her and yelled *"puttana"* — whore. To go out in the streets, to work, meant she had already forgotten her husband, that she had a lover.

Sometimes when I came home in the evenings I stopped by her storeroom to say I was back. Always I found her sitting in her doorway looking with glazed eyes down the dimly lighted corridor. Against the dampness of the basement and the chill of summer evenings she wrapped a crocheted black wool scarf around her head and shoulders and around her three-year-old daughter Rosa, who refused to fall asleep anywhere but in her mother's arms. They molded together into one hunched, almost cringing figure of passive desolation. Chichella leaning her head against the door jamb might have been asleep, except that her eyes were very wide open and the deep lines around her mouth spoke of bitter, frightened thoughts. If I asked her about them she was evasive.

"I don't think. In my position it's better not to think. I just go over and over my life trying to find what I did wrong; what made God punish me."

When she could stand no more self-torture she went inside her storeroom and crawled onto the bed she shared with the three children. There, in sleep, they wrestled with each other all night for it was not a real bed but planks straddling two iron stands. During the day, so that the neighbors would not know the truth, she covered and padded it into softness. One end of the little room was reserved for the owner's goods: stovewood, burlap sacks of grain and a wine barrel. The rest was a clutter of pots and pans, many filled with water, and a bread chest on top of which was a gas burner. One of the unexplained miracles of Chichella was how she kept the children as clean and decent-looking as she did. Vincenzo was seven, a thin, tiger-eyed boy whose gaze was fixed on the toes of his scuffed shoes. For more than a year he refused to speak to me. Some childish vision of cause and effect had given him the idea that, having taken his home, I was also responsible for his father's death. Luigi was six and looked exactly like Chichella, but there was something especially appealing about his brown eyes and well-formed head with its thick mat of dark hair tinged white from his mother's ministrations of DDT. She was so sure he played in "dirty" places that even the dire warnings on the box which I read to her did not discourage nightly treatments against fleas and lice. Luigi was ingratiating to the point of being a juvenile bootlicker. The parish priest was sure he would enter the priesthood; his teacher knew he wanted to go to normal school; the *guardie* saw him a policeman. They all spoiled him, but Chichella might have saved her DDT because he and Vincenzo with single-minded concentration spent their free time at the market snitching figs or peppers or persimmons when the vendors' backs were turned. Their memories of childhood will, I think, be of unrelieved hunger punctuated by lickings for stealing or wearing out their shoes. Rosa was only three but already had the wide-eyed look of rage that was her mother's face for the world. As long as she had a hunk of bread to chew on life was bearable. Only when she was left without it did she become a problem, wandering around the neighborhood, squatting wherever the notion hit her and eventually, after spankings from her mother for not lowering her panties, leaving a trail of Kelly green panties that had been constructed out of scraps from my curtains.

Chichella kept the three children clean and fed as best she could, but more than that, from the quicksand of her own despair and loneliness she managed to give them security.

By August the nights were chill and the air choked with the acrid smoke of burning wheat-stubble. We were preparing for our autumnal death, and often at night looking out my window, I imagined hell beyond, there in the fields, where the tongues of flame, burning the stubble, lapped in rows across infinity, making patterns like the seams of a gigantic, infernal patchwork quilt. Each day was less certain to bring sun, and the still, heavy rain that darkened each night extended itself farther and farther into the morning, veiling the old town in sodden mystery, but brutalizing even more the postwar eggcrate buildings, in one of which I lived. Chunks of plaster flew through the air as though prized out by a pixie with a malicious chisel. One morning without warning a balcony railing plummeted three stories into the courtyard below. Wind loosened roof tiles and sent stovepipes bounding, somersaulting away. What may have looked to be a charming, model housing development on the drawing board or in a plastic model in Rome was every day becoming more of a slum. Paved walks and trees had been planned — instead, in summer we had a garbage dump and dust bowl where pigs and chickens could browse. The winter promised gumbo. Maybe the poor should expect no better; as "they" always said, the poor were better off than ever before. But I found myself resenting, as my neighbors resented, paying a fixed monthly amount for maintenance I never enjoyed. At the same time I grumbled and snorted over a piglet who had been brought in from the cold to live under the stairs in the front entrance. In my rational moments I did not know whether my rage should be directed toward the omnipotent Roman bureaucrat who had planned housing without stalls or against the peasant who insisted on his right to keep a pig if he chose. More often than not I sympathized with the peasant, who faced a year totally without meat if he did not manage to raise his animal. Where the *average* income was between three and four hundred dollars a year, and much of that in produce, a man with a family was not finicky about how he increased the food that went on his table. I, the rich neighbor, was exasperated by the flock of diseased, half-starved chickens that pecked at my feet on the stairway or flew up spraying me with excrement and feathers. I saw no reason why the children, locked out when their families went to the fields, had to use the first two steps in the building as a latrine. The hazards of reaching my own apartment were increased when a faulty circuit blew out the hall lights. As the pig grew and showed signs of turning carnivorous, the adventures of the stairway became more titillating. Still the light could not be fixed because the government agency sent no one to do so, and it had been understood by all that anyone tampering with government property would be fined. Except when I was in residence and strung a bulb out from my apartment, the hallway of that building was in darkness for four years.

In the autumn of 1959 there was nothing encouraging in the molting that surrounded me. Even my work seemed to deteriorate into waste motion. I was still trying to arrange the myriad of contracts, but official summer vacations, staggered and extended, always meant that *one* official was missing. No decisions were ever final. As one obstacle was overcome, two more sprouted up to take its place: tax exemption forms, permits and agreements, applications for ministerial contributions, all in six copies — a bureaucratic snake pit of papers that taxed my ingenuity and daily made me weaker. I had progress reports to write for London headquarters, but they were more about efforts than results. The nursery building was finished, which might have been a relief had it not been for the complex final accounting with the contractor. In contrast it was almost fun to make curtains for the nursery, and argue with the carpenters about clothes racks and toy cupboards and cot closets. They wanted things hidden behind doors on high shelves where no child could touch them. That was the only kind of nursery they had ever seen; one where everything was carefully out of reach, new and shining, to be admired by visitors, not used by children. I fought the paper work, and tried to convert the carpenters to the new ways of pedagogy. When I could not convert, I had to order. I preferred to convert. I struggled on, discouraged and — I can admit it now — lonely.

The weather did little to help my spirits. I lived in a gray world where grayness could only become grayer; now all change would be for the worse and it was, except for my relationship with Chichella which miraculously changed too — but for the better. I was no longer merely tolerated. I had become a guest; she a hostess with all the duties and courtesies the word implied. She must divine my needs before I expressed them, and above all she must be sure I was properly amused. To her, one sign of desperation on my part was my picking up a book to read. No matter what she was doing then, she immediately stopped, pulled up a chair, and set about finding a subject that would hold my attention.

She had little to draw on except the story of her own life. I heard it in snatches — at times when I truly wanted to read, at others when I was in bed trying hard to die with a head cold, but most often on winter nights when her children slept and we sat over a smoking brazier while the wind and rain lashed at the windows. Her change was no sudden wave of sympathy. I remember the first signs of it very clearly. When I paid my rent at the end of the first month, I typed out a receipt and asked her to sign it. I sensed from the way she circled around the room avoiding me and my piece of paper that there was to be a problem about it. Finally she told me to leave it on the table, she would sign it later. When she left, the receipt had disappeared. Next morning she brought it back signed (with her maiden name, that is; she could not write her husband's). It was not enough that I had read the receipt to her; she had wanted someone else to read it too. For a couple of months she was docile about signing, but one cold October day she came wrapped in her black shawls that were beaded and glistening with mist, and sat down across from me at my little worktable. I bent the light so that it shone only on my notebook. Chichella's face became a death's-head shrouded in black. She put her hands on the table, palms up, fingers slightly curled in her habitual gesture of repose which always suggested a temporary rejection of her cares and with them the world. Only in those brief moments did she seem vulnerable, as though by turning her callused hands to reveal the pink, tender underflesh she were revealing something as private as her soul.

"I think it's time we talked. You know now what I am; I know what you are. We don't need receipts. I know you'll pay, you know I won't claim you haven't. But there's something else more important. When I rented to you I thought . . . well, it's all right for a couple of months, then we'll see. If I don't like her, I'll put her out. But I don't feel that way now. I just wanted to tell you you can stay as long as you want to, for years if you like. My house is your house until you leave — and even after that."

The shadows veiled her expression, but a strained thinness of voice betrayed her tension. Having made this awful commitment, I think she longed to take it back. Instead she rummaged in her pockets and up her sleeves for a handkerchief while I talked quietly about receipts, the changes "we" had made, her kindness in taking me in and her greater kindness in offering to let me stay. The danger was in being too matter-of-fact: I might diminish her sacrifice when I wanted only to ease her sense of absolute loss. She listened, pleating and unpleating the handkerchief, and when I had finished she sat silently pleating and unpleating until she made up her mind. Then she said:

"You don't understand what a house of my own means . . . or what it means to give it up." She was no longer sitting but crouched over the table as though ready to spring at me. "You don't know where I lived before, the places I've lived all my life, until three years ago . . ."

"When I was born," she began.

Mamma and Tanname* had moved up out of the Rabata to Via del Tramonto — under the tower right outside the gate of

---

* Tarnese for "my father," "Dad."

the Convent of San Felice. The houses used to be for the peasants who worked the convent land, but now, the way the nuns treat us, you'd think we didn't exist. All uppity and prissy picking their way through the streets, holding up their skirts and looking like they smell something bad. Just because they have a few girls who *pay* to study. Old Don Orlando, the parish priest, made the *corna* against the evil eye whenever he saw them coming. "Upset a man's liver, they do!" he used to say. They wouldn't have anything to do with us, but the convent bells tinkle-tinkling and clonking all day never let us forget them.

I was born in that house in 1925 and my first baby was born there on New Year's day 1951. It was a foul, one-room house of rough stone — not plastered really, just in spots like all the others. An outside stair led up to a long narrow room with a stall for the donkey partitioned off at the back. The roof looked solid but rain or snow dripped right through on us. There were no windows so air and light came from a slit grill above the door. We didn't wash the floor much because it was of humpy stone slabs with dirt between and turned into a mud swamp. Mamma's bed was in the middle with a cot at the foot of it. As the family grew it got harder and harder to find places for all of us to sleep. There was always a cradle, hanging by ropes over Mamma's bed, hooked up so she could swing it back and forth if the baby cried or she could lower it to nurse him when he was hungry. It sounds dangerous, but it wasn't really — the baby was so bundled with swaddling he couldn't move. Every night we pulled out sacks and put them on benches and crates. I was a girl so I got a crate. Eventually there were too many of us and two had to sleep in the stall with the donkey. At least it was warm back there. You see, there were eight of us and Mamma and Tanname; six boys and Tina and me. I'm next to the oldest now, but my brother's no good so I'm really head of the family. That's why I have my father's nickname Fascide. If you'd called him Pietro Andressano nobody would have known who you were talking about. He was Pietro Fascide. A *fascide*, in dialect, is a cheese form, but he'd never had anything to do with cheese. He was a vineyard keeper. The name came from his great-grandfather who was a shepherd boy. Every night when he brought his flock back to Torregreca, he went through the streets yelling, "Oy, anybody want this nice little *fascide* of ricotta. I've got a nice *fascide* of cheese. Made today! Anybody want my *fascide?*"

Night after night he hawked his cheeses that way until people started saying "Here comes *Fascide* again!"

And that's how it began, maybe a hundred years ago, and we're still called that. There was no registry office and nobody bothered with last names. Nicknames became real names to us and even today with the registry office you can't find anyone in Torregreca unless you know his nickname. That's just the way it is here. Everybody knows Chichella Fascide; no one knows Chichella Andressano.

Between us we didn't have enough clothes to need a cupboard. If we did have an extra pair of shoes we banged nails in the wall and hung them there. The walls were covered from floor to roof with pots and pans, strings of garlic and peppers and corn, hoes, ropes, cheese forms, grain sieves — everything you can imagine got hung on nails just to keep it off the floor. When we were lucky and had a pig to kill, the lard and sausages and salamis and hams hung from the rafters on chains. Some years we couldn't manage a pig, but the chickens that roosted under Mamma's bed tided us over — three hens and a big red rooster as I remember it. Tanname called the rooster Garibaldi and the hens he named for the three women he hated most: Teresa — she picked and pecked at the others — for Donna Teresa, his padrone's wife; Celeste for Sister Celeste, the Mother Superior of San Felice — she was very proud and strutted around with her head in the air; and Elena for the Queen. We never knew what he had against *her.*

There was no kitchen in the house, but an old, arched fire-place served for heating and cooking. At the side of it there was a hatch door into a little niche big enough for a pan with embers and on top of that a pot of sauce could be left to simmer. We called it the "oven" but it wouldn't bake anything. On either side of the fireplace were heavy, battered wooden benches that we dragged out when we wanted to get warm in front of the fire. Not that we kept one burning all day; just at night for cooking unless it was very cold. God, how many times I've sat with my bare feet stuck in the ashes from the night before, hoping I could get them warm! We never seemed to have enough shoes to go around; rag bindings are not the same, but that's what we had. And the smoke. That fireplace belched smoke like the fires of hell until our eyes streamed and our throats closed. We were smoked hams when spring came.

Everything was harder in the winter, but laundry was the worst. Somehow we always did it, but it was a hit-or-miss thing and if we got the clothes clean, we didn't bother with ironing. The problem was always the same; one change of clothes, no water and a room full of people. I'd send the little ones to bed to get them out of the way, but they were really still there. There was no privacy. I'd take off my dress, wrap a shawl or somebody's jacket around myself and start washing. The dress got hung in front of the fire. If it dried by morning, fine. If not, I stayed in 'til it did.

When it came to hiding sanitary rags it was harder; the men mustn't see. I found a hole in the wall, a secret hole, where I could stuff my rags at night, then the next morning I'd sneak out and wash them. That way not even my mother knew for years, but it was a good thing my grandmother had warned me, had told me about a lot of things — otherwise I wouldn't have known what to do. On Sunday mornings, if the weather was good and Mamma didn't have something for me to do, I'd run off to my grandmother's to watch her comb people's hair. She wasn't a real *pettinatrice,* but she did it for her friends and she'd let me watch if I stayed quiet and never, never told anything I'd heard. Fair Sundays she took two stools outside her door and sat in the sun with her back against the wall until someone came. She didn't knit, or anything, she just sat there with her hands folded in her lap and the comb hidden under her apron. When one of her friends came, she'd make her sit on the other stool and she'd take down her hair. It took a long time. They all wore their hair long, done up with bone pins, and it was only combed once a week. When it was all down, she combed and combed until every strand was straight and shiny. When I was big enough she taught me to squash the lice between my thumbnails. It was slow, patient work, but I remember how proud I was when she said I'd done it right and gotten all the gray-white balls out.

My grandmother was old then, but she still wanted things done the right way, the way they were done in Torregreca — that was her way. She told me things Mamma never had time to explain: how there were places bigger than Torregreca where everybody was rich like our padroni. She thought they had a right to be; they always had been and God meant it to be that way. She told me about Naples and Rome — how she imagined them to be — and about America where she had a brother who was a priest. He got rich there, but he never sent any money back to his family. She said that wasn't Christian and for me to remember that under their skirts priests were just like other men. I didn't believe her until a friend of mine went to the seminary. I knew what he had under *his* skirts! For her, priests weren't important — God was. She told me practical things, too, about "those days" every month and how I was to keep myself clean and I wasn't to be with a man then. I didn't understand, because she said I must never refuse my husband and the two didn't go together. She didn't like anything that was fake, and she didn't like the way the Torresi pretended they had a lot when they didn't. There's one thing she said I can remember word for word:

"Chichella, don't worry about people knowing how rich or how poor you are. They can always tell from the copper hanging in your kitchen or the sheets on your line. Just remember you're richer with one *clean* pot and one *clean* sheet than with a dozen pots and a dozen sheets you don't know how to clean. And another thing . . . never leave the house with an unmade bed. Only a slut does that!"

Those Sunday mornings were a week's entertainment for her. She heard the gossip and gave advice and had a laugh with the other women. For me they made the whole world look different. She was the one who told me to hide my sanitary rags and to sneak them out the next morning, but it was always a mess. I never had a minute to myself or a chance to do anything alone.

We even ate out of the same big plate unless there were too many, then we fixed a second; there were never less than five to a plate. Tanname gave us each a spoon for the pasta or potatoes or cornmeal soup — whatever it was — and then he propped the big round loaf of bread against his chest and sawed at it with his work knife until he was about to slice off his chin — then snick — a big oval piece fell off; one for each of us to begin with, but we always got more. Bread was the important thing about a meal, even if it was made of chickpeas.

There was no light in the house, no water and, of course, no toilet. For that we went up near San Felice to the public latrines, the stand-up kind. Those houses still don't have water, so it's men to right, women to the left. I'll never forget the stench or how scared I was of the old man who hung around trying to peek under the door on the women's side.

Everybody lived that way except the rich, and don't think we didn't know how they lived. We did. After the Great War Tanname got a contract as a vineyard keeper with Don Pasquale

Acquaviva. Mamma was part of the contract. She did all the work in the house and the chores for Donna Teresa — not that they paid her, except maybe a half kilo of yarn or a dress length at Christmas. Tanname was the one who was paid — by the year — a certain amount of grain, salt and olive oil, a little money and two hectares of land he could farm for himself. As the vineyard keeper he got a bit of wine too, but not much. Then there were all the things he had to give Don Pasquale, the presents on his name day and Christmas and Easter. Bad years we were lucky to eat; there was nothing left over for shoes.

The first thing I remember is going with Mamma to the pa-drone's house every morning. She could leave the babies in swaddling at home. The boys were bigger and could run loose, but she had to take me with her. Before she knocked on the big double doors at the palace — and it was never later than six-thirty — she always warned me: "Now, Chichella, be good and if you get hungry, remember I have bread in my pocket." Donna Teresa was very strict about that; we must never touch any of their food.

The double doors were only opened for carriages or carts, but there was a little door just big enough for a man to step through in one of the panels. One rap from Mamma and it would open. We wouldn't see anyone, but Donna Teresa's threatening voice came from behind it:

"You're late again, Carmela!"

That's what she said every morning. It never changed and neither did she. Even in the summer she wore a blue wool robe spotted with grease and she had a pigtail of gray hair down her back. Mamma said she dressed in the afternoon and was very fine, but I always think of her as old and toothless in that robe and brown slippers that flopped when she walked.

Sometimes I was allowed to stay in the courtyard. That was the best because there were chickens and rabbits and goats and one old carriage horse named Dante that Don Pasquale never drove because he didn't want to wear him out. If it rained I had to go inside straight to a chair in the kitchen that Donna Teresa called "Chichella's chair." It was a low wooden chair with a rattan seat and a hole in the middle of it "just in case Chichella wets herself." I hated it because my bottom slid through the hole and left me sitting with my knees almost to my chin, but it was better than all those dark, dank rooms and spooky furniture. Mamma did the cleaning and the laundry, made their bread and their pasta, carried their water from the fountain and their slops out to the street drain. She had to fix their lunch — there were twelve people counting the sons, their wives and children — and then later, after she'd fed us bread and oil at home, she went back to do their dishes, got more water and emptied the slop jars again. All their food came from the locked storerooms under the palace and Donna Teresa never let the keys out of her sight, but I dreamed of hiding in one and eating and eating until they found me. I was hungry all the time — that's why I can't get too mad at my children when they steal food.

Summers weren't so bad, but in the winter God turned off the sun. There was nothing to do but huddle over the fire, cursing the cold and the damp that never went away. Sometimes for days no one passed our door and I thought everyone else was dead, that we were alone in the world. I cried and cried, not for the dead, but for us. Mamma used to say "Silly Chichella, don't worry. The first time the sun comes out you'll see we aren't all alone. You'll see!" I got the idea that God lived in the sun. If we sinned, He turned it off — it stayed off most of the time.

Mamma was right. The first clear day the men wrapped themselves in their cloaks and went to stand in the sheltered corner of the Piazza. They just stood there all day, but the women knew better. We had until sunset to get the laundry soaped, rubbed, rinsed and part way dry before the fog came in again. First it rolled through the valleys below town, then slowly it crept up and up, street by street, and choked the chimneys and made the paving slabs glisten. Everybody was dead again. It was cold and still and lonely.

One spring when I had just begun to feel happy again, there was an earthquake — in the middle of the night. Funny crackling and rustling noises woke me up. I lay there trying to think what it was; then I heard it again and things began to shake. Voices in the street yelled "Fascide, Fascide, your house is falling! Fascide!" In the dark we couldn't find the door; when we did we couldn't get it open. Finally Tanname, Mamma, Tina and Antonio pushed out into the street . . . it was Tina who made it first. She always did. She's like Tanname, belligerent, quick with threats, but no good when it came to a fight or hard work. Even as a little girl she was only interested in Tina — Elisabetta as she made us call her when she was putting on airs. Either by force or by rolling her blue eyes she always got what she wanted and that was all she cared about. It figured she'd beat the rest of us out that night.

They were in such a rush they forgot the little ones sleeping in the back with the donkey, but I heard them crying and grabbed them. Out in the street Mamma was praying to Sant' Antonio for help in saving the donkey. She'd forgotten about us; lost her head. She was like that. Couldn't take surprises, but when it came to work, she worked. She was calm and patient and shrugged off an argument, but she'd yowl and scream to the saints if there were any kind of crisis. All she cared about that night was the donkey.

He was happy and safe in his back bedroom and the house was all right — it didn't fall, but after that it had a big crack in it. We tried to get the owner to fix it, but she wouldn't. She was the daughter of a witch anyway! We paid two hundred and fifty lire a year rent, but every year we stayed she wanted more. The extra she took in grain or wine. One year two hundred and fifty lire and a quintal of grain; the next year two hundred and fifty lire, a quintal of grain and a barrel of wine . . . somehow it was always more and still she refused to fix the house. After the quake Tanname said he wouldn't pay unless she plastered the cracks, and she said she'd sue him if he didn't pay. When she threatened to sue, Tanname decided we needed help. Don Pasquale told him the only honest lawyer in town was his own brother, Don Peppino, and gave Tanname a note of recommendation.

At home they talked about it a long time before they decided to see Don Peppino. I didn't know what Tanname meant, but he said "people like Don Peppino" always took advantage of "people like us." He didn't trust them. Mamma said we trusted Don Pasquale; we'd have to trust Don Peppino. In the end Tanname agreed to go, but he wouldn't take any fancy dealing and to show them he meant business he planned to wear his uniform. Mamma told him he couldn't, that she'd give his corduroy suit a good brushing. That's the way it always worked out. He blustered, then Mamma told him what he was going to do. He was big and blond and ferocious, people said, but it was all noise. He knew how to fix everything; if his bluff worked, he told us we'd never get along without him. If it didn't, he left us to clean up the mess.

While he dressed, he told Mamma what he was going to say to Don Peppino and how he should settle the witch, but when it was time for him to leave, he lost his nerve and told Mamma to come along with him because she'd never be satisfied he'd done right. I guess she wanted to go; he didn't have to ask her the second time!

When they came back, she told me about it. She was impressed. She said Don Peppino must be very important because he had a big waiting room with chairs, lots of chairs, and all of them were taken. When Don Peppino had read the note, he'd let them in ahead of the others. Tanname said, after all, that was the way it should be. They both talked about the carved furniture and the gold and the pictures; one of the King, one of the Duce, and one of the Bishop. They agreed Don Peppino must be important; he had even let them sit down. Tanname had explained about our rent and the grain and wine, but he got mad when he was getting toward the end and couldn't explain very clearly. Mamma had to tell the rest.

Don Peppino looked very serious, Mamma said, and pulled down three heavy brown books and started to read. When he finished with one book, he opened another and read some more. She thought he'd forgotten them sitting there, but finally he took off his glasses and just looked at them for a long time. Then he sent them home, said they had nothing to worry about, he'd take care of everything.

Tanname was full of himself; he'd arranged it all, he'd show people they couldn't take advantage of us. In the end he was right — in a way. The judge said we'd paid too much rent and could stay in the house for free. It was just a one-room house, but we didn't have to pay rent anymore; instead we had to pay Don Peppino.

We stayed on living there and I took care of the babies. There was so much to do at home that I never went to school. I'm the only one in the family who didn't, but when it came to work, I did my share. The year I was twelve I worked by the day, starting out before dawn, coming back after dark. Sometimes we walked eight or nine miles out to the fields, then eight or nine miles back. Until I knew every ditch and swamp Mamma made me carry my boots strung around my neck so I wouldn't get them wet, so both ways I was hiking barefooted. Before the summer was over I could do the trip with my eyes closed. Then, the next summer, 1938, when I was thirteen, they hired me out on a "season contract" which meant I stayed on the place from March to September. They sent me to a *mas-*

seria near Irsina where I was the youngest on the women's squad. We did what they called the "light work," hoeing broad beans, then hoeing the weeds out of the wheat and finally reaping, stacking and threshing the wheat. We weeded down one row loosening the dirt, building it up around each plant, until we came to the end and started up the next row. We were never done and the hoe that weighed five pounds in the morning weighed fifty by nightfall. They paid us two and a half lire (about thirty cents) a day and food. If it rained, we got food but no pay.

The boss on my first squad was an old girl, Concetta. She was, maybe, fifty and it was hard work for her to keep up with us, but she knew how to train girls. In a gruff way she was good to me, telling me not to gossip, showing me how to work. She talked to me all the way out to the *masseria.* The trip took a whole day. It was March and the wind cut like a knife. I remember we stopped behind a rock to eat our bread and peppers at noon and I couldn't feel my feet any more, that's how cold it was. We moved right along, the rest sang songs they all knew and on we went, but it was still after dark when we got there. The factor was waiting for us and he was mad because we'd held him up. Concetta whispered I should stay with her; she'd explain where we were and what I should do.

From the outside the *masseria* was like any other I'd ever seen, but bigger. There was one long, rough-stone building they hadn't wasted much whitewash on. The middle part of the building had two stories with a stairway leading to the second floor that formed an arch over a big door on the ground floor. It was like those houses we put in Christmas crèches, only bigger. I couldn't see that night, but the next day I found out there were two long wings that went back from the front of the building with stalls for the work animals, woodsheds, grain sheds, a room with a wine press, a room for making cheese, another for storing it, and pens for pigs and chickens and rooms for hanging sausages, hams and lard. It was an independent town on its own, even if it really was one great farm that belonged to one padrone — one of five or six the padrone owned.

Concetta led us up the stairs into a dim little hall where the factor was waiting to look us over. He had a big wool muffler wound around and around his throat and wore a black felt hat and a long black cloak like Tanname's. Later I found out he always wore the hat. The cloak came off the first of June, never before, and the muffler stayed around his neck until August. One of our jokes was that he slept in it.

"That's the factor's room and in back of that is the padrone's, but I bet he's not here yet," Concetta whispered to me, pointing off to our right. "Come on in here and get settled. No fighting over places, now, there's room for everybody."

She took us into a big, bare loft with room to sleep all of us and more. It had a rough, pebbly floor and an unfinished roof. Even by lantern light the tiles shone through the supporting beams. At either end were doors that were kept closed at night, but led onto balconies. I found out soon enough that they were always closed except in the morning when we were clearing up, so in the summer it was hot inside and stank of people and dirty, sweaty clothes. We did our penance sleeping in there. At the far end of the room were two wicker grain vats almost as high as the ceiling, and nothing else except a hand basin on a three-legged iron stand with a pitcher beside it, and four or five low chests, each maybe a yard square. Over the basin there were towel nails where some pots were hanging, but there was no place to cook and there were no beds.

Concetta told me to put my stuff — a sweater, my sanitary rags and a comb — in one of the chests and then go get my sack from behind the vats. She helped me drag it down almost to the door and put her own right next to the door to be sure she heard anyone who tried to sneak out; that was part of her job, to keep an eye on everything we did and block our way to the men. It wasn't enough that we were upstairs with the factor next door; Concetta had to sleep with one eye open.

When the sacks were all down in one long row and the bundles stowed in the chests, Concetta told us to line up and be counted; there were twenty-two. She gave each of us a big chunk of bread and then called the factor. I was surprised to see him carrying a bottle of olive oil. He was still wearing his muffler and hat, but I could just see the tip of a tie. I had never known anybody who wore a tie on ordinary days. He seemed very gentlemanly, more like a padrone than a peasant.

"Stand still," he ordered, and counted us again. "Now stick out your bread." We held out our chunks and he went down the line, dribbling oil as he passed the bottle lightly over the bread like a priest giving the benediction. "That's all. See you're out by dawn," and he left us to our supper.

While the girls dug around behind the vats for plates, Concetta went downstairs to make bread soup. She'd added water, pepper, garlic and a couple of shriveled tomatoes to a pot with our bread in it. That was dinner. I hated soup then; imagine how I feel now. That bread soup was dinner every night I ever spent in a *masseria* — until after the war. I had years and years of it and I'd starve now rather than eat it, but that night I was hungry enough and cold enough to eat it.

I don't remember going to sleep, but I woke up in the dark, numb and shaking. It was black. Everyone was asleep, and we seemed to be covered with one long piece of canvas . . . all of us under the same stiff sheet of it, and on top of that were some old, chewed-up blankets. It was the floor that was so cold. There were drafts under the doors. I did the only thing I could think of. I crawled out, took one of the blankets and stumbled around until I found the chest my things were in. I wrapped myself up in the piece of blanket and curled up like a snail on top of the chest. So what! I was cold. It didn't matter to me that my knees were up under my chin, if I could get warm. I slept on the chest every night until hot weather came; the girls called it my "nest."

It was still dark when Concetta lighted the lamp and got us up. It didn't take long to drag the sacks and the canvas strip back behind the vats, but there was a lot of arguing about whether or not to open the windows. Finally it was decided not to until we got dressed, which didn't take very long either because no one ever really undressed. We took off our outside bits and slept in the rest. Concetta gave us each a kilo of bread; that was the day's ration. We could eat it whenever we wanted, but there wouldn't be any more. She told me there'd be some cheese to have with it at noon in the fields — how much we ate before was up to us. That's the way it always was, a kilo of bread and fried peppers, or cheese, or anchovies or sometimes some potatoes, but always something to go on the bread, because eating in the fields we couldn't be fancy and cook. We sat down wherever we were and ate, and then went right back to work. If we could sneak time out, we pulled up weeds and stewed them that night at the *masseria* for lunch the next day. The only times we ever had hot lunch were the days it rained; then we'd get the men to let us cook downstairs in their place. That was the good part of a rainy day; the bad was not getting paid.

Now, when I think of it, it's a miracle we're alive. We didn't eat much; we were cold a lot of the time and we never washed a plate or a bowl. They say now that dirty plates can poison you, but we figured why wash them? We'll have to use them again tomorrow. The most we ever did was a quick rub with grain dust. There! That's clean. Clean a fork? No. You wiped that on the corner of your towel; the men wiped them straight on their pants. There wasn't any water in the house, and in the spring even the well went dry so we had to drink the same brackish water the horses had. It came out of any old ditch or pool and was foul and green. We had to drink something, and you know, we didn't get sick either. Now that everything is clean we get sick, but we didn't then.

That's how I lived every "season" for fourteen years. Always with the whole squad sleeping, eating and working together. When I was boss of my own squad I had to work harder. I had to do my own chores, see the others did theirs and make bread for the whole lot . . . and I didn't get paid much more for it either.

The men's quarters weren't any better than ours. They slept on the ground floor in one room with one little window. The floor was dirt; no one bothered to sweep it. The quarters didn't really belong to anyone and there were always arguments about who was supposed to clean it up, so in the end no one did and the fights went on. Over half the room would be filled from floor to ceiling with tiers of little platforms set in the wall, four to a tier. They were the bunks and if the men wanted some kind of mattress or covers, they brought them themselves. I never understood why, but the platform-bunks weren't ever very long, so that even a woman my size had to sleep with her knees bent. There wasn't much other furniture — maybe a battered table, some stools and a cupboard for plates and supposedly for pots too, but they were always sitting near the fireplace, collecting flies.

The men cooked there, ate there and slept there. They worked on a year-to-year contract and when the place was good and the padrone fair, they stayed sometimes all of their lives. They did the general work, the plowing, the sowing, the wood cutting, that sort of thing, but no matter what the work, they got a fixed rate for the month. It changed a bit after the war, but before the war they could count on fifty kilos of grain, one kilo of oil, one of salt and about eleven dollars a month. That wasn't a lot to live on, so they brought their families out during the winter and spring when there wasn't extra help tak-

ing up the bunks. That way they saved for wood and food, and
the padrone didn't mind if it kept them on the place. In fact,
sometimes, the padrone wrote it into their agreement . . . but
the mess of the place! Men and women in bed together, children playing on the floor or peeing in the corner, dogs scroung-
ing bits under the table; everything went on in that one room.
Someone was always sick and someone was always drunk. Babies were born with just anyone who was around helping. They
tried to put up blankets, or bamboo canes to divide one tier
from another, but it didn't help much. There wasn't any privacy, and there were fleas and flies from the animals, and
everyone fought all the time. I made up my mind early I wasn't
going to marry a contract hand and spend my life fighting in
one of those shit-holes.

I'll never forget my first summer at the *masseria*. Everything
was new to me and for the first time in my life I had a little
money. I remember I bought a shawl — I'd never had one of
my own before — the kind with fringes called a Venetian
shawl, and I was still wearing it when I got married, too! It cost
me two weeks' work. Then there were the shoes. There was a
man who drove a broken-down car from *masseria* to *masseria*
selling shoes, in fact he still does it, and even if you didn't want
shoes he was a treat to watch. We all turned out to listen to him
and his show. He'd tell a couple of stories, mind you they were
always the same ones we knew by heart, and then he'd go into
his spiel.

"Shoes, the latest models! Shoes! Anybody want shoes? City
quality, friendly prices. Step right up." Then he'd hold up
different kinds until people spoke out asking for their sizes.
He'd give you *one* of your number to try. If that didn't fit, he'd
give you another number — always one so you couldn't get
away without paying. He never stopped talking and he could
listen to ten people at once. Well, the first time he came I didn't
have any money, but the second time I did and I borrowed the

rest to get a pair of brown shoes with buttons. He gave me my number to try and when I said they were all right, he gave me the other shoe in exchange for my money — ten lire. All that money and they had buttons, but don't think they were pretty. Not with buttons, low heels and curled up, pointed toes! They weren't much, and to make it worse the second shoe must have been a size smaller. It was too tight, but I fixed that. I got them good and wet and just kept them on my feet until they dried; after that they fit fine.

Fourteen years is almost a lifetime. Every year in September when I went home, I tried to find work cutting and hauling wood — at least until the snows came — and that gave me another two or three months' work, so it was really only two or three months a year that I just sat in town. All that time I had an agreement with a boy in Torregreca, Giovanni, that we'd get married — someday. He wasn't quite like the others. He always looked cleaner and when he came to the house in the evenings he wore a white shirt and in the winters a real suit. He was smart, too, and worked hard, but his mother didn't want me. I didn't have a dowry or land or even enough clothes. I wasn't good enough for her son. I saved everything I could to buy sheets and blankets and slips . . . there's a regular number you've got to have before you can get married. The boy's family sends a judge to look everything over, to make sure you've stuck to the agreement. If you haven't, the wedding is put off. We never got to that stage, though; his mother wouldn't come to talk to Tanname. It wasn't enough that we'd decided; the deal had to be argued out by the parents and before they met, a formal "ambassador" had to put the idea to the girl's family. His mother wouldn't have me; called me a *cafone*. I wasn't good enough for her son because they had a little land and a house, a real one with windows. Still he came every evening to sit by the fire with us. I remember how his belt buckle winked and twinkled at me in the light. He was very proud of it. It was the only thing his father ever sent him from America. He'd been there for years; some said he had a new family there. Those evenings Mamma dozed by the fireplace, but there was always Tina to make sure we were never alone. She set out after Giovanni — did everything she could to get him. She sang and told funny stories and asked how many dresses his mamma had and how many hectares of wheat he planted. He told me once she had a mind like a cash register, but he talked to her, all right, even if he was watching me all the time. Every time I looked up from the mending he'd smile. I won't ever love anybody else, but it was no good. In the end his father wrote from America that he wanted the family to come over. Giovanni said he'd send for me, but I told him to forget it; I knew what would happen — nothing. He could just pretend I'd never existed. Either we got married before he left, in spite of his mother, or I was through; I was not going to wait any longer. He didn't believe me, then he got mad and threatened to slash my face with a razor so that any man who came near me would see the mark and know I was "Giovanni's woman." He'd set a mark on his property. He was as good as his word. He came all the way down to the *masseria* looking for me, but I hid from him and every night I crawled up in the pigeon loft to keep watch . . . every night until I heard he'd gone.

By then the war was over. I'd been working for "The Turk" down at the station for years. My big brother, the only one who ever amounted to anything, had been killed by the partisans. They called him "The Notary" because he'd been all the way through school, the only one who had, and he'd worked for a notary. He was gone, Tanname was dead, and Mamma was an old woman though she wasn't quite fifty. All day she'd sit outside our door, looking up the street, waiting for the men to come home. They wouldn't, anymore, and my brothers didn't seem to have any spine, so I took over. I made the contracts with The Turk for the whole family . . . even made Tina work. God, how he hated her. She talked back and slipped away from work. She caused all kinds of trouble, but I made him take her. I was the squad boss, the one who slept by the door to make sure the others didn't go romancing and the one who beat them to work. My brothers were taken on as shepherd boys, then laborers, but they spent everything they got. We had to live on what I made . . . and on what I could save or filch. Oh, I took what I could get. I figure if the shopkeeper doesn't know how to keep shop, he better close up. I got enough extra bread out of every batch I made for the *masseria* crew to feed Mamma in town. For a while I walked off with a plank each afternoon — found a freight car loaded with wood and no one watching it, so I'd shoulder a piece and march off. We got some furniture out of that. The Turk had connections with the black market. Shoe soles, overcoats, uniforms . . . things we hadn't seen in years . . . arrived from Naples in the middle of the night and he sold them. I did most of the selling, took the chances, so I made him give me a cut on every sale. Things hadn't changed much. We still lived in the loft, slept together and ate bread soup for dinner more times than I like to remember. And in the winter we were in the same one-room house in town. As Mamma said, no one ever moved out, more moved in.

It was Tina now who wanted to get married, but she'd give the boys a bit of her sharp tongue and they'd bust the agreement. Finally she had one trapped. She called him her "little peanut" and that's about what he was. A smart, ferrety little guy, our Nunzio. He was a barber by trade and now *he* came in the evenings to sit by the fire while Tina sat in the shadow pretending to sew. He talked about his customers and politics. Nunzio always said he was too delicate to work in the fields, but I think he was too smart. He picked easier work and he had pretty good trade for a while. His customers were all Communists. He was a Demo-Christian because the padroni all were

— he'd do anything to get in with the right-thinkers — and
when the elections came and he wouldn't change parties to suit
his customers, they left him. He had two or three left, regulars
with "subscriptions" — three shaves a week and a monthly
haircut — and even they didn't want to pay up at the end of
the month. He blamed everything on politics and sat by the fire
talking and explaining about it — to Mamma of all people.
She'd cock her head one way, then the other, and make little
noises — she was the perfect audience — and he forgot she
couldn't hear a word he said; she's been stone deaf for the last
twenty-five years.

After Giovanni left for America, I swore I'd never get married and Tina was always at me to give her what I'd saved and
my sheets and things. She said after all I wouldn't need them,
and she'd spent all her money on scarves and belts and fancy
shoes with heels. I'd fed her for years; now she thought I
should pay for her getting married. There was one winter I
dreaded coming home. Tina'd start about money, Mamma
about getting married, and they'd go on until I either left the
house or went to bed. Nunzio said flat out they'd have to live in
our house if they got married. My older brother wanted to get
married too and he was always at me for money. That was the
year I learned I had some rights and if I didn't fight for them,
no one would. I figured sooner or later I was going to get out of
Torregreca . . . until I did, no one was going to push me
around. Sooner or later everyone grows up; I did that winter, in
all that cold and silence.

So Tina got married and I sold the donkey. We didn't need it
anymore and we did need the room and the money. Nunzio
cleaned out the stall, set up their bed there, and pretty soon
they had a baby. And a second. Nunzio said Tina was the only
woman in town who could get pregnant while she was nursing
a baby. She said he ought to keep his pants buttoned. There

was no point in arguing, the babies were born. Mamma and me, three of my brothers, Nunzio, Tina and their two babies were all jammed into that same one room. The "season" was almost a vacation for me.

Every morning we scrambled out of bed to get the house cleaned up and the razors set out in case a customer showed up. Almost no one came. One of the new ones was called Michele the Neapolitan. He was tall and strong-looking with sleek black hair and very black eyes set back under shaggy eyebrows. You could tell he'd grown up in a city; he read a newspaper and told Nunzio's Communist customers they were *cafoni*, sitting letting the world go by while people in cities made money. Michele was very fussy about his moustache, how it was trimmed, not that I could see anything so special about it. It was just square, right up under his nose and went almost to his upper lip. He wanted scent after his shave and he always sent one of my brothers off to get him a coffee . . . I don't know who ever paid, but Michele didn't. He didn't have a job, said he'd come to Torregreca to see his sister and was just waiting for his fruit vendor's license in Naples to get straightened out. In town they called him the Poor Man's Lawyer because he told the men what they were entitled to under the insurance and if they weren't getting it, he'd write letters for them. In the end there were foremen who'd pay him not to work, just to keep him from stirring up the men.

I didn't like him much; he was too sure of himself, always taking advantage of people and bragging. He told everyone he was going to marry me; I said he wasn't, he said he was. Mamma said, "You got to get married, Chichella, you got to." I guess that's how it happened, really. It looked safe. I said we could be engaged to get Mamma off my back, but I knew we couldn't get married — that's what made it safe — because he didn't have a job. If he was telling the truth about the license in Naples at least I'd get out of Torregreca. I thought things could go along that way for years; maybe they could have, but he wouldn't let them.

I was working down at the Turk's hoeing beans, and I was to have a week off the first of April between crops. I told Michele I'd be back. He'd been pestering me for months: was I like God made me or had I been fooling around? He figured I slept with the Turk. I'd done everything else for the Turk, but I'd never slept with him, and I told Michele I hadn't. He'd just have to take my word for it. He wouldn't, and he kept trying to insist, said he'd see for himself, but I'd managed to throw him off each time. Well, so the first of April I started from the *masseria* at dawn, alone, to walk to Torregreca. I was in the wooded part just outside town when the mist got so heavy the trees looked as though they didn't touch the ground. It was like being wrapped in cotton wool and living all alone in a world where everyone was dead. It was quieter than the cemetery at night, until I heard footsteps coming toward me. I peered around, but there was no one in sight — still the footsteps — then suddenly the mist cleared, sort of unfolded and there was Michele.

"This time we're going to settle it once and for all . . . my way!" That was all he said before he grabbed me. He didn't give me time to run, but I fought . . . God, how I fought. I clawed his face and tore his shirt, and I knew enough to try to kick him, but I never made it. That morning I didn't get by. He got me down and settled it his own way. He found out I was the way I should be, too, that I'd told him the truth, and he didn't have much fun finding it out. We were both shaky and I think even he was a little scared — frightened at what he'd done and maybe ashamed too — but he covered it up being nasty and pushing me down the path in front of him. All I could do was stumble along. I couldn't talk. It was like a paralysis. I was trembling and scared and I hated him for what he'd done to me. I hated myself too; most of all I was scared.

By my schedule something should have happened by the fifth or sixth of the month, but nothing did. By the end of April, when there was still nothing, I knew I had to tell Michele. He was smart. After that morning he never tried to see me alone. We only saw him in the evenings when he came to sit with the family and it made it harder for me to catch him and tell him. When I finally did, all he said was, "The pleasure's all mine. We'll just get married." He was glad; I wasn't.

I tried everything but I couldn't get rid of the baby. They didn't sell the "gadget" then. Now it's easy. You buy the black plastic tube from the pharmacy — ten thousand lire. It's illegal, of course — and the midwife sticks it in. All you have to do is promise not to tell where you got it if you hemorrhage. But then they didn't have them and I was getting bigger and bigger. Michele had to go to Naples for his papers, so he borrowed all the money I'd saved and went off. He didn't come back and he didn't come back. Finally the end of June he showed up in a new suit and new shoes and a new suitcase . . . and without a lira left. I said I wouldn't get married in Torregreca where everybody'd remember when the baby came too soon, so we had to borrow money to go to Pompeii. It was June of 1950 and hot as hell; that was my first train trip and I'm not apt to forget it. We rode all night — me and Michele, and Tina and Michele's brother. They had to come too, to be the witnesses. Tina complained all the way. "Why couldn't you get married in Torregreca? You should have hired a car so we didn't have to stand on the platform for two hours waiting. You better make this trip fun or *guai à te*." On and on she went. Michele got mad, said we were *cafoni* and he wouldn't be seen with us. We had to wait hours for the church to open and then I fainted in the middle of the ceremony and they dragged me out into the sacristy. Michele ranted and didn't want to tip the sacristan who'd taken care of me. Then we had to get a room. Michele said he knew a place, and walked us miles and miles in the heat until I thought I'd faint again. He made the deal with the people; all four of us in the same room and the place smelled like a garbage dump. My God, I'll never forget the flies in there, either! Michele took us to a wine shop for something to eat and got drunk, so drunk he picked a fight with the owner of the place and then turned over a cart in the street outside. He said it was all our fault, we were nothing but *cafoni* and he wouldn't stay with us another day. We were going back to Torregreca. We rode all night again, missed the bus at the station and had to wait all day until the five o'clock trip. When we got home, Nunzio gave us a potato and two turnips for our wedding dinner!

Michele and I slept in a little hayloft above the old stall. Somehow he'd gotten a bed up there, but once you climbed the ladder you had to slither under the roof beams and lie still. Toward the end my belly was too big for me to clear the roof and I had to sleep with Mamma and one of my brothers in the big bed down below. I had the baby there, a little girl, with the whole family looking on. Then my breasts got infected and I had such a fever they wouldn't let me nurse the baby. Maybe what they fed her was wrong, or maybe, like the doctor said, she had bad intestines. I don't know, but she died in March. Michele didn't have a job so I went back to work, and he spent the day standing in the sunny corner of the Piazza, in his office, as he called it, giving advice about how to take the employers.

Everything got worse. One winter I kept us alive on what I'd gleaned the summer before. Michele worked sometimes, but he never brought the money home. He drank it up in the wine shops and then whispered to me up in our loft that he had evil spirits in his stomach. Sometimes I could tell it really hurt. Then one day he bled all over the bus going to Matera, and they put him in the hospital and cut out part of his stomach. For a year he was better, even worked, and I worked too until I was pregnant again. Michele said his son wouldn't be born in that "family flophouse," that's what he called it. He wanted a house of his own. Every time he said it, I said we couldn't pay the rent and he'd come back at me with, "We can pay when we're dead. Right now I want to live." I couldn't talk him out of it. Anybody who looks for something he can't afford will find it. He did. He found a house. It belonged to a relative of his who had the nerve to ask two thousand lire a month. Michele was beyond reasoning; he took it — two thousand lire worth of double mule stall, that was our new home. No one had ever lived in it. There was no window, no light, no floor and only the water that ran down the walls. We won't even talk about the smell; there was a "perfume" no amount of whitewash could kill. Michele bashed a hole in one corner for a flue and made a rough fireplace under it. For a toilet we had the outdoors, but we were lucky the *case popolari* up on the hill hadn't been built then, so we had a private latrine . . . breezy but quiet.

We took our bed out of the loft at Mamma's. She gave us an old commode and let me take the table a carpenter had traded me for that lumber I stole. Tina gave me a rush-bottom chair and Michele's mother gave me another. I found a beat-up bench-chest on the side of the road; it was falling apart but it was useful for flour and bread. And so we moved in. In less than a week the walls were black and running with oily tar . . . Michele had made a mistake about where he put the flue and it wouldn't draw unless there was a huge fire. We didn't have enough wood and what we had was too wet to catch at all without a lot of coaxing and teasing.

My gleanings didn't carry us through that winter. Michele needed good food and special medicines and the work I could find in the winter wasn't enough to keep us out of debt. We had to ask for credit. Lucky for us that our insurance books

were still up to date — even Michele's — so we didn't have to
pay the doctor and occasionally he gave medicines the insurance would pay for. The good ones aren't on the insurance. My
book as an agricultural worker was enough to get me a fifteen
thousand lire [$25] prize when Vincenzo was born in May of
1952. They explained it to me . . . something funny like a
premium for having a baby (as though I could do anything
else) . . . but I think it was meant to pay for the fifteen days
I had lost at work. When I heard about it, I started planning
the things I could buy. Why not get a real bed at last? At least
the headboard and foot. As soon as they paid me I went down
and bought the only one I could get for the money. It's the
same tin one I have still. Oh, I was excited! Even without
springs, with the mattress on boards, I knew I'd sleep better in
my new bed. Michele said I was trying to kill him by keeping
him from getting the right medicines. He got drunk and came
back home to beat me, but I'd do the same thing again today.
It was worth it to have a real bed.

I had three babies in that house; Michele worked when he
could. I worked. We were alive. He went back to drinking wine
and stronger stuff even though the doctors had told him not to.
Oh well, there was nothing I could do to stop him. Every night
he'd wake me up to boil rags for his stomach. That meant lighting the fire again. After one of his attacks he went out and
bought a three-ring burner that cost twenty times what a hot
water bottle would have. It made me laugh because most of
the time we couldn't use it . . . we had to pay cash for the gas
bomb.

For a couple of weeks he didn't go out, didn't drink anything, didn't smoke. He took care of himself and you could tell
just looking at him that he felt better. I began to hope. Then
one night he woke me up, gasping and strangling.

"Air! Give me air!" It sounded like he vomited, but in the

dark I couldn't be sure. I got out of bed and stumbled around feeling for the lamp. There weren't any matches, so I dragged the door open. It was still black outside. I saw a shadow. He's up, I thought. I got around to his side of the bed as fast as I could, but just as I reached for him, he fell over on the ground and dragged me with him. I couldn't leave him there. I pushed and pulled and heaved until I had his body on the bed and I could lift his legs around. He began to come to, but felt bad again and sat up. Then he threw up all over the bed, the sheets and the blankets. When it was over, he fell back and just lay there. "It's gone off now, Chichella," he said. "Get Mamma. I don't need anything. Just get Mamma."

I grabbed Michele's jacket and ran off barefooted for town without thinking that all I had on was a slip. It was still dark. Nobody would see me if I wrapped his jacket around me. It didn't take much to wake up his mother and his brother, Vittorio. They came back with me. We had almost reached the house when dawn came . . . that dawn when it's still night but it's day too . . . and Vittorio could see me for the first time.

"Hey, you're barefooted and there's blood all over your legs. Slut! Foul, filthy slut! Nothing shames you." He thought the blood was mine. I don't blame him, but I started to run.

"Gesù, it's Michele. Michele's blood. He's bleeding to death!" We all ran like the devil was after us. Vittorio lighted the lamp and then we saw what was on the floor, the bed, the walls, everywhere. My God, I never saw so much blood in my life. There were pools of it that had begun to jelly with bits of flesh in them. Parts of him had come out with the blood. While his mother and Vittorio tried to talk to Michele I started cleaning up. I swabbed with the dirty sheets, I mopped into a pail, I scrubbed the walls and the floor and in the end we changed the sheets, his mother and I, while Vittorio held Michele. Then

I tried to wash myself off; I was covered in blood. My slip stuck to me! Thank God I couldn't stop to think about it because they were sending me back to town for the doctor and I had to hurry.

When I got to the doctor's house it was light and people were beginning to move around in the streets. It was the same doctor who'd taken care of me when the baby died and he'd done his best with Michele, lecturing him about his diet, giving him medicine and the certificates we needed for treatments and pension applications and for insurance payments when Michele couldn't work. He'd had his fill of us. We didn't pay him; he got nothing but the government fee, but still he promised he'd be along to see Michele.

He didn't come until eleven that morning. Vittorio accused me more than once of not talking to the doctor, or, if I had, of not explaining how sick Michele was. When he stuck his head in the door he was all smooth-faced and jolly.

"Well, well, Michele, how are we this morning?" Michele could only wave toward me. He wanted me to explain.

"I told you, I told you this morning. He was dying. He vomited blood all over the house; it just kept coming!"

"Now, don't exaggerate, Chichella! You're just cross at me."

"I'll show you. Look at the sheets over there . . . and see the blood in the pail. Take a good look in the pail and then tell me if I'm exaggerating."

He came over. "Why didn't you tell me it was this bad?"

"I did, I did. You didn't listen. I did tell you."

He shrugged. "I thought you meant a little bit. Get him to the hospital . . . right away, do you hear?"

I tried to hire a car to take Michele, but the Torresi don't let sympathy get in the way of business, and as soon as they heard I'd have to pay later, they had things to do or all of a sudden their cars wouldn't run. No one would help me. The best we could do was load him on a flat cart Vittorio borrowed from a vegetable vendor in the market and push him down the main road and through the Piazza to the hospital. We were ashamed of doing it that way, but we had to get him there and we couldn't even wait until it was dark to do it. He stayed in the hospital for weeks and when he came out I think I knew it was all over. He lived almost four years, but he never was right. We already had three children to feed. Then in 1956 there were blizzards . . . not snow, blizzards that went on for months. People starved; airplanes dropped food and Michele's mother and brother came to live with us. You add it up . . . all of us in a double stall . . . would you like having an audience for every action of your life? If it rained, you did your business in the house in a clay jar — with everybody sitting there. Sometimes I couldn't put Michele off — with his mother and brother in the same room almost on top of us.

Oh sure, we got out of the stall before Michele died, just two years before. Rosa was born here. They finished these *case popolari,* twelve apartments. *Twelve* for hundreds of applications! There was a regular war to see who'd get in; the law said they were for the ones with the lousiest houses, but nothing works like it should here. Guess I was lucky with the inspectors; they saw how things were with us. The big cheese sat down to write something and got his pants wet; accused me of sopping the chair with water. In the end I convinced him that stall was an indoor swamp and we'd rot there in the damp . . . us and the chairs — everything. It was too late for Michele, but he got to *die* in a decent place.

Do you know what it means to someone like me to be able to close the door and sleep in my own room? To have a room for the children, to cook without spreading things on the bed, and to use a toilet where there's a lock on the door? I never had any of that until three years ago, when we got this apartment. Now to live I have to give it up. I just wanted to tell you it's yours for as long as you stay. But you've got to understand what a house means to me — what giving it up means.

She sat looking at me, her eyes large and brimming with honest tears. Once again her hands were turned palm up on the table as though, disconnected from her body, they had been laid there to rest on their own. I have no idea how long we sat mute; she, glazed by her encounter with her past; and I, shocked by the disparity of our lives. I tried to imagine what I would have been in her place, and then wondered if she had ever tried to imagine herself in mine.

VI

TODAY AND YESTERDAY

EVERYWHERE I went people watched me. In shops they bunched around the counter to listen to my requests for soap or two hundred grams of cheese as though I were going to say something of moment. Each morning as I went to the furniture store to beg a newspaper, people turned and pressed themselves into the sliver of shade next to the walls of buildings that they might watch my progress. Strange that I bought a paper, stranger still when they found I never bought the same one two days running. The next stop was the bar for a coffee — into the black, black cavern with the sparkling pink-and-gray plastic counter and the new machine that hissed importantly. Men watched me from the street, and inside the men in cloth caps who were already hunched over the only table playing *scopa* looked up in surprise. Women were neither expected nor welcomed. The proprietor, a leathery-skinned man with a long, sad face, had worked in Africa for years and fancied his few words of English. He bowed from the levers of the coffee machine and announced, *"In piedi!"* (On your feet!)

The men shuffled away from their table and with their caps in their hands, their foreheads gleaming a translucent marble white, they lined up along the bar facing me. The proprietor wiped the aluminum chair seat and tabletop with a greasy rag and motioned to me. The levee was mounted. The men stood silent, watching me with veiled eyes; theirs was motionless anticipation, the quiet before the dancer begins to tease. I always disappointed them. I drank my coffee and read my newspaper without enjoyment but with decorous self-possession. When I left, the men all bowed. I persisted in thinking that, in time, the novelty would wear off and the card game would be continued in the back room. Instead the cardplayers were joined by the curious until I had an audience of twenty, sometimes thirty men who lined up along the bar, caps in hand, to watch me and bow me out.

Shattering as the performance was, it had one great advantage. In a very short time everyone in town knew about me and my connection with the new housing and the nursery. Comments in wine shops and whispered conversations at fountains had announced my influence. A walk through the Rabata or the Saraceno meant a string of invitations . . . "Come in and see my house. Then you'll know I should have a new place up by the nursery . . . If you want to, you can get it for us . . ." "Come in . . ." And that was exactly what I had to do. I had been given a list of one hundred and sixty-four families who had certificates that proved they were qualified in every way for the new housing. They did not possess land; they had large families; they lived in unsanitary housing. Only thirty-two could have houses. Their need had to be rated on a sliding scale by the committee. Visiting each applicant was the only way an estimate could be made. Conditions were medieval. There were a few houses with ceilings so low I could not stand up straight. No one had water or toilets. They all lived on top of each other in one room, at the most two. One family of eleven people and two goats lived in a windowless room eight feet by ten. The old father, a young stepmother, a son and his wife and their two almost grown sons had bedded down in so many different permutations that the five younger children might have been fathered by any one of the four men. None of this surprised me as much as the truculent ill-will of the men and the fear of the women. They were hostile and resented yet another intrusion from which they knew in their hearts they could expect nothing. The invitations were a dare, a challenge. Come in and see where I live, then see if you've got the guts to deny me a house. They were bitter and powerless. They were afraid to refuse information, and at the same time convinced that any they gave would somehow be used against them. In their minds power gave me the right to be arrogant and they were ready, bristling with resentment. I could understand their suspicion and antagonism; I could understand insults or silence; but I was nauseated by the toadying that was the ignoble end of too many of the visits. Pride evaporated in the stinging summer air. They wanted to indenture themselves to me as serfs . . . they would do my cleaning, my shopping, keep me in eggs. They wept and whined and I loathed them, myself and the system. At night they skulked through the courtyards trying to reach my house without being seen. If they could present me with salami and gain a promise, they were ahead of the others. They lurked in the dark shadows of trees on the road, at the garage where I kept my car, even behind the big hall door of my apartment building. They wanted a word, a promise, a smile, anything that would commit me as a champion of their case.

I dreaded the house visits and the unavoidable relationships they set in motion, but I forced myself to stick to a daily quota and to ground rules I had made for myself. I tried never to be in a hurry. I tried to remove the inquisition air so natural to such visits. I never wrote down anything in front of the people except the noncontroversial birthdates of their children. I asked nothing about the education of the parents. Even in 1959 there was no middle school in Torregreca. I could imagine what their schooling had been; the rest they told me themselves as they talked about their children, or what work they did, or what they might have been. They were mystified at times. I seemed to be interested in the land and crops, in the lack of water and sewers, in the dialect and nicknames, in weaving, in rush bas-

kets, in wine. I did not stick to my subject. The visit disinte-
grated into a social meeting. They talked about themselves. In
the end they were not satisfied, but I was.

My notes were made while I stood in streets three or four
levels away from the last house visited. There was always a
stone wall or a stairway where I could loiter. Sometimes I just
looked out over the cascade of roofs with their tufts of singed
moss and their cockled chimney pots. My eyes took in more
than I knew. Houses separated themselves from the tile-and-
plaster mosaic and I saw what I had not been able to see before: these were not real houses, they were caves that stair-
stepped up the hill in such a way that part of each roof was the
alleyway on the level just above. Of course there could be no
windows in such a house; the back went into the hillside and it
was logical too that sewage dumped in the streets or even into
those pipeless drains should filter down the walls of the houses
below. To the drone of flies and the audible sizzling of stones
and dirt drying in the sun I wrote my cryptic notes.

✳   ✳

TEDESCHI, Paolo fu Angelo — 6 children, between 6 months
and 11 years (birthdates listed). One room, no window, back
wall oozing brown, tarlike substance. Roof leaks, ceiling stain
over bed. One bed, one hanging cradle visible. Jesus, St. Anthony, Grandfather with light, and framed dollar bill over
bed. Four chickens and a rabbit in shoe box. Fireplace, no gas
ring, twigs piled in corner, sink surrounded by water pots, two
strips lard hanging on hooks. Unglazed brick floor weaves
when walked on (stall underneath belongs to someone else).
House very neat, but stench incredible. Curtain by door covers
slop-feces chute. Only two chairs; borrowed one for me from
neighbors. Query — do children eat standing? Sharecrop ten
acres hillside 6 miles from town — wheat 12 quintals for one of
seed. Rent house 48,000 per annum. *Children* — three eldest in

school. NOTE see to X-ray Maria — pigeon-chested, black circles, fever and cough. TB? Paolo square, red-eyed (!) diffident, then aggressive, opinionated. Divides world into Us and You — probably Communist. Evasive. Wife thin, quick-eyed — wanted impress me with church devotion. He learned to read, write — Army; she illiterate though speaks better.

DEMA, Giuseppe di Giovanni — town crier, paid 200 lire (32 cents) each subject (chickens, bleach, etc.,) for two rounds daily. Two rooms, one window in back where his parents stay bedridden. Both blind, rice-paper skin. 4 children (6 yrs. to 25), youngest Mongoloid. 8 miscarriages. 4 beds front room, gas ring, radio (blaring), grain sacks piled corner, no sink, hand basin on stand, water jugs. Motorcycle!! Basket of eggs, six hens under "matrimonial" — chairs piled on top. Interrupt water sloshing on stone floor. Dema thin, 50ish, toothless. Fears lose job, speaks no Italian. "Times changing," 2nd grade. Wife blond, prolapsed, kidney pains (uterus? talks of suppurations) smiling, but shy. Calls Mongoloid her "stupid son" (*ciutto*). Air of defeat. Eldest son ferret-faced, white shirt, tight black pants. Has motor-scooter, refuses to work — does not want to be a peasant. Wife brought 6 acres in dowry, transferred to son to qualify for housing. He left it fallow. Probably Demas unable adapt to move. Try another visit when son not present.

MISEO, Pancrazio fu Giorgio — sharecropper, vineyard keeper. 4 children, all married. One son, wife and 4 children 2 months to 6 yrs. living in house. Miseo in fields. 1st room wrought-iron double bed with olive branch stuck over Madonna above, fireplace, fire lit, bean pot bubbling, twigs beside, peppers, garlic, etc., hanging, no pork, no window, floor broken bricks — clean — slop jar, water jugs, no smell. Radio-alarm clock doesn't work. Battered dowry chest. Rosina, round, greyhaired, long skirt, boots, won't have chickens in house. In stall with donkey — stall latrine? Sometimes the children, she says. In corridor to stall, down two steps is double bed — tin — sacks grain, potatoes, no window. 2nd room off corridor ten steps down ladder, no window. 4 children of "underworld" sleep on 1 bed, 2 benches with sacks. Mushroom-cellar bedroom for the babies, tar oozing down wall, dirt floor. Down snaggled stairs to donkey stall . . . no window, no outside door. House was padrone's, rent 44,000 lire per annum. Son and wife both day workers: harvest. Rosina says husband Monarchist, too old to change. Son Communist, worries mother. Children bright, hopes all will be teachers!! Get along fine, she says, good land, padrone thief, 15 quintals grain for one seed, wine, cheese, (run goats, sheep) but house brings rheumatism. Pipe in children's dungeon broken — "tar" seepage from sewer. Recommend son, wife and children get new house. APPLICATION.

CAPPELLA, Antonio di Angelo — landslide destroyed last house. This house 50,000 lire per annum. One room, window, roof caved in, mold one wall, 7 children 6 yrs. to 18 yrs. Double bed, army-neat, cot at end, 2 chests (beds at night) table, four rush chairs legs wired X brace, plates clean in racks on wall, pots ditto, peppers, tomatoes, etc., hung walls, curtain hides clothes on nails, slop chute but no stench, no sink, gas ring, cheese on raffia platform across rafters. Antonio 45ish, square, strong, ragged but clean, wants go Germany. Sharecropper. Wary, leaves talking to Filomena, black, high coloring, energetic. Both literate, they say. Turns out they can sign names. No formal schooling. F. seamstress, no machine, earns bit embroidery, knitting. *Mario* (6) *twisted foot*. QUERY LUCA. Angelo 7½, needle-thin, chronic bronchitis!! Catarrh, nose yellow. Forced one boy to swear vocation — got him into seminary. 18-yr. old works electrician's assist. 200 lire a day. Impressed cleanliness, plans children, alertness. Antonio says won't get house — Communist and has a "half-conviction" against him. *Investigate Registry Office, Comune.* Same reason hasn't applied work Germany. Why not Turin? Good material.

*　　*

And so it went. I prayed that some of them would *not* end up in the *villaggio*. New housing would not make them neater, more responsible or more enterprising. Worse, it might convince them that the less they did, the more someone else would do for them. I came to think that new housing, in the face of such general need, should be treated as a premium for those who had been pig-headed enough to make a life out of what they had. They were the mothers and fathers of the children who would come to the nursery. I hoped they would still have some initiative rather than just their full quota of negative resentment.

Every Sunday morning in August and September the Mayor, the members of the housing committee of the town council and I swooped down on houses like well-fed hawks ready to pick a fresh cadaver. This was the official version of my own informal house visits and was without exception the most embarrassing duty I have ever been asked to perform. While men shouted presumptuous questions at the man of the family, who was neither deaf nor dumb, others snooped in drawers and behind curtains. "*Tu*, what party did you vote for?" "Are these children yours, or does your wife take visitors?" "What do *you* know about how selection is made? You, *tu*, you can't read. You can't write. Leave that to your betters." I talked to the women, told them not to worry too much, asked about their children or what they were having for Sunday lunch. Anything that came into my head. The committee was trying to prove to me how methodical its procedures were; we visited families in rigid alphabetical order even if it took us from the bottom of the Saraceno up and out to a stall on the Appian Way and then back down to the Rabata. As we clambered up stairs and through piazzas the men discussed the politics and connections of our last victim. I tried to divorce myself from the group, lingering behind to scratch fleabites that speckled my body.

One day a list was delivered to me by the town messenger; fifteen names had been struck from the list of one hundred and sixty-four because of penal records. After each name was the notation "March 1944" and nothing else. Luca would know what had happened then that involved so many men, but I forgot to ask him until one evening when we were pacing gently along in the *passeggiata*. It was just at twilight. The sky was purple and pink with ribbons of deep blue skywriting. Even the houses way at the tip of the Rabata were tinged red and had taken back the three-dimensional quality they lost with the morning's light. It was a halcyon end to a halcyon day and Luca seemed more at peace than usual.

He shook his head at my question. "No, it's a long story. A forgotten one . . . tragically forgotten. On a day like this it hardly seems it could have happened, but it's not important now. It came to nothing." I insisted it could not have come to nothing if, fifteen years later, men were to forfeit their right to houses because of it. Finally, weary and a little irritated with me, he said "All right, I'll tell you about it, but I'm going to be comfortable while I do it and I'm going to tell it my own way. When we get to your place, we'll go in and you can just listen."

Luca had sprawled in the armchair and was loosening his tie when the door opened and Chichella came in, red-faced and puffing.

"Evening, Don Luca, Signora . . ." She went right through to the kitchen, dragged a chair to the door and sat on it. She was saving my reputation once more. The lines at the corners of Luca's eyes tightened. He slipped his tie back up, sat straighter and laughed.

"Well, now that we're all here, maybe you'd like to get us two bottles of beer, Chichella?"

"What's that, Don Luca? I don't listen, you know, I just sit." He repeated his question. "Sure, but you don't expect me to leave her . . . here . . . do you?" She pointed at me. "Just be patient, I'll get it." She marched through the sitting room and out onto the balcony where she bayed, "Vincenzo . . . Vinn-cenn-zzo-o-o-o-." The child's name echoed through the neighborhood. "Vincenzo, Vinn-cen-zzo-o-o-o-." Until a small voice answered, "*Oyee*, Ma. Whatdoya want?"

Beer came. Chichella settled down with a piece of black material and a large needle that she poked into the stuff by diving from above, and then yanked through from underneath with such force I could not imagine she was seriously sewing. Much of the time she snoozed.

"Before I can tell you what happened, you'd have to know how things were in Torregreca before the war. I remember it best the first night after I came back from Milan . . . when I had finished my medical training. It was the summer of '38, perhaps, and I hadn't been home in five years."

Twenty-four hours traveling had dulled Luca's original sense of anticipation. There had been a new electric train as far as Rome; then back to wooden seats, closed windows and no food. It was July. To escape the oppressive closeness of his neighbors he pretended to doze and had just achieved an uneasy separation of mind and body when the conductor shouted "All out. Latrine stop. All out." He had stumbled down with the others and performed in the predawn chill like an obedient child. After that Luca had looked out the window, waiting for the first light to play over the rolling hills he remembered so well. It came, but what he expected to see was hidden under a webbed camouflage of erosion. He had forgotten. Time had played its gentle tricks; he might have been on the moon. The sun flicked at white, stair-step houses high on the ridge. The glare from a windowpane burned Luca's eye. With a jump and a shrug the train stopped. He had arrived. The station master's wife was doubling for her husband. How surprised his Milanese friends would have been by the sight of this heavy woman with the red and gold cap squarely on her head, a trumpet and a flag under her arm and a baby sucking at her left breast. She had a message for him. His father had been unable to meet him, but had arranged for the bus to wait. As he stepped off the platform gray-blue thistles grabbed at his trousers. How many times as a lonely boy he had listened to them gossiping in the wind, and had wondered what secrets they told. Now they dipped lower and seemed to hiss, "Nothing changes, Luca. We're still here . . . still here." He was beginning to remember.

His Uncle Girolamo's house, though only one level below the Piazza, was so entwined with its neighbors that light and air reached it secondhand from tunnel passageways and dim air shafts. It was small, but enough for his needs; three rooms and a musty kitchen with a toilet-closet hidden in one corner. He was no lover of the modern so his sitting room still had the traditional geometric stenciling in deep red on a sepia wall, and the floor was of unglazed brick. Old bedspreads were thrown over chairs to hide tattered upholstery, and dog scraps were hardening on plates in the corners. Still, heavy carved oak cupboards, a fireplace and papers strewn over a tapestry-covered table gave it a feeling of comfortable disorder. Visitors here were an intrusion; the only exception was Luca. For him Don Girolamo had aired the spare room next to his own at the top of the precipitous stairway that twisted up out of the kitchen. It was a bare room and dank, but the mattress on the big brass bed was new. The last minute concession of a second chair brought up to the sitting room fireplace did not disguise the tentativeness of Don Girolamo's welcome. Luca could sense that his uncle and Assunta, the peasant woman who came each day to rearrange the confusion, had girded themselves against changes in their daily routine. It was their house; they issued the orders. Luca was sent to bed for the day and told that the barber would come in the evening. He enjoyed the fuss after so many years of lonely independence.

The grumble of their voices from below woke him up. He smiled happily to himself. His pessimism had given way to elation. Pouring water into a basin, he thought of his father striding across the Piazza that morning like a portly gray bear. Had he always worn spats? Caught up first in a woolly hug and then swept on by his father's enthusiastic introductions to everyone in sight, there had been no time to think. "This is my son Luca. He's a doctor now — a medical doctor!" They knew him and he knew them, but they had shaken hands and smiled to please the old man. Squads of little boys had taken his bags, his hat, his coat, his book, and with stray dogs gamboling about, feinting at their heels, they processioned down the Corso to Palazzo Montefalcone.

His mother had been waiting for him in the musty *salone* saved for weddings and funerals. There, in a sea of chairs with dingy red plush seats, she perched on the edge of a love seat, the center of a royal tableau, with Matteo standing at one shoulder and Titti at the other. They were so stiff and ill at ease that even Donna Filomena seemed relieved to escape to the dining room once she had Luca's promise to sit by her for the ritual coffee welcome. He had watched them moving his mother. They were not so positive as he remembered. They apologized to him for everything, like waiters, and tried to hide their self-consciousness with solemnity. These tyrants of his youth came into focus as drab creatures protected from the world and from Torregreca by this crumbling, fusty house. Suddenly he was free. With them, at least, he would never again feel inadequate, for he saw them as timid spectators of life. He might reassure them as they had never reassured him. Matteo, for instance, with his hands clasped in front of him, well away from his body as though making allowances for the paunch that would, in time, swell out to meet them, was already a make-believe priest in his high-collared seminary uniform. Yet he was flushed and his glance that darted from face to face hinted at nervous uncertainty. He was no longer the bullying squad leader who marched the little boys of the *Ballila* relentlessly around the Piazza, but was he, perhaps, unsure of his vocation?

On the other hand, Titti had lost none of her self-assurance. She had tried to impress Luca with her intellectual prowess. Teaching would be her career and she already spoke in resounding absolutes.

"Luca, Luca," she had called across the confusion of moving their mother. "You don't realize how low the standard of teaching is here. When I have my degree, I intend to introduce the newest methods. In five years the school system will be totally different. I will . . . Matteo, not that pillow. Mother wants the green one. Now, Luca . . ." She interrupted his thoughts about her moustache; maybe wax would improve it — it was hardly appealing. "Luca, pay attention. I was saying I intend to give my life to teaching. Marriage is such a waste of intellect." Ah, that's good, he thought, then later she won't need an excuse. Plump, but still hawkish, she seemed little changed. She met all overtures with aggression and wrapped herself in dowdy clothes and righteousness, but for the first time he felt her to be pathetic.

"Glad to see you dress well, young man." Don Manfredo's interruption relieved Luca of finding a tactful answer for Titti. "Nothing makes a better impression. Even here, little touches of elegance make a difference . . . I see you're eying my spats. A bit eccentric perhaps, but the Duce wears them and they're very good for protecting the ankles . . . against fleas . . . speaking with all due respect, of course." Luca had almost laughed at this maidenly refinement. "Come along, Girolamo will be impatient to see you. Wouldn't come to the house, you know, always considerate of your mother. I'm sure you understand."

On the whole his mother was the most amiable of the lot. So thin she was almost gaunt, her nose was bonier than ever and her wide, luminous eyes still had that ambiguous sparkle that might come from malicious amusement or deranged fervor, it was impossible to be sure which. More than once Luca wondered if her conversational reversals of subject might be a private escape from boredom, mixed of course with mental vagueness. He knew she was far from normal, but there was something still of her old shrewdness. The household revolved around her and her comfort.

As he dressed he decided it had been a successful meeting. His plan to stay with Uncle Girolamo was considered very practical for the simple reason that no one would be incommoded. He would have lunch each day with his father and mother. Otherwise he was free. And now he was impatient to get out to the Piazza. As he came down the stairs he heard Assunta say:

"He's got that passionate look like his uncle . . . and he's a *signore* too. I can tell by his shirts . . ."

The barber's pace had been slow. He was meticulous about his arts — shaving and gossiping. Methodical as a lawyer, he enumerated the steps of each "crime" as bald fact and not fantasy. Today his subject was Don Mimmi Mangiacarne. Don Mimmi, he revealed, was the father of his serving girl's child. No question she was pregnant. Easiest thing in the world in the privacy of the shop's back room. And Don Mimmi's long evening conferences with Dr. Delle Monache? Why did Don Mimmi go to Bari? On his return Rosa had taken to her bed.

Aborted, they said. So what did Don Mimmi buy in Bari? Poor
Don Mimmi, thought Luca, he has made two mistakes; he is
shaved by the postman and he keeps a shop for his own amusement, not for profit. It was beyond the Torresi's understanding
that a man might have a hobby, might long for the masculine
peace of catalogues, card games with friends and the aimless
dickering with salesmen from whom he did not intend to buy.
Nothing was so suspicious as the obvious. Only a fool accepted
it. The simplest event, to be understood, must be analyzed and
reconstructed until it was a lacework of deception and evil intentions. Distillation had revealed Don Mimmi's store as a
cover for his sexual adventures. The same acrobatic imagination had discovered that Luca was setting up practice in Torregreca. His objections and denials were met with gentle cluck-
ings meant to soothe a tantrum.

Luca had escaped to the Piazza for air. The gray buildings
were golden in the setting sun and a feeble breeze teased the
dust of the cobblestones, ruffling it one way, eddying it another.
People were beginning to stroll out, blinking in the light,
hunching their shoulders in a half stretch as though stiff from
too long a nap. Even the dogs were awake and snuffling around
the bars for tidbits. Before long, thought Luca, the Bishop will
amble into the Piazza with his secretary and will nod to the
Podestà, Rocco Dabbraio. Yes, Dabbraio's already in his place
by the monument, surreptitiously polishing his boots on the
back of his trouser legs. It was like seeing a film a second time;
he knew what would happen, but remembered details were now
replaced by others that seemed more important. The light on
the face of the clock in the church tower was dim compared to
the glare from the *Circolo dei Civili* that sliced out a wedge of
the Piazza and claimed it as private property. Children skirted
around it; men passed on the other side of the monument. So
many women in mourning; so many priests. Suddenly as
though he were seeing them through inverted binoculars, they

were little black ants bowed down by enormous loads. Back
and forth they stumbled, never tiring, always following some
invisible leader. If you could break the hypnotic procession of
their days, maybe harness that wasted energy . . .

His uncle had come up then and taken his arm. Had the
barber come? Mustn't let Giovanni's gossip upset you. He has
too little to do, so he imagines things — never about the poor,
knows too much about them. Always the wicked rich. Sometimes he's so sure of their ruin I think he's surprised to see his
victims going about in a normal way. Come, we'll have a coffee
at the *Circolo*.

The long narrow room was veiled in opalescent smoke that
did not entirely hide the blistered, stained paint of the walls.
Six or eight men, their hats pulled down on their noses,
slouched in rattan chairs ignoring each other. They paid no
attention to Luca and his uncle. Some subliminal buzzer set
them talking at the same moment. They argued and snarled.
Then silence again. Luca understood little of the discussion. He
knew the men; landowners, lifelong friends of his father's and
his uncle's, but he had never before seen them hibernating with
their own sullen thoughts. More machine-gun comments, then
silence. Would they hang a crucifix, as the Bishop had ordered,
seemed to be one of the questions they debated. Luca could
just make out pictures of the King, the Queen and Mussolini on
the back wall. Then there was the question of Fiore, Luca's
childhood mentor, the veterinarian. One of them said, Better
not disturb official waters, let him be a member. Waters be
damned, don't need a police spy, spat another. There was a
long, sucking snuffle of disapproval from one nicknamed Dry
Nose. He turned his back on the others to offer Luca and Don
Girolamo a coffee, then banged and tapped on the wall with
his cane to signal his order to the next door *caffè*. They waited
in silence until a crippled old man brought coffee on a tray
swimming with water. He stood close in front of his customers,

his face expressionless, watching the cups as though afraid they would disappear if he took his eyes off them. He snatched them back as quickly as he could and disappeared.

"How about a quick hand, Girolamo?"

"Not today. Luca wants to see Torregreca, wants to see if it's changed any."

At the end of the room a lawyer who had never practiced but was famous for his ability to "fix" anything, suddenly straightened up and called, "What sort of change? Sounds interesting."

"What kind of change indeed?" said Dry Nose, and blew into his handkerchief. "What do you expect? Crops are worse, the peasants stubborner, money's tight, but we get along." He sighed. "Death and malaria are here to stay. The rest takes time. No point rushing change. Leads to mistakes. We keep things steady here. You won't find change, Luca."

And he had not. By contrast to the *Circolo* the Piazza was alive with people and their chatter. Luca and his uncle paced back and forth in front of the monument. A man muffled in a gray scarf joined them and told a joke about what the Neapolitan prostitute said to the policeman who arrested her in front of the Milan cathedral. Don Girolamo countered with one just as old about the Sicilian peasant in a Naples whorehouse. Promising to meet his uncle in an hour, Luca struck out on his own along the Corso. A friend of his father's stopped him to say that his wife — and of course his daughters — would be expecting him to call. Luca remembered them with a shudder. Shopkeepers nodded to him as though they saw him every day. One stopped him for a halting conversation about "supplies," which meant nothing to Luca until he remembered the story of his setting up practice in town. Pancrazio, the friend for whom he had stuffed the dog, did not recognize him and was shy when Luca insisted on walking with him. Pancrazio was a mule handler now and this seemed to mean they were no longer friends. At the pharmacy Luca found the cathedralesque gloom he had remembered. The floral and gold labels on porcelain drug jars glimmered in the flame from an open burner, and the spool screen that protected the pharmacist from his customers suggested the confessional. In the backroom, behind a laxative display, he found the town's four doctors sharing a bit of medicinal brandy with the pharmacist. Dr. Delle Monache, the dean of the profession, was effusive in his welcome. His courtly, white-haired exterior did not quite hide a petty disposition which turned vicious if his importance or his opinions were questioned, but that evening he was determined to welcome Luca. There was a tense silence. The young surgeon, Armento, smiled but did not speak. He seldom did at such gatherings, for there were no operating facilities in town and most of his work was clandestine abortions . . . not the best of professional subjects. He was very handsome and his pastimes might have fascinated everyone, but these he never mentioned. The other two doctors were discouraged, middle-aged men in no way remarkable except in their submission to Delle Monache and their private vices. Di Martino drank, and Minutillo went twice a year to Naples, each time returning much calmed, but gray with exhaustion. The pharmacist, Ferdinando Perrone, was the shrewdest man in the group. Small and nervous with wispy blond hair and ill-kept clothes, he nonetheless had a tidy, blunt mind that penetrated the clouds of side issues to reach the only point of any conversation.

"Hear you're setting up practice." He had said what the others were thinking and had given Luca a chance to make a direct denial. The group became almost jolly. Another pill glass was brought out for Luca and a desultory conversation started up about an outbreak of flu in one street in the Rabata. Flu in July? Luca thought it had the earmarks of typhoid. The surgeon left and Luca felt the quiet settling in the shadows. The men drew closer together. Ferdinando Perrone explained they were wrestling with a moral problem. What Armento did in a medical way was his affair. He would be answerable to the provincial board, but on moral issues each citizen had a duty. Don't you agree? A duty. Delle Monache was smoking a cigar with his eyes half closed, shamming detachment, but Luca saw that he was examining each face, assaying their strength or their weakness, perhaps, never missing a word. Perrone had agreed to receive Armento's mail . . . not an unusual precaution between men of the world . . . but lately there had been too many letters from the same person, all postmarked Torregreca. The time had come. The time had come to speak against a colleague in defense of their moral beliefs, in defense of their homes. As Luca watched them steam open the latest letter, he was chilled by the thought that each man feared his wife or his daughter had betrayed him. The bell on the counter rang, and Luca sidled out behind Perrone saying he would look in again soon.

Uncle Girolamo was waiting for him, in the sense that half of Torregreca was standing in the Piazza waiting for something to happen. Men drifted up to them and then drifted away. Others lingered nearby as mute satellites to the changing group. Don Manfredo came freshly shaved and acted as master of ceremonies as his friends, some with their wives, came to welcome Luca back. The Piazza had become a playing field with teams lined up, one on either side, leaving a no-man's-land in the center. The *civili* clustered along the shop fronts on the ground floor of the Ducal Palace. From time to time one group melted into another and reformed in two different sections. There was little talk but what there was seemed animated. The old jokes Luca had already heard suggested that the men would not be saying anything of great importance this evening. They were waiting and would go on waiting until something happened or it was time to go home. Luca stood with his uncle and his father between the *civili* and the monument. On the other side of the Piazza dwarfed by the bell tower, three times as many *ca-*

foni stood watching the *civili*. Occasionally a comment rumbled from neighbor to neighbor. It was dour wit that brought sneers to their faces but never distracted their eyes from the men who chatted so languidly across the way. Resentment was the glue that bound them to each other. For the first time, that evening as he watched them, Luca felt the threat of their resentment. One day it would turn to hatred that no meager offers of work could calm. Then what happened would be up to the *cafoni*. And the very men who would lose their world stood across the way with Luca, chatting, thinking that force — the old, tried-and-true method — would work again. The frustration of those peasants was a physical miasma that clung about them like the smoke from their cigarettes. No wind would blow it away; it would choke them first. Luca had shivered. It must come soon, he thought. It will be violent, but will it be violent enough? He found himself praying it would.

Luca had been so taken up with his own thoughts that he scarcely heard his father's proposal of a stroll. Later, at supper with his uncle, and in bed when sleep would not come, the faces of the *cafoni*, bearded and slit-mouthed, interwove themselves through his father's soliloquy. He could not hear the words without seeing the faces, nor see the faces without hearing the words.

"I've had time to think recently about myself and you and life in Torregreca. Men have reasons for what they do, Luca; if you live in one place long enough you'll understand what I mean. When I look around this Piazza, I know what every man is trying to hide . . . and that is the key to what he does. Towns like this poison men, make them worse than they are, but that doesn't mean that men like us don't have moral obligations. You and I were born with two duties; one to preserve the holdings left to us, the other to lead those *cafoni* over there." He had spread his hand in a large gesture toward the other side of the Piazza. "They don't know what is right. They must be led. It takes time and strength and neither must be wasted on the pettinesses of friends." He stopped, looked around and sighed. "You may think this a strange time to be saying this, but I don't want you to mistake familiar things for important things. Remember the land, Luca, and the enforcement of just law . . . all else will fall in its proper place. See old Bruno over there. He killed his son-in-law. He was never tried because *we* believe he was right; it's not important what he did. There's the judge. He sleeps with his clerk's wife — that's not important either. Raffaele drinks. Pancrazio administers two convents and steals from both. Still it is our task to cover up for them in front of those men standing over there watching. They know no law, no order, we are the symbol of it. Wherever we go, we remain the symbol of it. That is enough for one lifetime whether you're a doctor or a landowner or a skeptic like your uncle." He had stopped, exhausted by his own outpouring. "Try to be on time for lunch tomorrow. It means so much to your mother. Good-night." And he had marched off toward the Corso walking with his head down.

"That was the first and only time I ever saw the situation clearly," Luca said . . .

Even the next day my ideas were fogged by bits of daily life that blur any crisis and make it seem unreal. But that's how things were in 1938. The *cafoni* waited, not so patiently I suspect, until the winter of 1944. The Germans had been pushed north, Mussolini had fled and the new government was having a hard time organizing what was left of a hungry, defeated country.

The *Podestà* was the same Dabbraio who cleaned his boots on the back of his trousers. He owned some land, not much, and as *Podestà* had his first, and probably his only, chance at power. He was young. He thought Fascism would go on forever, so for him being *Podestà* meant he was czar for life and he made the mistake of being cruel, pointlessly, brutally cruel. Suddenly Fascism did not exist. For a while it seemed that nothing had changed. He was still *Podestà*, directives still came to him, but he must have felt uneasy. He decided to collect all the unpaid fines and taxes. If the new government asked for them, well and good: if not, he had a little nest egg of his own. But he had underestimated his people. They were starving. There was no work, pensions and subsidies were not paid, and every kernel of grain went into government warehouses to be realloted to the peasants in ever smaller quantities. The old men stood around the Piazza "fantasticating" as they say here. Maybe if such and such happened, we could . . . *ma nò*. They were too constipated by fear and hunger and tradition to do anything but fantasticate . . . and refuse to pay taxes to a nonexistent government. But the women talked too and they were younger, with their lives still to live. Fear meant nothing to them because the police can think up no hell that could be worse than the hell of each of their days.

One morning, there was a rumor — no one knows just where it started — that the *Podestà* was collecting his papers and planned to flee that night. Without plan or signal the women poured up out of the Rabata shouting and yelling "To the *Comune!* To the *Comune!*" In an hour there was nothing left. Chairs and tables went out the window. The records poured down on the Piazza like snow. Bonfires were lighted; everything was burned. The men still stood in the Piazza. Then the women charged to the tax offices, to the *dazio*, to the land registry offices . . . destroyed the furniture, but most important of all they destroyed the records, every piece of paper that could incriminate any citizen of Torregreca. They were going to have a clean start. They set fire to the *guardia*'s office and were about to take carabinieri headquarters when the shout went up "The telephone lines! Cut the lines before they send for help!" And one of the older women did climb the pole out at the junction of the main road! She cut the lines and gave the Torresi three days for their rioting.

Once it was safe, the men got into it. They broke into the grain stores, looted the mill and the shops, but their real vengeance they saved for the *Circolo dei Civili*. They splintered everything and set fire to it. That led them to the padroni's houses . . . always cautious, the men . . . they didn't hurt anyone, but they broke into the storerooms and took cheeses and salami and wine, all the things they hadn't seen in years.

The women had gone to carabinieri to get a particular *maresciallo*, one of those who had specialized in the rubber hose and castor oil treatment. When they were through using their pitchforks he was a sieve. But all the time they were really looking for the *Podestà*. They caught him trying to sneak out of town and tied him to the monument in the Piazza. Two men were set to guard him, but they turned their backs when stones were thrown, and they baited the kids to twist his nose. Dabbraio took kicks in the groin until he was almost dead and then someone brought sticks and kindled a fire under him. He was so scared he wet his pants. Everyone had a high old time. Someone had Don Gaetano barricaded in the Post Office; every time he tried to sneak out to go home he got a pitchfork in the belly. He was stuck there three days . . . until the Army came.

"That was my Aunt Giulia," said Chichella from the kitchen. She had dozed through the first part of Luca's story, but when the riot was mentioned her eyes had opened and she had listened quietly to every word, nodding her head. "She had the family organized so that someone was on guard at the Post Office day and night. She still laughs about how pale and shaky he was at the end. Every few minutes he'd call from behind the door, 'Hey, Giulia. Let me out of here! I'm hungry.'" Chichella stopped.

Luca motioned her to go on and she lifted her chin in that

silent "no" that seemed so final. "Go on, go on! Tell her what happened. You were there. I wasn't." Luca's words were insistent, but his voice was gentle and he was smiling at her.

She smiled back and then came out in the middle of the sitting room and stood with her hands on her hips. There is no way to imitate her telling. It was not just words, but actions, voice, mannerisms that changed with each person she told about . . .

Don Gaetano shouted, "Giulia, you know I haven't eaten since yesterday, let me out!" Giulia's answer was always the same.

"Don Gaeta', you've got a while to stay before you know how it feels to be hungry. Just keep your face in there."

"Now listen, Giulia, there's no point blaming me because the subsidy money didn't come. Let me out. I order you to let me out! You let me out and I'll get you something to eat."

"You let me go hungry for two months. You didn't care then, now shut up and try it yourself."

There'd be nothing but shuffling of papers for a while, and then he'd be back at the door calling to Giulia again. He said his wife was sick and he had to go to her, but that didn't work. Then he needed his medicine or he'd die. Giulia yelled back, "My pleasure!" Oh, she had a good time getting her own back and scaring the old man. Of course he's still there, still postmaster, and he's got his children in there working too and he's still a Fascist. He's made Giulia pay for those three days she kept him in the Post Office. She's the last to get her pension, they close the money order window when they see her coming. They tell her they don't have any stamps. They do everything they can to pay back those three days, but she says it's worth it.

It all happened because of the women: we started it, and we were the ones who wouldn't stop. The men would have stopped after they had the grain. Late in the afternoon on the

third day, great Army trucks full of troops arrived and that was
the end of it. They weren't dumb, either. They made all of us
go to our houses, and we had to stay there. No one was to be on
the streets; there was a curfew. They must have worked fast at
getting names because their very first night in town they
started around, knocking on doors, dragging people out of bed
and down to the police station. The men and married women
they kept, but they didn't have anywhere to keep the unmarried girls, so they were sent home after questioning. The first
night they picked up my Giovanni, and he got word out to me
the next day that we were in trouble. An old enemy of Tanname's was in there and had sworn that my brother Nicola and
I had been in on the beating of the *maresciallo*. He'd got me
mixed up with Tina. She'd been right in the middle of things
from the beginning, but that didn't make much difference because they wouldn't keep me or Tina. Somehow I had to tell
Tanname to hide Nicola without letting him know who'd
warned me. He hated Giovanni, said he was making a whore
out of his daughter. I went rushing home and tried to talk so
fast, he wouldn't stop to wonder.

"Hey, listen! Listen! I got a message from the jail. They're
going to call Nicola in. Baffone told them Nicola and I were in
on the beating. We've got to do something quick!"

"If they send Nicola to prison, I'll fix Baffone. Just you wait
and see. We can hide Nicola so they won't find him. Quick, run
down the street and see if Aunt Rosa will take him for tonight.
In the morning we'll get him out of town. Quick now, get moving."

And that's where he went, to Aunt Rosa's. The carabinieri
would never look there, because she was ninety and blind and
not likely to be part of a riot. That night we did everything just
as usual. We'd all gone to bed when bang, bang at the front
door. It was the law.

"Who is it?" Tanname called.

"Carabinieri. Get up and open the door."

"Get up, Chichella. Get dressed. You out there — wait a minute."

I was so scared, so scared. Bang, bang again.

"All right, all right. My girl's coming to open the door. What do you want to do, scare her out of her wits? I'm sick in bed. Can't get up. She'll open up, just wait a minute."

Tanname was always looking for a fight, but he never could keep calm about it. I opened the door.

"Does Andressano Nicola, son of Andressano Pietro, live here?"

"Yes, sir."

"Where is he?"

"He's not here." It was the truth.

"What do you mean he isn't here, where is he?"

"If she tells you he isn't here, then he isn't here. He's been in the country for twenty days," Tanname yelled from his bed. "If you want him for something, you'll have to go out and find him."

"Back in there, what's there?" asked one of the carabinieri. He was looking back toward the recess where the donkey still lived.

"Another ass just like you," answered Tanname. "Want to see him?" They went and looked in. "The way you're acting you better come and look in my bed too!"

"Come on, let's go," said one of them. The other had seen a little trapdoor that went down below into a little compartment where we stored wood.

"What's that?"

"Keep wood in there. Want to see it?" Tanname got out of bed and headed for the trapdoor. He didn't look very dangerous in his long underwear, but the gleam in his eye put the carabinieri off. They decided they didn't have to see it if we'd tell them where Nicola was. "Out at Don Pasquale's old vineyard, and if you've got the courage to go all the way out there, go ahead." Tanname knew they weren't from Torregreca and would be scared of the hills at night.

The next morning before it was light, Tanname hitched the donkey with panniers, called Nicola and sent us out to Don Pasquale's . . . me, Nicola and the little ones. Nicola had to stay doubled up in one of the panniers with a load of hay on top of him for the whole trip. I prayed to God the police would be too busy to stop me and inspect the load. I had Nicola in one side and nothing but rocks in the other balancing him, so I was fried if they stopped me. Tanname had given me orders before we left.

"You stay out there 'til I tell you to come back. The door is strong and if the law comes, you remember what you're to do. Don't open the door. There's the hatch in the door, open that. The carabiniere will stick his face right up to it. You take the sickle and cut his head off and don't worry about it. No one will send you to prison. There's a strike on. How can you know who it is? You've got to protect your brothers and sister. The rest we'll fix later."

Nobody stopped us on the way and nobody ever came looking for us either.

Luca had encouraged her, nodding at points, laughing at her carabinieri. When she stopped, he said quietly, "What happened to the others?"

"Oh, they spent three, four, five months in prison. Aunt Giulia got five months for Don Gaetano and the Post Office; Giovanni got four. They had them in jails all over the province; Matera, Irsina, even Montescaglioso. Concetta — the same Concetta who was my first squad boss — was the only one who got more than five months because they could prove she damaged government property. She got a year for cutting the telephone wires, and she can't vote or emigrate or get a government job because she's got a record. A lot of people who'd been the worst didn't get anything, but the pitiful ones were those who'd had nothing to do with it and ended up in jail just the same. You see, it's kind of a vendetta. If someone sees he's being dragged in for questioning, he figures what the hell, if I'm going to get it, so are all the others and he names everyone he hates and wants to get even with. The police don't know better — they don't have the town mentality. They don't understand the trick, so they haul in everyone who's accused by the others. Out of the hundred and fifty they sent to jail, at least forty of them had nothing to do with the riot, but that's the way justice works in Torregreca.

"It's hard to tell what the riot did. The police took over the grain stores and distributed it bit by bit. There wasn't a mayor but something called a commissioner. They never did rebuild the Club in the Piazza — maybe because there weren't any padroni left after the land reform took all their land away from them. They say the priests wanted to take the Club for themselves, but the Bishop wouldn't let them. It was funny . . . almost as though we'd swapped one set of padroni for another. The real padroni disappeared and all of a sudden the priests were in everything. You might say the chairs became stools and the stools chairs, the way things worked out. There aren't any real padroni anymore, even the ones who sold us grain at twice the right price ended up in rags without a penny. The land reform took what they had left and gave a bit to everyone . . . now nobody has enough. We die of hunger just the same, only they say it's more dignified than before. Instead of the reign of the padroni, we have the reign of the priests . . . that's Italian democracy!"

"Want some beer after all that talk?" Luca stuck one of the bottles out at her.

"No, you had me on talking . . . now it's time for you to go home. Time *we* had some dinner and you showed up in the

Piazza." She bustled off to the kitchen and reappeared with a pot that she took into the bathroom to fill with water. Luca had been watching her, not with any resentment.

"She's smarter than we are. And she's reminded me of something. Concetta got a year for cutting the wires, but all the others, the ones on your list who are excluded from the houses, have been pardoned, not just once, but three of four times by amnesties. Their penal records can't keep them out of the *villaggio* . . . Chichella's right. It's time for me to show myself in the Piazza, and talk to the Mayor. That list can be voided."

As he left I thought he looked tired. His shoulders sagged and his eyes were strangely lifeless. The ghostly outlines of the old system were beginning to show through the cardboard democracy of the politicians. With the water boiling hard enough to steam the paint off the walls, Chichella came to stand in front of me.

"He's always been different. People trust him; but then, he's never had the courage to stay in Torregreca." It was an indictment. She and many others felt they had been deserted. She could understand him in her way, but she could not forgive him. It was useless to ask for her sympathy. She wasted little enough on her own kind and none on those better off than she. More to change the subject than anything else I asked what the war had been like in Torregreca.

"Eh . . . the war . . . it was just a war like any other for us." She shrugged. "We felt it in the gut."

VII

CALABRIAN GAVOTTE

THE list excluding men involved in the riot of 1944 was withdrawn, but combined with one other incident it was enough to put me in bureaucratic purdah. I was proving difficult: Anglo-Saxons do not understand the Mediterranean culture. Although it had been Luca who questioned the validity of the list, I was the one credited with upsetting the Pharisee. Then the following week I had a late evening caller, a forestry guard who had a disconcerting way of popping out from behind trees or parked cars to waylay me. He was a handsome, slender man with white hair and a slow manner of speaking that made long pauses either normal or insinuating depending on the state of the listener's conscience. With me his conversations were always straightforward and consistent; he had taken special interest in the nursery, checking at night to be sure everything was in order . . . it was unwise to leave a building untended . . . therefore he thought . . . was sure, in fact, I would appreciate . . . well, thought I would want to recognize . . . I heaped him with praise, but refused to understand his more tangible hopes.

Hat in hand he stood on my doorstep smiling gently, lecherously. He was very sure of his welcome.

"Just thought I'd come by . . . for a little chat. You must be very lonely. We can have pleasant evenings together."

"Signor Soldo, you know quite well that no decent woman receives a man at this hour. Good night!" and I slammed the door. Just in the nick of time too, for I started giggling. So

Victorian at my age! Next I would hear myself saying, "Sir, you are no gentleman!" or "Unhand me, you cad!" But at least in principle I had been right; he could make no sly half-statements to his friends in the Piazza.

The next morning I twitted Luca and the Mayor for not warning me of the gayety that awaited a lady cast up, so to speak, on the beach of a Torresi housing development. To think no one had prepared me for gentlemen callers! They were in turn mystified, then amused and finally very serious. They insisted on knowing my caller's name. The situation was quite out of hand, but I told them the story, still treating it as a joke. In retrospect I can only explain my fits of frivolous humor as reactions to the somber *serietà* of living in Torregreca. This was my first experience, but there were so many others that in the end I wrote down whatever struck me as funny, and never mentioned it aloud. In fact I have an entire notebook of such incidents and phrases — all apparently to be accepted as normal. The salesgirl who told me, "Tissue paper is out of season now!" The peasant man who said he could not work because he suffered from "hot flashes of the testicles," and another who explained he had turned down the job of street sweeper because the doctor had told him not "to breathe." Then there was the eager man who traveled from Salerno once every two months to read our light meters. Rather than disturb me, he endowed me with a sparkling array of American appliances that would have blown all the fuses in town and then estimated my consumption. *Useful information:* in Italy one must pay a bill *before* one can protest it. For me the system had one advantage: I did not pay another bill for two years. The utilities were always capricious. For instance Mastro Carmine cut off the water at the nursery in a fit of pique at not being asked to the inauguration. Another time a plumber assured me he could install a very efficient gas water heater in my bathroom, but, of course, I would have to remove the glass in the window . . . to avoid explosions.

There was an aged gentlewoman, one of the town notables, who had had a stroke, suffered from elephantiasis, could hardly walk and still insisted on going to church each morning. On occasion I saw her home. She was a sweet, smiling woman wrapped in a cloud of black draperies. Her greatest joy in life seemed to be that the doctor had told her she suffered from an "extreme case of infant diarrhoea." It was her sister, almost as aged, who sent me a large package of phosphorescent madonnas and rosaries to distribute among my "heathen friends in America." And then there was a nurse who protested she could not shave under her arms because she would "lose her sexual powers." She seemed so convinced that for one desperate moment I though I might be confused, not she. In time I accepted myself as eccentric and gave up hope of sharing what amused me.

When shown an icebox of walk-in proportions bought for the express purpose of chilling water in the summer, I admired the icebox and made no comment on the lone bottle within. I was gentle with a sixty-year-old woman who insisted on special consideration because she was a war orphan, and I listened with straight face to a man no more than ten years older than I who raged against the American government for cheating him of his pension from the Spanish-American war. I was surrounded by people who felt that all of life, or at least that part which had to do with a social worker, must be deadly serious. Amusement was unbecoming to my profession, and those tidbits that brightened my days brought convulsive shame to my hearers.

I understood how complete was my isolation when Soldo, the forestry guard, was suspended for six months without pay. The same authorities who had ignored two earlier criminal complaints filed against him, one for fraud, the other for theft, had acted with lightning vengeance when he made "inappropriate overtures" to me.

The way I found out had a certain element of comedy too. One rainy morning as I walked across the Piazza, vaguely aware that an unusual number of people had turned to stare at me, I was attacked by two women in black, wielding umbrellas as lion tamers brandish chairs.

"You're the bitch!" the younger one howled at me, and poked me in the stomach. The older woman's jab fell short of the mark, but she made up for it by clawing at her hair and unleashing a banshee wail that chilled my blood. The younger one dropped her shawl and lunged, hands outstretched, for my head. It happened too fast for me to have any idea what was going on, but in raising my arm to protect myself I clipped her under the chin with my elbow, which gave the spectators just enough time to grab my attackers and haul them away.

Mastro Pancrazio, galvanized to hysteria by the scene, dashed back and forth apologizing to me and cursing them until he was forced to referee a free-style wrestling match between the ladies and their captors.

A sensible man near me had explained that they were Soldo's wife and daughter and when that failed to mean anything to me he went further. "You *do* know he's been suspended for six months for his improper behavior with you? I would like to apologize for every man in town. It was an insult."

The carabinieri and Lieutenant Mazzone appeared and urged me to file a charge of assault, which I refused to do as I refused the escort they offered. As the good lieutenant battered at them with warnings, I left the Piazza and went to the Post Office. When I came out, the two Soldos were waiting for me with sheathed umbrellas and unsheathed tongues. They followed me in and out of shops, through a long list of errands, yelling "Bitch," "Whore" and worse, probably, that I could not understand. Windows were flung open, balconies crowded and the streets jammed with people. I ignored the ladies; they followed me. We were better than a circus. When they ran out of expletives they chanted "You'll see. We're very special friends of Don Luca's. He'll see that justice is done." Something cruel in me longed to eavesdrop on that scene, and my curiosity was only whetted by a comment I overheard. "Watch out for that bunch. That girl's husband knifed her one night in the middle of the Piazza. Jealous fit they say. They're all wild."

Overnight I was a person of power to be handled with care; like a case of TNT, I might explode if jostled. Instead I was suffocated in a featherbed of super-respect. There was a logical side effect. If there were any possibility of my pristine conscience being brought into play, I was circumvented. So it was that the notices of the housing committee meetings never reached me, or if they did, they were never less than a week late. My presence would have been inconvenient.

The *villaggio* was to be a community of thirty-two housing units. There was no question that all one hundred and sixty-four families on our list needed new housing for one reason or another. The same could have been said of almost everyone in town. However, when the official rating of families in order of need was posted, it was obvious that a great many compromises had been made. The troublemakers had been taken care of; old debts had been paid; and then a few of the most desperate cases had been thrown in for flavoring. In the thirty-two families finally chosen there were forty-six children between three and six years of age who automatically had a right to the thirty-two places available in the nursery. In the same thirty-two families there were one hundred and sixty-two children under the age of twelve. Two of the women were certifiable. One man, an alcoholic with seven children, officially made his living as a sharecropper, but had found that renting his bedroom to clandestine couples paid much better. There were two active cases of TB and one paid Communist agitator, who had promised to shut up if given a house. The family of eleven people living in one room expected to move in a body to their new two-bedroom establishment. I battled until they were forced to divide the troop; the son, his wife, their two grown sons and four of the five young children eventually came to the new house. Then the mother immediately delivered herself of twins! It was hardly a great victory, but the atmosphere was somewhat healthier than before.

Simple mathematics showed that forty-six children would not fit in thirty-two nursery places, and after counting and re-counting, the best solution seemed to raise the age limit of the children from three years to four, so that they would be assured of the continuity of two years of nursery life, and more important, nursery food, before they went into the first grade.

A month after the list was posted, it was announced that there would be a delay in the consignment of the houses because the *Comune* was unable to pay for the outside connections to the main light and water supplies. This was to hold us up six months and, indeed, even then, when I finally opened the nursery there was still no current. I could postpone the actual opening, but I could not postpone the official inauguration which had been set for early October. Ambassadors, their aides, Italian ministers, prefects, and regional commanding officers do not have elastic schedules. The nursery building itself was ready. At times my life seemed to stretch in front of me as an endless roll of curtain material and I dreamed of mountains perforated with windows and doors, for in my absence the painters had thought to surprise me with a "superlative fake-walnut finish" on all the woodwork. Still, on the appointed day, I had finished the curtains and had transformed the windows and doors with three coats of gray enamel. I had arranged for flowers from Matera, sandwiches from Potenza and police escorts for everyone. The nuns were to provide a formal banquet.

The Bishop would bless the building. Engraved invitations had been sent out, but in a moment of folly and brotherly love I paid the town crier to invite the Torresi to attend the inauguration ceremony. I could not guess that once the ceremony was over they would invade the nursery, stuffing their pockets with a supply of sandwiches and pastries that must have fed them for a week. There are, however, some very amusing pictures of exactly that. I console myself that there is never an official production without some hitch.

The day of the inauguration was dark and foggy. At 6 A.M. I slipped and fell down the front steps of the Matera hotel where I had taken the Canadian delegation the night before. Back in Torregreca I found two television crews, one Italian, one Canadian, who had to be housed and fed. The Ambassador and his party arrived early, and the ladies asked discreetly if they might retire. It was then I discovered that Mastro Carmine had turned off the water. One of the women, who had slaved at scraping the floors and tiles for the final cleaning, was hilariously drunk on Campari sodas stolen from the refreshment table and wanted to entertain the company with a striptease. All in all it was a very jolly party that produced a letter I shall always cherish.

From London headquarters I received a note from the chairman of my Foreign Relief Committee, who was also a lady-in-waiting to the Queen. "Dear Ann: The enclosed was passed on by Buckingham Palace. Should we do something about this lady? I did not know we gave away houses. Best wishes . . ."

The enclosure read:

Dear Queen of England:

I, the undersigned, Maria Oliva, born of John Oliva (deceased) and Carmela Oliva (deceased) in the township of Torregreca, Province of Matera, Italy, on the 10th day of June 19— bring to your attention with this present letter the disgusting fact that your social worker, known as the Brigadiera has refused to give me a house or a mattress or a bed. The beforementioned Brigadiera has done this and more for her friends while ignoring me, a poor widow with three children and no pension. You should know she gives immoral parties at the nursery too. Now that we have democracy in Italy, I want to see justice done. Trusting in an immediate and positive answer from you, I send my most respectful greetings.

(*signed*) Maria Oliva

P.S. I would take a blanket.

Maria Oliva was a dressmaker who lived across the courtyard from me in a low-cost apartment. Her three children were of age and working; her *amante* paid the rent. Needless to say she did not get her blanket.

Even though I could not open the nursery for the children on schedule, still I had plenty to do. We had another demonstration nursery already in operation three hundred kilometers to the south in the province of Catanzaro. I spent several days there every month and arranged for my trips back and forth to cover a number of other commitments. In some isolated mountain villages elementary school teachers were interested in possible after-school projects which we particularly encouraged when they could be combined with supplementary feeding programs. Mountain children seem never to have enough to eat. I had, as well, a regular round of visits to institutions that received American surplus food supplies through us. They were all small institutions with ten, maybe fifteen girls or boys, and because they were small, were often unknown or forgotten by larger agencies. Of course I was supposed to check that the foodstuffs were properly used, but it was never that simple. I tried to invent new ways to use "processed" American cheese (a mysterious item in Italy where cheese is cheese), and insisted that jam, chocolate or even ersatz coffee flavoring would make the chalky powdered milk more palatable. Everyone begged for clothes, warm clothes and blankets. The children were shivering and blue. I have never forgotten a sweet young nun who asked if I thought it was "immoral" for her to put hot-water bottles in the little girls' beds at night!

In one hamlet, Ezzito, we were even trying to convert a room into a school. Conversion would seem a simple matter, but there was no road, and building materials had to be loaded up the mountain path by donkey. Electricity was unknown; water from an open stream had to be carried two miles in small barrels. The building rented by the government as school premises was a two-room peasant house with a wobbly floor and a roof that collapsed, dribbling tiles down into the room below. The teacher, his wife and little girl lived in one room, with two windows. Classes were held in the other, where light was provided by the open door. The latrine was a clump of slue grass under the bedroom window. Once I spent the night sharing the double bed with the teacher's wife and three-year-old daughter. Over my head athletic rats chased each other along the rafters and the little girl interrupted my nightmares with *"Mamma, voglio far pipi,"* at which her mother lifted her over the edge of the bed and there was the gentle splash of *pipi* hitting the floor. At dawn the room was black with flies. After that I walked the six and a half miles up the mountain and the six and a half miles back down in one day.

Occasionally, in remote settlements, I met teachers who were convinced against all odds that there was a point to teaching. They, unlike their colleagues, did not show up each morning simply because they had to if they were to be paid. Their ingenuity was heartbreaking. One young man in Roccanova had weathered the collapse of two different classroom floors that had cascaded him, his pupils and their desks into the room below. Undaunted, he taught a dreary civics course as an experiment in city planning. "After all, they have to come to school, but it doesn't mean they have to be bored to death." Since they knew nothing about cities, he suggested they re-plan their own village, which led to questions of public facilities, water supply, natural watersheds, sewerage, schools, duties of the individual and so on. The boys, sons of shepherds who would themselves be shepherds, had made a topographical map of the area in clay, showing all the unknown hidden springs, and had devised a collection basin and gravity aqueduct that would have changed this waterless town into an oasis. Of course it was a pipe dream, just as the teacher's hope of showing them a real city was a pipe dream. But sometimes dreams should come true. Fifty dollars took the boys on a bone-crushing trip to Taranto and then, miracle of miracles, to swim in the sea which they had never seen.

The day we worked out the plans, the teacher was as excited as the boys, and to celebrate invited me to watch a performance of *Tosca* on the only television set in town. It was brand new and a sign of progress like the three-room hotel in which I was to spend the night. We did not go to the *caffè*, as I had expected, but into a stall and up a ladder into an old loft where forty peasant men sat on three-legged stools, popeyed at the witchcraft of the television screen. They were in a state of cataleptic enchantment. As aria followed aria, the tension mounted until striking a match made them start like deer at the sound of a rifle. "*Mo, mo* she'll sing . . ." then a nervous voice croaked the words. They knew the themes, tempi and words — better than the performers themselves. "Ssst . . . the best is coming." Their courtesy to me was Victorian. Each offered his stool, no one smoked without first asking if I minded, and they took turns telling me exactly what would happen next. Never once was I made to feel there was anything unusual about my presence. In an intermission a man crawled over our knees and down the ladder. When he came back, he brought a bottle of beer for me. No one else had anything. En masse they walked me through the frosty silence of midnight to the miniature hotel and I had a chance to ask how it was that the television set was in the loft.

"We bought it for our headquarters . . . out of party dues," came the answer.

"What party?"

"The Communist party, of course, and now we have to beat away new members. We've raised the dues, too."

Not even my mattress of corncobs or the raucous squeals of a pig sale that started at dawn dimmed my delight with that evening. I was not, however, terribly surprised the next morning when a fresh-faced carabiniere wanted to arrest me as a Russian spy. "It's a well known fact that you're traveling on a fake American passport."

By contrast Torregreca was cosmopolitan. We had two television sets, a cinema the shape of a sheep dip, and the panache of the Bari Band coming to perform at our festa. As I drove into town after that trip to Roccanova, my eyes discovered a new refinement. There was grace in the curved line of the roofs sloping off toward the point of the butte and an orderliness, even elegance in the whole that had escaped me before. I eased along toward the Piazza until carabinieri headquarters came into sight with laundry draped all over it. It looked like a three-masted schooner under full sail. That strange telepathy of kinship told me the sheets, towels and underwear were my own. With a chill I imagined Lieutenant Mazzone viewing the Piazza through a peephole between my brassieres and girdles and so rushed off to find Chichella. She, far from ashamed of her deed, was hurt by my lack of appreciation. As always her reasoning had been very clear; even if the town were without water, the police would not be. The story she had told the *maresciallo*, who was very sympathetic, was that I had a fetish about cleanliness and she would be fired if she did not, somehow, manage to wash my laundry before I returned. Over the years she invented a number of personalities for me that suited her purposes and I was expected to shut up and go along with her. I usually did.

Torregreca was changing. That fall the first middle school (6th through 8th grades) opened in temporary quarters in the *case popolari* across the road from ours. The boys' classrooms were in one apartment; the girls in another on the floor above. Equipment was at a minimum. Desks were discarded relics of the grade school. The only bathroom in each apartment had to serve one hundred and fifty youngsters. There were no cupboards, no bookcases, no books — in short, no *plan* for a school. It was a simple matter of statistics — Torregreca, for its population, had to have a middle school.

The *preside,* the principal, asked if I could help, and she, the home economics teacher and I went to work. Back to window painting, and curtains! I bludgeoned several fathers who were carpenters into covering the writing surfaces of the desks with linoleum, and then inveigled them into making blackboards from plywood painted with opaque black paint. We tried to arrange for a hot lunch program, but that took a number of years to materialize. Athletics were on the required curriculum, but the Appian Way did not seem a suitable gym. The director of schools in Matera ordered us to use the front hall of the new hospital which was a labyrinth of scaffolding and open troughs for pipes. I found a kind man who gave us an empty garage. No matter what the problem, my solutions were greeted with "It can't be done"; but it could be, and it was.

In reply to my letters, publishers sent a startling variety of books; schools, travel commissions, and governments all over the world answered the children's letters. The gaps were filled, but the bathrooms had become Augean Stables, and the janitor referred darkly to their cleaning as the job of the "other janitor." On paper the school rated two janitors and, indeed, was charged with two. It just happened that "the other" was too busy as chauffeur to the regional director of schools to do more than collect his salary. We had run head-on into "the system," that frustrating and still invincible network of official privilege. But I am glad we battled to make the place decent, for the school stayed in those quarters for seven long years.

I had other problems. The Mother Superior of the Convent was in a state of prostration at the idea of the orphans walking half a mile to the school. After a lot of careful questioning I understood that it was not the distance that worried her, but the possibility that they might be "contaminated" by contact with little boys. *Ahimè!* To protect her eleven-year-olds from this deadly peril, she wanted me to ask foreign organizations for a bus. Instead I suggested we try to set up a camp for the little girls who had no relatives to take them in during the summer vacation. Then I was in the camp business too.

So there was more than enough to do even with the nursery closed. I was trying to fight the indolence of the public health officer and insisted that he examine each school child as the law provided he should. He saw no reason to clutter his days, so I cluttered mine with convincing the mothers that they must insist on an actual examination. Then, too, Luca and I had a scheme for adding a pavilion onto the hospital, which had been planned without a maternity or pediatrics section. Yes, there was more than enough for me to do.

The fogs of early October gave over to torrential rains which were eventually to flood all of the lowlands and leave Torregreca isolated from the world for two weeks. The streets were deserted. The town crier no longer bothered to tootle his little brass horn and screech the day's special prices. Mud was everywhere and the drumming of the rain was as irritatingly monotonous as a dripping faucet. I had been farsighted enough to install a clay stove, a charming one whose firebox was bordered by a frieze of cavorting wood nymphs. Each seemed to be slipping away from her draperies into a freedom that threatened to be Arctic, because the stove would not draw if asked to burn anything larger than a toothpick. I had pulled my worktable right up to it so that, by lowering my arm, I could feed it a twig. Whatever heat it produced warmed my near side. It was there, in constant attendance on the fire, that I ate my meals and wrote up my endless notes by the white glare of a small gooseneck lamp.

One evening late in the month Chichella came in shrouded in wet black shawls and thumped down in the chair opposite me. She seemed tired, and from the way she sat rolled over on herself I thought discouraged, but she did not say anything. I felt that perhaps intuition should tell me what she wanted, but my mind was blank. Finally she said, "In a few days it's All Souls'." Then a long pause. "I paid the last of the money today; they'll put it up tomorrow. Will you go with me to the cemetery? It would help . . . maybe. They all say it's an insult to Michele, but I couldn't do any better." It must be the tombstone, I thought, and asked why it was an insult. Because, she replied, it was the cheapest kind that would still have a porcelain medallion with his picture.

"He wanted to be buried wrapped in a sheet. That shows he didn't care about the trimmings, but the funeral cost me a lot of money just the same . . . 45,000 lire by the time I paid the Confraternity to walk in the procession, and the sacristan who rang the bells, and the priest. I had to buy the casket, a new shirt for Michele, a pair of shoes . . . We made do with his wedding suit but it looked awful, all stripes and tight-waisted. I didn't mind anything but paying the sacristan to ring the bells . . . There's one way of ringing them for a poor man, another for a rich one; you can tell if he was married or not, young or old. There's a special ring for each one . . . and even after he got paid, he rang the poor man's call. Now they say I'm insulting Michele with the cheapest gravestone. What would you do if you owed more money than you'd made in your whole life?" She did not expect an answer, but she thought for a long time.

"Maybe if you went with me, they'd feel different," she said.

I promised I would, even in the rain, but still she sat there, dejected and far away. Finally she said, "Well, it's late . . . I'll see you in the morning. They told me they could spare the boy from the shop at two. Do you mind going then? I'll get your lunch early."

The next morning a torrent of rain bubbled along the tin gutters above my windows and in its rush to the ground rattled the down spouts against the building. Then, suddenly at noon, it stopped and a gusty wind came up to play tumbleweed with the clouds. I offered to take everyone — us, the boy and the headstone — in the car, but Chichella was scandalized. The tradition of self-flagellation was too strong, so we walked to the marble works which were really nothing more than a shop with several sets of water sprays and grinding devices. Professor Angerame, the proprietor, was scanning the road through a peephole wiped in the milky dust that clouded the glass door of his shop. "Wants to get home to his dinner," mumbled Chichella. He had a lean, fox face that always looked hungry to me, but worse, he had the surly tongue of a man who has no competition in a self-perpetuating market. The grieved were given to understand that their order of a tombstone was an imposition on his time for which — naturally — there would have to be a suitable charge. He got rich on those reluctant favors, but his indifference was known for what it was — a pose. No one had forgotten his one term as town councilor. It had been right after the war when there was a movement to rename the streets of Torregreca after the great benefactors of humanity. Angerame and a carpenter who specialized in caskets had blackballed Sir Alexander Fleming as "a man who had impeded the growth of commerce." Most recently he had received a temporary appointment as the design teacher at the temporary middle school. He had given himself the title of Professor.

"Hurry up! Did you think I'd wait all day?" He had opened the door and was motioning to Chichella. "Ruining my dinner was not included in the price of the stone. Now pick it up and get going. I'll send the boy up . . ." I had been hidden by the opaque glass and when he finally saw me I was looking at my watch. It was exactly two.

"Ah, Signora, what an honor! What an unexpected honor! Come in, come in, let me show you around my little shop." His voice was gentle, coaxing. He turned away: "Hey you, close the door. Don't want freeze the Signora, do you?"

Chichella leaned back and relaxed her weight against the door which crashed home in its frame. Angerame pretended not to notice, but he must have felt her scorn. He led me slowly around the shop showing me cupids and cherubs he had copied and handsome baroque sconces so heavy they would have pulled down all but the most medieval of castle walls. In answer to my questions about cutting and polishing, he called out for Gianmauro, who appeared from behind a monumental piece of machinery where he must have been hiding to eat his lunch. He looked as though he had wedged an entire loaf of bread in his mouth and his eyes popped in an effort to manipulate the mass around to a chewable position. Indeed his eyes were the only human things about him. His eyelashes, his hair, face, hands and even his clothes were of white marble. Before Angerame could berate him, Gianmauro flipped some switches, and words and thought were lost in the squeal of motors. Water splattered everywhere and dust spewed out from the round saw wheel like grain from a harvester. How could we ever stop the Sorcerer's Apprentice? Fortunately he stopped

himself, probably because he had swallowed the giant mouth-
ful and felt he could face his padrone.

"Absolutely fascinating," I announced, my enthusiasm a bit
muffled by the dust. Angerame glowed with pride. "Now really
we must go. I know you're hungry for your lunch. Is that our
stone over there?"

"Yes, beautiful isn't it? I took particular pains with it." It was
gray, polished, lettered. I could see nothing different about it.
Chichella rubbed the dust off the porcelain miniature with her
shawl and then looked at it as though it were a decoration she
might or might not buy. Michele's was the long, heavy-boned
face of a big man. Thick eyebrows accentuated the downward
slant of wide brown eyes and suggested pain — or was it disappointment? His mouth was full, a bit too large, and the moustache about which he had been so particular seemed to increase his dignity though it was the square, slightly comic
brush beloved by peasants from Hitler down. He would have
been a stubborn, intelligent troublemaker and I could imagine
that, unlike the rest, not even hunger could force him to accept
an underpaid job.

"It's very dignified. I'm sure Chichella will be proud of it.
Now if you'd call Gianmauro to carry it, we'll leave you to have
your dinner in peace." I turned toward Chichella who was
winding a folded towel into a doughnut. It would be the balancing pad between her head and the stone. "Don't worry
about that, Chichella. Give the pad to Gianmauro. He'll carry
the stone." Professor Angerame signaled me that she had no
money; I wigwagged back very firmly that I did. Gianmauro
was sullen as he took the pad and hoisted the stone to his head.
Chichella had not protested or changed her expression in any
way, but from a quick wink I knew she was enjoying the little
scene. Ours would be a stately march led by a paid beast of
burden. The neighbors would have time to wonder at the maj-

esty of the arrangements and would, I hoped, forget the price of the actual stone. It was a mile to the cemetery.

"Signora, you have a car. We could . . ." Gianmauro had to turn like a stiff robot to speak to me.

"Sorry, it's not working. You go in front, we'll follow."

It might have been a funeral procession. Chichella pulled her black shawl tight around her face and hung an arm through mine as though she needed support. Staring at the road just in front of our own feet, we paced away from the shop.

"They'll never believe this," she muttered. "We're really doing it in style. Don't look up, but Gino's already spotted us from the balcony. There — he's gone to tell Tina. She should have come with us, but she wouldn't. Said she was ashamed. Nunzio's there and now Tina too. You ought to see Concetta gape . . . Oh, now Carmine's seen us too . . . well, they won't have anything more to say." Her satisfaction was almost worth that cold, dreary walk, but as her comments became more and more bitter, I wondered if this one bit of mummery could purge the gall of so many silent months.

In the end victory was hers. One by one women wrapped in fringed black shawls fell in behind us. Tina and two of her little girls. A sister-in-law and then another. Carmine's wife and the famous Concetta, who had cut the wires during the riot. Chichella repeated her instructions that I must not look back until we reached the gates of the cemetery where they would leave us to go alone. They chanted softly, their words blurring into a moan of agony that clung to us like cobwebs and then was wrenched away by the wind. Michele could never have been more alive — or more dead — than he was in the mourning of those women.

VIII

PROPHECIES, WITCHES, AND SPELLS

I KNEW a man in the Abruzzo, a foul, drunken hermit who claimed he had seventeen spirits who did his bidding. He babbled nonsense by candlelight (the number of candles having an occult relationship to the number of spirits needed to solve your case), brewed great flasks of murky liquids, and spent long hours in a trance, as he said, communing with his spirits. He needed several consultations before he opined just the right cure. It might be a powder of dried ox blood and herbs to be taken at the dark of the moon, or a little phial of one of his liquids to slip in your lover's soup or a verse of saints' names and magic words to be repeated nine times, in nine different houses on nine different days. He was a *mago*, a *stregone*, a witch. Every village has one, often a woman, proficient in the art of casting and uncasting spells, of healing mysterious diseases and driving away evil spirits. It has always been a respectable, lucrative profession, but it does not attract the young of today. The idea has been embarrassed underground. Medicine has improved. Spells have softened into superstitions and the evil eye has become a generic explanation for anything not understood. "Our mothers, our grandmothers believed in that sort of thing. We don't." Strange, then, that everyone in the province of Matera, doctors, lawyers, peasants, waiters and bus drivers, refers to one town as *Quel Paese* (That Town) rather than whisper its name. He who dares, even if he touches iron as he says it, must forever avoid the town for he has invited the curse of the evil eye. There is no antidote. Calamity awaits him in *Quel Paese*. Superstition, I said, and never avoided the name. In fact I looked forward to *seeing* a town of such power, to *feeling* it, since such malevolence must create physical vibrations, but I had to wait almost a year. Barricaded by mountains, itself perched on a high rock spine, it was not a place on the way to any other. You went there on purpose or not at all. When I did, I was not disappointed. *Quel Paese* gave me a day I will never forget, not because what happened there was important, but because it had never happened to me before — or since. All my luggage was stolen.

Once in Torregreca I met a surveyor, a charming, bearded Venetian who was jubilant at the idea of talking to "a sensible person," as he called me. He felt more foreign than I, for this was supposed to be his country, yet it seemed darkest Africa to him. If he "gazed on" a mother nursing her child, the family went into paroxysms of counter-spells. "Dammit, I don't want to 'gaze on' them, but they will haul out their breasts in cinemas and office waiting rooms and bus stations. What am I to do?" Shaving his beard might have helped. It is a well-known fact that if a stranger's hair falls on the breast it clogs the tit. Still, as a stranger, his envy was a threat to the milk. In passing he could snatch it up and take it with him. What irritated the Venetian surveyor most was *Quel Paese*. "Rot, nothing but rot and my boss expects me to believe it. He's ordered me not to mention the name in his hearing. Eh!" he threw his hands up in the air. "What do you do with these people? They're back in the dark ages." A Northerner's sense of humor is as quick as his irritation. Soon he was telling stories in a bad mock-Southern accent and planning another meeting when next he came to Torregreca. I never saw him again, but he sent me a postcard from Matera. "I take it all back. Had to go to *Quel Paese* alone — no driver would take me. A mule threw me. I landed on an iron stake that pierced my chest. They say I'll be all right

— three weeks in hospital followed by six months sick leave. Guess where I'm going! VENICE. Best wishes . . ."

Enchantments, *affascinazione*, sudden passion, strange physical symptoms, infertility, falling hair, cross-eyed babies — everything can be blamed on a spell that has been cast or a potion slipped into food. Casting spells may be the speciality of one witch; breaking them the art of another. The problem lies in choosing the right one.

The human being is surrounded by danger. It floats in the air. The glance of a stranger, a neighbor's jealousy, a spiteful thought, the moon's beams or the dark of a shadow — they are all threats. An adult protects himself as best he can, but a child must be defended. For centuries the campaign has been a delaying action. Mothers teach their daughters how to distract spirits. Their wiles are concealed by the yards and yards of swaddling that truss a baby from the time he is born until he is a year old, sometimes older. This living mummy can be taken anywhere, like a package, dumped in any field, left on any shelf, and he is always protected by the charms slipped between the layers of his bindings. The twice-daily unswaddling and reswaddling is a ritual that takes skill. The baby is placed in a nest of old, soft rags. His arms are forced to his sides, his legs held straight out, then with a quick swirl of the wide band he is immobilized. Another quick wrap and the charm sack can be placed roughly where the mother thinks the genitals might be. The sack is not so important as its contents. There will be a length of hairy string, a few grains of wheat (any number so long as it is odd), perhaps a rough Cross, an image of Sant' Antonio, San Rocco or the Madonna. If the evil spirit can be tricked into counting the strands of string, or the wheat kernels, he will forget his wicked errand. Each saint has his own sphere, of course, and his very presence might put the spirit to flight. The sack in place, more swaddling is wrapped around, and then a pair of scissors, open to cut the evil spirit before it can reach the sack, is slipped between the folds. Now the bundle is ready for the final neatening-up. The outside layers must be very even and close together, so that the baby's head seems to stick out of a cocoon of striated linen. He is slipped into a cotton envelope with coarse lace that tickles his chin, and he is ready for any eventuality.

Only certain people can make charms, ones that are truly effective against curses. Chichella's grandmother, her mother, and later Chichella herself were considered masters of the art. No one has ever been willing to explain why one person has the right personality and another does not, but there is some undefined relationship between the person and the spirits. It may be the courage to defy their powers or it may be a subtle affinity created by invisible wavelengths, but whatever the unknown attraction is, it cannot be acquired. One is born a charm-maker, or one is not.

The nursery children all had charms pinned onto them somewhere, and when I said they would be expected to change in the nursery to play clothes supplied by us, I found that the charms were no longer pinned in but sewed onto their wool undershirts. Some mothers felt that all the child's clothing was blessed by the charm and, to keep me from removing anything, literally sewed their children into their sweaters and pants and dresses. Quietly, when they thought I was not looking, they eased into the kitchen to ask Chichella if she would make a "special" charm, one that would protect even if I took off all the child's clothing.

It was one subject she never wanted to discuss with me. Another was the strange power she developed during menstrual periods — when other women avoided planting or making bread for fear they would "sour" whatever they touched. Apparently she reversed the cycle, excelling in those things she normally did well. The women knew it and came begging her

▲ Figures in the landscape

▼ Worker

Worker

Children at the nursery

A meeting in the street; bread aloft

Festa in the street; San Pancrazio aloft

▲ *The living room in the street*

▼ *The keeper of the myth: Chichella, 1967*

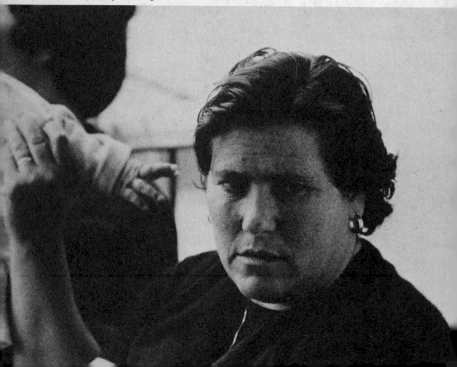

to do them a favor, something they particularly wanted to turn out well, when she had her next period. I think she did most of them, and they were favors in the sense that she was never paid for them. But she did not want to talk about it. Naturally, I did. She usually had her own way. She could not remember, she would say, or, No one believed in that sort of thing. It was rare that I could lure her into any comments on magic, curses or her own minor powers; but I remember one winter morning reading a book called *Sud e Magia*,* while I waited for the fog to lift. Chichella was busy in the bedroom, then in the bath cleaning, but she bustled back and forth more than usual. Keeping an eye on me, I thought, as I read:

Our analytical discourse becomes more conclusive when we try to draw a psychological significance of what we have indicated as the power of the negative in the Lucanian regime of existence . . . a negativity more serious than any lack of one particular element of well-being; it brings to light the risk that the very individual existence can disappear as a center of decision or choice . . .

"Chichella," I called, stopping her as she disappeared into the bathroom. "Did you ever hear anything like this?"

> *Sope 'nu tempetille*
> *c'era quatto voiarille:*
> *'a cap'e ranule 'a scazzavane.*
> *Fucitinne ranele da la vocca:*
> *La chiave de la Chiesia non si tocca.*

> On top of a little hill
> there were four little steers
> who squashed the head of a frog.
> Flee little frogs of the mouth [i.e., cankers]:
> The key of the church cannot be touched.

---

* Ernesto de Martino, *Sud e Magia*, Milan, 1959.

"What's the matter? Your liver off?" was her answer.

"No, why?"

"You're always funny when you read too much."

That seemed the end of the subject. I turned back to my book. Chichella does not like to be ignored and she had more to say. She planted herself right in front of me with her hands on her hips.

"Your *professor,*" — her scorn covered the whole profession. — "Says it's like that, so it *must* be. But the words are wrong . . . and he doesn't understand about church keys." She closed her eyes, frowned and then started singsonging the real Tarnese words in a high nasal voice which had none of her normal huskiness. It was a trance voice; I could feel her trying to reach a particular spirit. She chanted on through different verses — as best I could understand, against infant diseases, cradle cap, hernia and rough, thorny skin. She stopped as suddenly as she had started, opened her eyes and looked at me in surprise, I thought. Without a word she turned to go back to the bath.

"Don't stop."

"Nobody believes in that sort of thing anymore."

"Didn't you take Luigi to a witch when he was little?" I asked.

"That was different. The doctors didn't know what to do and I was desperate. Besides the witches have all died off now. They were old."

"Here . . . take a look at this picture." I showed her my book with its picture of the witch of *Quel Paese.*

"Looks like Ucculich right here in Torregreca. She's old now, doesn't do much, but I did hear her daughter will help . . . sometimes . . . as a favor." She blushed at giving herself away. The rest of the morning she was too busy to talk, and left with a short *"Buon giorno"* to me.

The fog went on for a week. We draped our faces with

scarves, like Arab women, to keep it from searing our lungs, but it stung our eyes and prickled our cheeks. Once or twice a day there might be a tear in the gray cotton revealing a sunlit patch way far below in the never-never land of the valley we thought no longer existed. A blink and it was gone; the mirage of a mind laid seige to by fog. The cobbles were slick, stone walls shimmered. Clothes clung, then mildewed on our backs. Finally late one afternoon a gale blew up to sweep the skies clear again and release us from prison. People streamed out of their houses and the babble of life began again. We wanted air and reassurance. For mine, I walked through my own land of make-believe — across from town and around the end of the butte to the mountains. As I walked, I wondered about spells, for I could find no other explanation for my own enchantment with the deep red of saturated tiles studded here and there with diamond beads of moisture, or with those houses I knew to be mean and squalid, but which were, for me, a gleaming copper fall of light, shadow and geometric pattern of mysterious beauty. Valleys stretched hazy and blue as far as the eye could see, with here and there a trailing veil of mist that had hidden from the wind. Stumps of grapevines, cruel and black in their deadness, tangled with their own shadows to cast a grotesque net over hillsides. In the wheat fields twilled with furrows the earth was gray, almost fertile looking, but no silken green sprouts had dared to announce a future. On beyond, the mountains — purple, red, blue, violent in their cleanliness — were more than ever the insurmountable wall between us and the rest of the world. Never had they been more beautiful or more threatening. Unmasked by clouds their challenge was brutal. Still, men had built that proud sentinel tower I saw glowering red in the sunset; maybe they could fight on to some kind of victory. I hurried back to my fire.

Late that night I was awakened by pounding at my door. It was Chichella, hysterical.

"Luigi's dying. He's dying right in front of my eyes and I can't do anything about it. It's a spell. He's always been under a spell . . . no one's ever been able to break it." She babbled on while I dressed. Down in her storeroom, in bed with the other two children, was a very feverish little boy shivering and crying, unable to swallow, unable to breathe.

"It's a curse . . . nothing to do . . . it's a curse."

"Have you called the doctor?"

"What doctor? I need the witch, the right one who understands the curse . . . I've never found the right one." She howled on. A linen towel wrapped swami-fashion hid Luigi's head and much of his face. When I pulled it aside to feel his cheek, Chichella turned lioness, clawing me away from the bed.

"Don't touch that!" she screamed. "Don't . . . touch . . . that!"

"All right, Chichella. Calm down and stay here. I'll get the doctor, but you could bathe his forehead and his face. He'd be more comfortable . . . and for God's sake stop babbling about a curse."

"He won't come . . . you know he won't. Besides . . ." She thought better of it and I left before she could tell me again about the witch.

I cursed the cold, the spells and the fancy language of anthropologists . . . *negativism*. That was not just negativism; it was stark terror. I would get the doctor out. He would come for violent fever or diphtheria. That last word was enough. He pulled his clothes on over his pajamas and in less than ten minutes we were back at Chichella's. It was a strep throat, and someday . . . soon . . . there will be a new saint, Sant' Antibiotica, famous for protecting children and exorcising curses.

It was gentle, rabbit-faced Dr. Neri I had dragged out of bed, the *medico condotto* who cared for the official poor list. Afterward, as I drove him home, I asked what he thought of spells that seemed more powerful than any God or medicine. He answered slowly without contempt or medical bluster, offering me an idea after he had peeled off its rind of prejudices as he might the skin of an orange.

"We all try to explain our misfortunes, you know. Theirs are so violent, so sudden. To us a landslide, the collapse of a roof, or a disease . . . TB, ulcers . . . don't burst into existence like lightning. We see the symptoms . . . causes if you prefer. Life has a certain reasonable order to us, but to the peasants it's a series of somersaults. Each jolt is so unexpected it could only be caused by malevolent spirits and their curses . . . and they outrank God, or the disaster could not have happened. Take Luigi. His throat's been brewing for days, but the crisis tonight was the first anyone knew of it. A curse is the most logical answer for Chichella . . . a curse or God's vengeance. *You* seek comfort in God; *their* lives are spent trying to stay on the good side of all the gods." He paused as though working out a problem. "As doctors we could do a lot to change their faith in curses and spirits, but I wonder if we will. They're too convenient . . . they cover up all the things we don't understand. If your patient believes in the evil eye, you feel safer. Maybe I don't make myself clear. All of us in the South, not just doctors, but all the educated class have encouraged ignorance in the peasants for our own protection. Times have changed, so have the peasants. They're not afraid of us and they're less afraid of spirits every day. One wonders where it will end." He shook himself. "At this rate I'll be seeing ghosts pretty soon. Must be the night air. Won't you come in for a cognac?"

I thanked him and drove home.

I heard no more from Chichella about "We don't believe in spells now. Our grandmothers did." It was a bad winter for her. There was no work. She was trying to live, feed and clothe her children and pay her husband's debt on what I gave her. Once, for a week, we kept a record of everything the children ate.

Originally I had wanted to do it for a month, but as Chichella said, it was a waste of time because they always ate the same things. The breakdown is without specific quantities except for bread. Each child ate one pound of bread a day. One was three, one six and the eldest was seven years old. Chichella herself ate a kilo, two and one fifth pounds of bread a day.

Breakfast	Lunch	Dinner
Bread, persimmons	Spaghetti, oil, cheese, bread	Bread, persimmons
Bread, persimmons	Spaghetti, tomato sauce, bread	Bread, persimmons
Bread, sausage	Spaghetti, oil, bread	Bread, dried figs
Bread	Macaroni, beans, bread	Bread, persimmons
Bread	Spaghetti, oil, bread	"Pizza" (flat bread with garlic on top)
Bread, persimmons	Greens, beans, bread	Dried codfish, potatoes, bread
Bread, codfish	Macaroni, dried peas, bread	Bread, dried figs

On that kind of diet it was not surprising that the children in Torregreca were often small, potbellied and listless. Teachers prided themselves on how well they kept order in their class-rooms without realizing they had not overcome a problem; they had simply failed to recognize one. It is not natural for nursery children to sit like lumps for eight straight hours. If they do, something is wrong. Ours certainly would not have accepted such inactivity, partly because they were more stimulated, but mostly because they were well fed. After following hundreds of children through the three years of nursery school, seeing them wake up and become alert, curious little monsters, I do not think the effect of diet can be exaggerated. Even Torregreca's elementary teachers, who may not have thanked me, admitted they could tell within the first class hour which children had been in our nursery and which had either stayed at home or gone to the traditional sedentary, minimal-food nurseries. Ours were not just pestiferous. Their manual dexterity, their use of words, their ability to reason and concentrate were more advanced. Food made fifty per cent of the difference.

On the diet their parents can afford, the children are lethargic. As adults, their strength will not last for long periods of heavy work. Their pace must be slow if it is to be constant. Young or old, they have little resistance to infectious diseases, especially those of the respiratory system.

Chichella did the best she could on her budget. She seldom bought greens (spinach, chicory, broccoli, lettuce and the like) because they were not filling enough. The fruit and vegetables she did buy were "surplus" — too poor in quality to haul to the market or too abundant to bring a decent price. Vendors shoveled "surplus" off the backs of trucks; the more you took, the less you paid per kilo. The years had a pattern for Chichella and her children. One month they lived on peppers; another on figs. When we kept our record, it was persimmon month. The children made off with twenty-two pounds of them in two days.

But it was always bread that was the filler, sometimes smeared with a blob of leftover beans, sometimes with a dried tomato or fig; more often than not it was softened with water and a drop of oil. Even Luigi, who was bottomless, got tired of it.

"Mamma," he asked one evening, "does everybody eat plain bread for supper?"

"Just leave it, if you don't want it," had been her answer. He did. Because they were always hungry, Chichella protected the precious extras she might have by carrying them with her in a patchwork shopping bag. At times she left it in my custody; three dried sausages, an egg and maybe a packet of margarine

I had told her to take when I left on a trip. If the bag were unguarded for a minute, the goodies disappeared. Still her expenses were twice her income, and I was not surprised when she jumped at the chance of adding even sixteen cents a day to her income by cleaning San Potito, the parish church.

She had to finish before the first morning Mass at six, so she got up at four. One morning, as she stumbled through the dark she heard what sounded like a baby's cry. She stood still; again the cry, but further away, to her left. She followed it; again and again came the cry. She went on, stopping to listen every few steps until she realized she was nearing the cemetery gates. Then she panicked and ran to the church, where she bolted herself in until the priest came. She knew and so did everyone else that she had heard the souls of the dead crying out in protest. At dawn they had to return to the exile of the grave. Morning after morning she heard the same cry, a wail that was fainter and fainter unless she followed it along the road toward the cemetery. Morning after morning it terrified her. Old hags brought special amulets. Still the souls cried. She wore one of her own sack-charms against the evil eye. The souls howled and wailed. Finally she could bear it no longer. She gave up the job . . . and the priest could find no one willing to take her place. One hundred lire a day is not enough for braving an encounter with the souls of the dead who resent their graves.

One morning in the Piazza I met Don Matteo, gay as always and plumper, judging from the way his cassock pulled under the arms.

"Ah, just the person I wanted to meet. Come along with me, Donna Anna, we'll have coffee . . . it's my only vice now that Luca's put me on a diet." He chuckled, pleased at having one vice no one could deny him. "I don't see nearly enough of you . . . and what are these strange goings-on up your way? Have you been courting the devil?" He waited to continue until we were settled at a table and the men had retreated to a re-

spectful gaping distance. "Now tell me, what have you been up
to with the spirits? They say even you have heard them."

I told him of Chichella's dawn meetings with the souls of the
dead and my regret at her giving up her job at San Potito. He
nodded kindly as he listened, and seemed so sympathetic that I
asked if he believed the spirits cried as they returned to their
graves.

"*Ma nò* . . . you mustn't take that sort of thing seriously.
They're always talking about spirits here. Old wives' tales, like
ghost stories; their imaginations get to work and pretty soon
they believe they've heard spirits crying." He hesitated a minute raising his eyebrows even higher. "But I *do* believe in the
Monached. You know what they are? The spirits of unbaptized
babies damned to wander the earth. They end up living with
people; they have to . . . Now don't laugh, I'm not teasing,
they do! There's one in every old house in Torregreca. Ours is
special, has a personality like no other. Of course he prowls at
night. Likes jam and throws pots and pans around and lately
he's taken a dislike to my new breviary . . . keeps pulling
pages out. He's misplaced my father's old Fascist medals. You
can laugh if you like. Father may be absent-minded, but not
about his decorations. The *Monached* did it. If you'd rented an
old house, you might have had trouble. They don't like change
and sometimes new tenants don't suit them. I suppose they'll
disappear with all this new housing. They won't move, you
know . . . absolutely won't. I'm *quite* serious!"

He was getting cross with me, so I asked about witches and
curses. His face turned to a mask, his eyebrows straightened
out and I saw for the first time what a sad face he had. I
thought he was going to dismiss the subject entirely. Instead he
said, "Fear makes them believe. Doctors don't have the right
cures. No one can explain the things that happen . . . finally,
rather than believe in a true God who has His reasons, they
believe in curses and witches. Enlightened priests — and there

are some — have fought it. Others let it go, incorporate the pagan in Catholic ritual. As for witches . . . they're like plumbers here . . . everyone is a halfway witch. Old Ida, our faithful messenger boy, for instance. When her spirits are just right, she's one of the more powerful. She's a bit temperamental. If she doesn't like her customer, she pretends she can't do anything, but if there's a spell to be broken, she's the girl who can do it. I've noticed she likes you, so anytime . . ." He smiled, but talking about the superstitions of his parishioners had depressed him. He signaled for our check and then leaned over and said very quietly. "Look at the men's faces! They can't imagine what we've been talking about. I'd better help them or . . . or their imaginations, you know. You must always be careful." In a louder voice, a public voice: "Have a nice trip, Donna Anna, and come back soon. There's still much to be done in Torregreca." Now what would they think? I was not going anywhere.

In Lucania if there is a sense of religion in magic, there is also a sense of magic in religion and, to complete the braid of common belief, a silken strand of the pagan. Serpents are draped over statues of saints; the Madonna is called on to exorcise evil spirits; grain sprouts, grown in the dark, are placed in Christ's coffin on Good Friday. A bride and groom's relatives, who prepare the marriage bed, hide amulets in the mattress against evil spirits and sprinkle salt on the springs, but the culmination of their work is the formal blessing. Later a plowshare, in these parts an ambiguous symbol of fertility, is hidden under the bed with a sickle — once more the blade to cut the evil spirits before they can do harm. The serious business of the wedding taken care of, everyone settles in to have a high old time, except, perhaps, the bride and groom. Until very recently they were sent off to bed while the relatives danced and drank in the next room — and, of course, banged on the door for

progress reports. Even now couples are barricaded in together
for seven straight days in what is referred to as "The Bride's
Week." Fortunately relatives may come to call; the first visit is
always that of the two mothers who bring coffee and remake
the bed — a courteous way of snooping for proof of the bride's
lost virginity. All they ask is a spotted linen towel to display —
and who can tell human blood from the blood of a chicken,
that noble fowl who has already supplied meat for the feast.
Small wonder that those who can afford it are married in Pompeii and spend a few days away from their village!

Sanctuaries in dank caves or in the crypts of churches still
hold a mystical attraction for the afflicted. Their subterranean
quarters make them both Stygian and churchly, uniting, as it
were, all the powers under one roof. Often they are so hung
with arms, legs, fingers, heads and other bits of the human ap-
paratus that they might be the parts depot of a wax works.
Each votive offering has been brought by a pilgrim to thank
the saint for driving the evil spirits out of a specific part of the
body. Often the vows are made for children suffering the dread
lassitude that signals infantile curses. The real malady — dys-
entery, worms or just plain malnutrition — is so persistent the
mother knows her child has been put under an evil spell. "Free
my little Angelo of these evil spirits and he will wear your cassock and rope for a year as a reminder of your protection." So,
for a year, if he is cured, little Angelo dribbles and spills on the
same habit, sleeps in it and trails it through the dusty muck of
the village streets. Sometimes the saint does not do his work
well. He is discarded for another saint and another sanctuary.
The power of curses is infinite; the power of saints limited and
capricious.

Superstitious and devout as they are, Southerners have a casual approach to their saints. In May, for instance, for the festi-
val of San Pancrazio, avenger of false witness and false oaths,
the Torresi simply ignore religious facts and rearrange things to

suit themselves. Of San Pancrazio's life only the end is known. In 304 A.D., during the Christian persecutions ordered by the Emperor Diocletian, he was stoned to death. He was fourteen years old. That is the official version, but for the Torresi he was the ever-faithful lover of Santa Filomena, the mystery lady of the Catholic Church. There is no agreement about *her;* there are a number of stories. One tells of a Santa Filomena found perfectly preserved in a green dress in San Severino Marche. Another tells of remains found in 1802 under a garbled inscription in the Catacombs of Priscilla. At first they were identified as those of a martyr named Filomena; subsequent analysis proved they were of some later lady hurriedly buried in the same grave. The whole affair turned into an ecclesiastical porcupine; anyone who tried to get to the meat of the situation was punctured by the dissenters' quills. From their resting place under the altar of a village church near Naples, the "wrong" bones were already producing miracles and apparitions and the parish priest had written an inspired life of Santa Filomena. Today it is considered a masterpiece of religious fiction, but it did much to confuse the issue at the time. The Church, in its wisdom, has decided there is nothing certain about the life of Santa Filomena. She *may* have been a Christian martyr who lived in the second or the sixth century. The Torresi are not so cautious. As they tell it, she was the beautiful daughter of a rich merchant of Bari. San Pancrazio saw her, fell passionately in love with her and asked her father for her hand in marriage. The father agreed. Santa Filomena did not. She knew her destiny was sainthood and her most precious purity must be defended at any cost. When, on her wedding day, she still could not dissuade her lover, she walked into the sea until she drowned. San Pancrazio was inconsolable. Through seventeen centuries he has followed in her wake, and though he may be no closer to his beloved now, he has become a special favorite with all women, particularly the unmarried.

Prince Charming *all'Italiana* had found his way into the religious calendar and had brought such joy that anomalies of whatever character were to be forgotten. This was to be a gloriously irrational feminine festa. I was startled when the celebration began the night before, with bonfires lighted in all the streets and alleys. People sat around them, gossiping and feeding the fires with twigs. At the sound of a footstep they called "Who goes there?" The answer "Friend!" brought greetings and the offer of a glass of wine. A few feet further on another fire, another group, another call "Who goes there?" On into the night they sat, watching by their fires until they judged all evil had been put to flight. This was the spring exorcism of the spirits that had coagulated in Torregreca during the winter.*

Next morning Santa Filomena led the procession, borne aloft, reclining like a china Elizabeth Barrett Browning on a gold baroque chaise longue with satin pillows and angels that bobbled at the ends of long springs. She was languid and either very frail or very haughty. Her herald was an old shepherd who tootled away on his bagpipes; her followers, the women of the town who were more dejected than elated by their lover's pursuit. They groaned an anthem whose words were lost in a babble of conflicting versions. Way at the back came San Pancrazio, a medieval beatnik scrubbed up and dressed for the occasion in tin armor and a satin mini-skirt. With each lurch his puttees rattled and his helmet swiveled around on his wig. His bearers were doing their best, but they had to follow the excited directions of a priest carrying a wax hand mounted on a golden column. When he raised the hand high in the air, they stopped and wobbled. Two waves and they staggered off. The

---

* This was as I first saw it in 1960. By 1967 *some* Torresi had found a more respectable interpretation. San Pancrazio was a vineyard keeper, a very careful one, and the sight of neatly trimmed vines gives him pleasure. So the fires are of vine cuttings and if there are enough to appease him, San Pancrazio will protect the vineyards from storms. Perhaps this version is slightly less pagan, but it certainly is not the traditional one.

pace was so slow there at the back that the men who followed
San Pancrazio had time for a glass of wine at the several shops
along the route. Soon their faces were flushed and their steps
uncertain.

Snaking through the alleys of the Rabata and the Saraceno,
Santa Filomena was usually one street higher than San Pancrazio. As I glimpsed them through the funnel of a cross-
stairway they seemed to pass each other going in opposite directions. Where it would end was hard to tell. For a while, as
we backtracked, I thought we might gyrate until the proces-
sioners had been dropped off, one by one, at their own door-
steps. Instead we drew up in front of the prison-like elementary
school. The statues were arranged side by side. No one spoke.
The silence was tense, expectant. The men took off their hats in
a half-embarrassed salute. The women, stiff, their eyes forward,
held their candles absolutely vertical. Nothing happened. The
priest brandished his wax hand again. Still nothing happened.
He went red in the face and wigwagged emphatically. Pop,
pop, pop, pop, pop, pause. Then again, all around us the not
very loud pop, pop, pop, pop, pop of firecrackers — lots of
them. And another pause. Bang! Bang! Long, long pause —
BOOM!

The windows of the school rattled and there was a big sigh
from the crowd. The festa was over. It was time for lunch.
People hurried off in all directions. In the scramble I collided
with a woman.

"Wasn't it a lovely festa?" she asked. "I always feel better
after we burn the spirits out."

"And San Pancrazio?"

"He's so handsome, but it's the fires that count, you know.
Well, good-bye. *Buon appetito.*" She hurried off to her lunch, I
to mine, though I already had a slight case of indigestion.

The festa season had begun. The next event was simply a
postponement from January to June. Sant' Antonio Abate, pa-

tron saint of animals, has had to wait until mules and donkeys are important and the weather more clement for the human being. His little church just outside town on the edge of the fields is used only once a year. The bell has been stolen and the brick yoke in which it hung is crumbling. Inside the smell of mold, dead flowers and sheep droppings add to the dejection of cracked plaster. No last-minute trimmings can mask years of neglect. Still, only this church can protect animals. During the Mass there is a frenzy of activity outside. Herds of sheep mixed with goats are driven around and around through the crowds of donkeys and mules resplendent in plumes, harness and bells. Each animal must make three full circuits around the building — no more, no less. And, to follow the magic of numbers, each human being must bow nine times to the Cross. Breugel never dreamed of such confusion. Unfortunately, quarrels and threats of lawsuits over watermelon stands upset by stampeding animals mar the Christian quality of the day, but most are satisfied that their animals are safe.

The rest of the summer is for work. In the middle of August Italy takes a holiday for the Assumption of the Virgin Mary, but not the peasants of Torregreca. To them a spring or summer festa is premature. Only when the harvest is in will they know how thankful they should feel. By late September they are ready to praise, extol, threaten or grumble at the Madonna . . . but not before.

There is nothing new in this domestic "if you've been a good girl I'll give you a candy" approach. Crauford Tait Ramage, a young English clergyman who spent the year of 1828 in Naples as a private tutor, encountered much the same treatment of saints when he went on a walking trip through the South. He was an observant, rather eccentric young man who must have startled the natives as much as they startled him. He was meticulous in the planning of his trip, even to an all-weather costume that avoided the need of carrying bulky changes. "I have

a white merino frock-coat, well-furnished with capacious pockets, into which I have stuffed my maps and notebooks, nankeen
trousers, a large brimmed hat, white shoes and an umbrella, a
most invaluable article to protect me from the fierceness of the
sun's rays . . ."* At the end of the first day he reports solemnly
that a band of women took fright at his appearance and "scam-
pered off in the utmost confusion." Alarmed at the sight of a
strange man, he thinks, and he persists in his idea that Southerners are ill-mannered because they stare at him. No behavior
offended him more than that of the well-to-do in Taranto.
Ramage had slipped into a ditch and when he appeared, pale
green and dripping slime, in the main piazza of the city, the
evening promenaders gawked in speechless wonder. Boors, he
snorts, all boors. Peculiar as he was, he penetrated deep into
country few foreigners had ever seen and made notes of the
strange things he heard and saw. While in Calabria he comments about saints and festas: ". . . I can see that the Cala-
bresi are urgent in their demands on heaven. If drought deso-
late their fields and no attention is paid to their prayers, it is
said that they proceed to put statues of their most revered
saints in prison hoping that humiliation may make their inter-
cession more effective . . ."

Norman Douglas, who endured fifty years of a Southern
affascinazione and was Calabria's most devoted explorer,
wrote: "South Italians, famous for abstractions in philosophy,
cannot endure them in religion. Unlike ourselves, they do not
desire to learn anything from their deities or to argue about
them. They only wish to love and be loved in return, reserving
to themselves the right to punish them, when they deserve it.
Countless cases are on record where [pictures and statues of]
Madonnas and saints have been thrown into a ditch for not
doing what they were told or for not keeping their share of the

---

* Crauford Tait Ramage, *Ramage in South Italy,* ed. Edith Clay, London, 1965.

bargain. During the Vesuvius eruption of 1906 a good number were subjected to this 'punishment' because they neglected to protect their worshipers from the calamity according to contract (so many candles and festivals=so much protection)."*

Everything in its proper place. The Torresi would harvest their broad beans, their wheat and their grapes before they committed themselves. In the clear light of the year's balance they would decide whether or not to pin a thousand lire note on the Madonna's skirt.

---

* Norman Douglas, *Old Calabria*, London, 1913.

IX

RES ECCLESIASTICA

THE two weeks I lived in the Convent of San Fortunato in 1959 and the years of cooperation, even sparring, that followed taught me a lot about religious life. I had imagined uniform austerity. I found instead that there were as many variations among nuns and priests as there are human beings.

My indoctrination came from Sister Clemente who used talk as an ego tonic against discouragement and physical exhaustion. At mealtimes in the little back dining room I was the ideal captive for her stories about herself, the other nuns and the townspeople. Soon she appointed herself my mentor, explaining, as though to an idiot, the subtleties of each situation and the action she thought appropriate. Her stories fascinated me, but her advice was the bitter steeping of prejudices, and useless except as an index to peasant mentality. I was careful never to accept or reject her strategies because by Convent rule she had to report every discussion to the Mother Superior. I was attentive but neutral, and in almost no time I noticed a deviousness about myself that Luca would have admired. Sister Clemente was a natural pipeline to official reaction. An artist of the *bell'imbroglio* herself and ever watchful, she was disarmed by flattery. Nothing pleased her so much as being asked her opinion. If I outlined a "half-formed plan" I knew that within twenty-four hours either the Mother Superior would call me in, which meant objections, or Sister Clemente would assure me of the brilliance of my idea and offer help. I could gauge my support or opposition without taking one irrevocable step.

This collusion had an inconvenient by-product. Sister Clemente was stricken by a Convent malaise, *amicizia particolare;* she had a crush on me. Wherever I went, her huge black figure was sure to appear. She was too outspoken, or maybe too inexperienced to be a good dissembler. Where someone else might have eased into conversations unnoticed, she burst in with a raucous, over-surprised, "What are *you* doing here?" The question was more appropriate to her. She should not have been in a bar. She had no excuse for coming to the carpenter shop in the bowels of the Rabata, nor any reason to lurk in the dark corners of the mechanic's shop . . . but there she was. She would throw her arm around my shoulders and kibitz my conversations. She never seemed in any hurry; nothing at the Convent needed her attention, or if it did, it could wait. Having found me, she would not be shaken off. She wanted to stroll the streets arm in arm, to tease me, to hold my hand and arrange things for me . . . in short, make me her property. I was not just embarrassed, I was revolted by the pawing. When I evaded her for several mornings, she developed a new ploy. She drove the jeep right up under my balcony in the afternoon, and honked the horn over and over again until I was forced to stick my head out the window.

"*Oyee*, just wanted to know if you were home. I've brought some flowers." Sure enough she had a huge bouquet cut fresh from the Convent garden, and was determined to bring them up. My neighbors were amused. Each afternoon when the horn blew, they stuck their heads out their windows, to call in their most seductive voices "*Yoo-ho*, Sister Clemente . . . come up and see *me!*" She pretended to ignore them, but she must have heard, as I did, their gibes. "Oh, it's just the Signora's lover," or "Sister Clemente's come a-courting again." She never knew their kindness to me, however. If my car was not parked in front of the door to give me away, they would yell, "She's not here, Sister Clemente. No point in blowing anymore. She left an hour ago." Cowering behind the curtains, I blessed them, and thanked them when they came to find out if they had done the right thing.

It was a ridiculous situation; still I hesitated about going to the Mother Superior. With her fierce pride and determination Sister Clemente was not a naughty child to be punished by a slap on the hand. She had bulled her way up, over and around every obstacle, to build a huge farm complex out of nothing. She had been determined to excel in her own pen and she had, but she found it lonely . . . she had made it that way. The other nuns were jealous of her; the rest of the world handled her with care because she made no secret of her basic disdain. Two premises governed everything she did: first, all civilians (that is, non-religious) were tricky swindlers; and second, peasants were a human subspecies who must be required, even forced if necessary, to do what higher beings decreed. Considering her background these were bizarre foundations for a religious life. She argued that she had been both (civilian and peasant) so she understood their vile motivations. There was no palaver about Christian charity and understanding. She would be a cynic and a nun at the same time. She was brash enough to push successive Mother Superiors until, their wills broken, they were her puppets. Special permission to break minor rules led inevitably to other special permissions, until she became a law unto herself. Impossible to keep in a religious community — yes, but it was Sister Clemente alone who had once defended the Convent against fourteen armed robbers. While the others whimpered and prayed, she rushed from window to window firing an old shotgun. Fearing they had stumbled into a community of gat-toting nuns, the bandits dropped their own guns and fled. After Sister Clemente collected their leavings, she announced there would be target practice for the novices. She might have become the captain of a female militia if the girls had not been so terrified. They petitioned the

Bishop. Reluctantly he brought the experiment to a halt, but not before he had praised Sister Clemente's courage . . . and her ingenuity. For twenty years a parade of Mother Superiors tolerated her willfulness because, quite literally, there was no way to replace her and she knew it. I did not want this little "love affair" to be the final blow. I became elusive, almost furtive. The Mother Superior made pointed comments about my disappearance, and still Sister Clemente lurked near the market in the mornings or came to the house with flowers in the afternoon. Then one morning Mastro Pancrazio gave me a message that the Mother Superior wanted to see me.

"You have been very tactful," were her first words. "But nothing escapes Don Evandro. I'm sorry you didn't come to me, however." She sighed. She looked tired and for the first time since I had known her, self-possession had given way to a weary sadness; still I was unprepared for her next remarks. "When I was young, I thought to be a Mother Superior meant the only easy life in a convent. Now I know how lonely it is. I pray God to give me strength, but sometimes I'm sure He finds me lacking. No human being can be right *always*—and yet that's a Mother Superior's job and she must do it by herself. Then I look at you and I marvel . . . no, no, let me go ahead. I never talk this way, but I want to tell you. The subject will not come up again. You are as alone as I and thirty years younger — presumably less wise and you live in the world with its temptations. For all that, you manage to keep a sense of perspective, you are fair, yet you never become entangled. My life, in comparison, is easy but I feel unequal to it. This is a strange thing to say but for the first time in many years I feel I can trust someone to be dispassionate. I can ask advice, I can talk to another human being as a human being. I wish I thought all the nuns in this Convent were as Christian as you . . . Now . . . I'll never mention it again, but I hope we can be friends."

She pulled herself up very straight, stretched her neck out of the stiff white collar, and resumed her calm, quiet, resolute manner. She might never have said any of it. We took up from her regret that I had not come to her.

"Convent life is not easy. In many ways it is unnatural. All things considered, incidents of *amicizia particolare* are surprisingly rare, but naturally there *are* rules . . . just in case. I tell you this so that you'll understand why Sister Clemente will no longer speak to you, or have anything to do with you. She will be forbidden to do so for six months. She will spend one hour more than usual in Adoration at the altar and must pray for forgiveness. There will be no explanation made to the other nuns. I'm afraid they won't need one, since gossip is the legitimate pastime of so many of them, but I hope you'll return to your old habit of coming down when you feel like it. You're always welcome . . . and as you realize, needed." She stood up. I was dismissed. When I tried to say something, she interrupted. "You have nothing to explain. Remember, I have experience in dealing with Sister Clemente. I know how hard it is to discourage her once her mind is made up. Now, will you come for lunch Sunday. I've promised the nuns you'll talk to them afterward. They enjoy you, you know. You make them laugh and you tell them about places they don't know. Come, we'll make it a party."

And so began an unlikely friendship which has limped along through disagreements and misunderstandings to the present day. It has had its disconcerting moments. When my mother, part of whose education was at convents, came from America to Torregreca for a brief visit, the Mother Superior startled her by taking over the duties of a waitress and offering every dish of a complex luncheon herself. She brushed aside my objections with, "By serving the mother, I show respect for the child. She will appreciate that." She did. Beyond mutual respect there was obviously a practical side to the relationship; we were useful to each other. I had access to supplies she needed but could not afford to buy. Every nun of the order spent six weeks in the Convent on a summer retreat. She could and did send them to see the nursery and urged them to ask my help. It would be naive to deny that we were mutually convenient. While we disagreed on many things, we listened to the other's side of the question. I will never approve of isolating girls from boys until they marry; she will never accept that grown women, teachers, can live in nurseries without chaperones. But we tolerated even bigoted convictions in a sincere effort to help and at times comfort the other. All the more astonishing then, during a period of revived interest in "The Southern Question," to pick up one of the most widely read Italian newspapers and discover that my own Mother Superior had had a number of disparaging things to say about me in a published interview. Hostilities have been suspended now. She says she was misquoted; I still feel there was no logical reason for my name to come up in such an interview unless *she* mentioned it and obviously with some malice.

Whatever the circumstances she will have had her own reasons. She does nothing lightly. No disagreement can detract from her skill in the difficult art of Mother Superiorship. If Sister Clemente is openly iconoclastic about her own behavior as a nun, she has thirty less obvious sisters. Wisely, each has been put in control of one section of convent activity where her eccentricities inconvenience no one except novices, who were born to suffer.

In another society Sister Giustizia, the Novice Mistress, would be called a do-it-yourself buff. She has developed her own didactic method to increase memory and minimize the use of books. No one quite understands how it works, but it is thought to have some basis in free, though not too free, association. Cards are fundamental to the system. Sister Giustizia shuffles and reshuffles great piles of them and then flashes one at her novices: Anti-Christ. The chosen victim must recite an entire lecture, Sister Giustizia's lecture naturally, on the subject. The Anti-Christ dealt with, she goes on to Transubstantiation, Circumcision and Purification. Each card should evoke an appropriate lecture. A true inventor, she is absorbed in her theory. She experiments with it, changes words and does test runs on the only material at hand . . . the other nuns. Convinced that they should be beyond the prompt-card stage, she pounces on them from behind doors or in dark passages and announces, "Purgatory, Sister Gioiosa." In ten years Sister Gioiosa has never been known to answer anything except "*O dio*, what a fright you gave me." One memorable day at lunchtime she glided up behind Sister Eufrasia in the kitchen and bellowed "Indulgence" at which Sister Eufrasia dropped a cauldron of boiling pasta and fled to the cloister shouting "Demons, demons!" They tell me she "had to be put to bed with the doctor" before she would calm down. Both novices and nuns react to Sister Giustizia's stimuli with mute bewilderment, but she does not abandon her theory or even simplify the words. Quite the contrary. Some perverse lack of understanding drives her to further elaborations.

As General Housekeeper, Sister Gioiosa can vent her passion for the preservation of fresh vegetables. She is the mistress of the linen, laundry, furniture and general food supplies. There would be enough work for two nuns, but she has never been willing to share the secrets of her inventory and so the full responsibility rests on her. No sheet can be taken, no bar of soap unwrapped before Sister Gioiosa juggles her keys and weeps over her registers. The problem used to be to find her; now everyone knows she will be turning, one by one, the potatoes, apples, persimmons and pears that cover the entire attic floor. She coos to them, encourages them, exhorts them to last. She scolds soft spots and shriveled skin. Occasionally she is elated at breaking her own record, but no one takes her chattering seriously. It has long been accepted that she is a harmless but compulsive vegetable turner.

The Doorkeeper-Nun, who had nothing to do but sew between callers, was usually aged and inactive. Her duties were not exacting. She released the latch by pressing a button in her little cubbyhole, then interviewed the visitor and rang the cloister bell the proper number of times to call the nun involved. Sister Michelina had seemed perfect for the job. She was aged, fat, a trifle vague — and as it turned out, had brooded over a secret resentment for years. No one understood about her feet . . . *parlando con tutt' il dovuto rispetto,* as she said, apologizing for her blunt reference to what genteel society calls extremities. She wanted a pair of handmade shoes for those feet, knobbled and stunted by years of walking on marble floors. Since her hopes were limited by the Convent budget, she buttonholed each visitor fate brought to the door. Innocently they took the matter to heart . . . at least the first time. Not knowing this was her *idée fixe,* and unable to ask exactly what she was wearing on her feet at the moment, they were at a disadvantage. Sister Michelina would describe at length the discomforts of all the shoes she had worn in the last thirty years. Nothing would stop her. It was to avoid such importunity that the Mother Superior interrupted her work, listened to the opening of the front door, and then gauged the elapsed time before the nun's call bell was rung. If the silence was too prolonged, she dashed to the visitor's rescue.

In fact the Mother Superior manipulated all these frustrated personalities. She had to judge eccentricities: were they a healthy safety valve, or were they slipping over into mania? Before they veered too far they must be smothered or replaced by milder distractions. Without allowing herself to be involved she had to know all about the petty squabbles that nibbled away like termites at the framework of her society. She was responsible for the food, lodging and education of one hundred orphan or half-orphan girls who lived in the Convent, for fifty old people bedridden in another wing, and for the proper training of twenty-five novices. She required self-discipline of the nuns, but knew that her own figure looming in the background was the physical reminder of conscience that averted chaos.

She was a self-taught financial expert. She knew exactly how many time notes she could sign per quarter and still hope to come out even — with the help of *Divina Provvidenza*. She paid the taxes, begged contributions from provincial authorities, searched new laws for helpful provisions, administered estates left to the Bishop, went to two Masses daily, spent an hour in silent devotion, and still found time to read stories to the orphans. After my arrival she added my conversion to her duties — for she was serenely confident that in time I should become Catholic.

She operated out of a small room furnished with battered leftovers from government offices. It was not hard to understand why they had been discarded. Three crate-wood desks had to be equipped with bread knives for unjamming the drawers. The only file cabinet, which towered in the air on a base of cupboards, had started life as a mail-sorting bank and had such deep pigeonholes that the Mother Superior had rigged a bamboo pole with a crossbar and hook as a fishing pole for papers that slithered to the back out of reach. None of the inconveniences bothered her as long as she had her typewriter. It was an ancient, tank-like machine that responded to nothing but brute force. Each morning for three hours the burliest nun in the Convent did battle with it, thumping away until picture frames rattled against the walls and the Mother Superior was driven to cover her ears with her hands. Together they flooded the world with letters pleading for help and were often surprised with their results. Through their efforts the Convent had been given a central heating system, which was a great addition, though it was found to be too expensive to run.

Then there was another piece of luxurious equipment, an elevator. It has been completely installed and tested by the company, but remains nonfunctional because no one in Torregreca is qualified to do the monthly mechanical check required for the operating permit.

At times the gifts were perplexing. The Mother Superior asked me if I had any idea what she could do about twenty-five of the orphans who could not be sent home or even to relatives for the summer holidays. I had suggested a camp and had found for it one of the Convent's own farms, high on a ridge overlooking the valley and mountains beyond. It was ideal. The tenant and his family lived in two ground-floor rooms of the house, which left two rooms above and a large, empty loft. Two nuns could have a bedroom to themselves; there was a large room that could be used as a communal sitting room and dining room and the loft would serve as a dormitory. I promised enough food for six weeks and a small amount of money for purchasing general supplies. Our calculations showed we had provided for everything except twenty-five cots. There was no question of moving the girls' regular beds to the camp, because they were needed by the nuns for the annual retreat. The Mother Superior and I outlined a heartbreaking letter for the secretary to write. We stressed the delicate physical condition of the children, how important it would be for them to be outside, to play with animals and be in the sunshine. The secretary was so familiar with the procedure that we left to her the choice of companies to receive the letter. I had imagined an avalanche of beds. Instead there was one answer announcing the shipment of "twenty-five articles" and apologizing because the "twenty-five articles," though entirely efficient, were not of the latest type. This seemed reasonable enough: the company could give donations from its back inventory, and after all how much could cots vary? In due course a crate with "twenty-five articles" arrived. One look sent us running to the files for our letter.

It was a masterpiece of grammatical and ungrammatical verbal gymnastics. After a preamble of thanks for past, present and future generosities came the meat:

> The Divine Provider has seen fit to lavish one hundred of His abandoned souls on this institution and we, His humble servants, do all in our power to nurture them. Now that the season of the Assumption of the Virgin Mary is about to carry them off into the dangers and temptations of the outside world, we find that twenty-five of these children of sin cannot, for reasons of inappropriate family atmosphere, leave the institution and be placed in contact with degradation worse that that of their fathers. Therefore, we propose to take them to a hillside where the air is good and the food healthy, but you, Dear Benefactor, would not want them to be left under the stars without protection for their little bodies, without SUPPORT . . .

The "twenty-five articles" were trusses. We laughed until we cried. The Mother Superior finally caught her breath long enough to splutter, "What kind of an institution would need twenty-five trusses? Now that I think of it, what am I supposed to be running here?"

Eventually we were able to borrow the cots. The trusses joined a collection of old chests, wardrobes and broken chairs donated by people who had wanted to get rid of them without paying a cartage fee. They cluttered one long corridor awaiting the time when they would be valuable in a trade. The trusses *might* be useful, sometime; they were potentially more useful than the vast supplies Don Germano kept under lock and key.

Don Germano was another of the Mother Superior's problems, one she could neither solve nor escape, for he had been instrumental in the rehabilitation of the Convent and had insisted on the establishment of the old people's home in one wing. At the time he had been a young man who looked more like a lantern-jawed prizefighter than a priest. His avowed philosophy was "global"; the larger picture held his attention, not the niggling details that so delighted women. Women. "Ah yes, women!" he would say, and throw his head back as though pondering the question. "If the world's progress had been left to women, men would still be running around in embroidered fig leaves." He translated his opinions into such epigrams and then repeated them until they passed as proverbs of antiquity. True to his philosophy, his life had been one of action and far-reaching projects. The very first had been a footbridge across the valley that would, if it could be finished before it collapsed, join the town with the hillside opposite. Since the peasants would have just half the distance to walk to their fields, he assumed they would be willing to give their work free. After all, it was entirely for their benefit. He was scandalized when they refused to cooperate. Their reasoning was as close as his was global. If they refused to work for nothing, he would have to pay them or give up the project. If he gave it up, they lost nothing they had ever had, or for that matter ever wanted. The work began in 1920. By 1960 the bridge was half finished and every man-hour of work had been paid for by Don Germano. It had been at about the same time that he laid the cornerstone for an immense Pilgrim Hostel which he argued would attract visitors to the miraculous but as yet unknown sanctuaries of Torregreca. The two ventures drained his resources, and so work had to stop. It would start and stop that way for forty years, but he was never discouraged. He turned to aesthetic matters — such as the veiling of two exuberantly masculine statues and the destruction of the fresco at the Convent that Luca had pointed out to me. The statues were Torregreca's only tangible rewards from Fascism. One had been mounted in front of the elementary school, the other was to have graced the athletic field; but the regime ceased to exist before work on the field was started. The National Arts Commission had ordered them stored in the school's basement and there they had remained forgotten by all except Don Germano. His blunt tenacity had won him the respect of everyone in town, but it was often inconvenient for the authorities. The Commission held out for years, until finally it was decided to humor him by ordering fig leaves for the statues. A local plasterer flung white cement in the general direction of the groin and plopped the fig leaves in place. Contrary to Don Germano's expectations the resulting blobs and smears were much more obscene than the original anatomy. The Commission was adamant on the matter of the fresco. There was no justification for destroying such a vast work by a painter who might yet become famous. Don Germano railed, but the members of the Commission would not budge. On the contrary, they became distant and too busy to see him whenever he applied for an appointment. They would not allow that the beheading of a Bishop was an insult to the present holder of the office, even if, as the priest claimed, it had not happened in the diocese, but was one of the more ignoble moments in Saint Anthony's life. Over the years the peasants, though still unwilling to give their work, had come to think of Don Germano as a flesh-and-blood saint of lost causes, a champion of the downtrodden. Now it was his honest stubbornness that was his defeat.

The Bishop had put up with the extravagant projects and the frankness that often bordered on revolt, but he could not countenance a priest who libeled the authorities. He talked to Don Germano gently about old age and the limitations of the flesh, explaining that he had delegated much of his own authority. He hoped his priests would follow his example. Don Germano refused to understand. He was more vigorous than ever, why should he retire? Since he would not do it voluntarily, it was done for him. He was relieved of parish duties and ordered to confine his activities to his private affairs and to the administration of the old people's section of the Convent. The Mother Superior became the target of his frustrated wrath. He renounced global philosophy and expected every match to be accounted for, its use documented. The nuns snatched my burned stubs from me to add to "Don Germano's pile." "You're an open-handed lot," he would say. "No wonder the Bishop thinks I commandeer supplies for my projects! You waste so much. I'll show him what administration should be." Each truckload of food that arrived was fought over; each donation to the Convent in general, he claimed for the old people. The Mother Superior could not win all the skirmishes, so his storerooms were piled to the ceilings with things utterly useless to the old. High rubber boots in children's sizes, dolls, school furniture, sixteen midget toilet bowls originally ordered for a new wing of the orphanage, two crates of left-footed tennis shoes and ten bushels of hog mash. Argue as she might, the Mother Superior could not persuade him to release these precious commodities. The hoard that galled her most was the salon full of powdered milk. He would not let the orphans have it to drink. He stuck to his idea that it was detergent, and issued a daily ration to the Convent laundry squads. The novices were happy to give up bars of yellow lye soap for this foaming delight and it was reported that not only did the brew wash well, but it starched at the same time.

Each morning Don Germano patroled the halls of the Convent with his keys. At noon he went home — with his keys — and dedicated the rest of the day to his business affairs. He had been left a number of houses by the members of his family and with the rents he purchased others, always one- or two-room hovels in the Rabata. Investment was a science. He was not interested in the new, so-called valuable real estate that required wealthy tenants. "There have always been the poor, there always will be, and they have to pay rent even for a pigsty. The definition of a good investment is one where the income is steady and the market sure."

Quiet days reformed the warrior and made him silent and hunched. He paced the streets peering into people's eyes as though in search of something he had lost or forgotten. His tremendous head with its bushy mane of white hair seemed to be all that was left of the old Don Germano — and at that he never threw it back and charged into verbal battle. He ignored his old "projects" and until he died three years ago it was assumed he had lost interest in them. His will made it clear he had not. The income from his real estate was left to the Convent on one condition: that the Pilgrim Hostel be finished within five years of his death. So he continues to be a problem to the Mother Superior, who must mortgage property of greater intrinsic value than the houses or forfeit sure income forever. His last statement, written in large scrawly letters, has been interpreted in various ways, but everyone agrees on one thing: Don Germano fights on. "Now that I am dead, I will, with the help of Almighty God, perform such miracles that even the blind will see the use of my Pilgrim Hostel."

Not all Torresi priests are so eccentric, but, as the Mother Superior commented, priests are still men, and they vary accordingly. Some are content to minister to a parish; others are too ambitious or too restless to accept the tedium of saying the rosary with old ladies and nagging children who duck catechism class. They seek out chances to preach, or study, or administer. Still, any discussion of the priest-man dead-ends in the polite quarantine we keep for people who are different. We cannot quite admit he is human, that he dislikes spinach and women in red dresses, that he suffers from constipation or has hobbies and non-physical passions. He is just different from other men and when we search for a reason too often the key seems to be the vow of chastity which, according to us, isolates him from "normal family life." To be fair, chastity relieves him of a wife and children, but not of his father, his mother, his sisters, brothers and all their children. A priest has as many problems and distractions as a businessman. What sets him apart is his devotion to *one* and only one cause. We dilute our efforts; he concentrates his, finding justification for any means that will further God's work. His is the just cause, but absolute dedication to one facet of a multi-faceted existence does not lead to a sense of proportion. And so the priest must be human after all. Italians keep him that way by crediting him with the most heinous sins they can imagine. You may be sure a priest is a saint on earth if you hear nothing worse of him than that he likes money. Priests have a monopoly on love affairs, especially with their housekeepers, but when it comes to perversions, sadism and craving for power the nuns come in for their share. From the gossip — given out as pure truth — they must rush from one debauch to the next without so much as a Hail Mary in between. It sounds a giddy life, thoughtless and fun-loving, until common sense cuts through the exaggerations. Most of those sins are invented by piazza idlers who resent everything in general, the Church in particular. Its power, too absolute for too long, is the target. Nuns and priests are neither more nor less depraved than others; the exception is just more conspicuous.

The Church's true immorality has been collective. In collusion with feudal landlords, it sapped the vitality of Southern Italy. When it was divested of its holdings in 1870 it was already too late. The process of exhaustion had been gradual but constant:

> No productive activity, no financial operation escaped the control of the religious agencies. The clergy, from 1500 on, seemed to polarize the economic life around itself. Within a few score years real property, pastures, farms and buildings were controlled by unchanging owners, the Clergy of Matera, and monetary wealth, pushed by the same centrifugal force flowed into the ecclesiastical safes making [sic. the clergy] absolute arbiters of the local financial situation.[*]

[*] Raffaele Giura, *I Beni Ecclesiastici nella Storia Economica di Matera,* Matera, 1961.

By 1754, in the province of Matera, which is a small one, the Church owned 22,408 hectares out of 31,083 hectares of land. (A hectare is roughly 2.5 acres.) This is exclusive of the Holy Patrimony and the land that supplied the annual payment due for the support of ecclesiastical organizations. The clergy were not enlightened landlords. They wanted return without investing in costly improvements, and because of the vastness of their holdings found it convenient to lease large tracts to middlemen who then split them into minute leases. So fractional pieces were offered to peasants willing to risk sharecropping. The chain was such that each squeezed out his profit as best he could. Nothing was put in, but each year more must come out of the same land. At the same period there was, always in the province of Matera, one priest for every fifty people. (At that rate there would be 200 priests in Torregreca today — indeed at times it seems there are.) The census shows that of 3,159 families, 2,791 were dependent on income from day labor or share leases. The other 368 families, which combined to form the upper classes, were: 8 patricians, 24 large landowners, 47 members of professions, 31 employees of the crown and 258 priests who were included because they did not live in the innumerable convents and monasteries that dotted the province.

Each year more and more land had to be relegated to pasture. The middlemen ran sheep; the day laborer became a shepherd. The Church got her rents. It was an extreme and strangling mortmain that continued and even grew right up to what we consider modern times. The social and economic force of the Church has never been progressive. Its temporal aim has been the preservation of its own power, and while it has succeeded, it must also take much of the blame for the poverty and degradation of Southern Italy.

From 1870 to the Lateran Treaty of 1929, the secular governments of United Italy slashed away at the octopus. First the Church lost her lands, then control of the schools, and finally in

1890 the tithe was abolished and Church charities were taken over by the State. The Church had been slow to learn and slower still to reform. Crispi, as late as 1890, was able to show that the Church was spending 90% of its revenue on Masses, candles and fireworks for gala occasions, and only 10% on actual assistance. Unlike the conquered in other situations, the Church has stayed to rebuild its power, this time not in real property but in services and favors to the needy. Its aims may not have changed, but its activities have. As the entrepreneur of the cradle-to-the-grave society it runs hospitals, nurseries, trade schools, old people's homes, orphanages, summer camps, counseling services, social clubs, young ladies' seminaries, and, perhaps most important of all, an efficient and victorious political party. The Italian government of today is obliging. It supports the Church's social work with its own welfare funds. The Church has come almost full cycle; the only visible bruise is the confiscation of her lands, but they are worthless now. *"La ricchezza d'Italia è nei suoi bambini"* — Italy's wealth is its children — and so it is on the children that the Church now concentrates. Parents are not insensitive to advantages. Children are enrolled in the society at birth. Membership can influence everything from care in an Infant Welfare Center to burial. Anyone who is not Catholic must be a Communist. Communists, as the enemy, are excluded from the network of benefits.

A many-talented staff is needed to run this black-garbed army. There is always room for a priest with initiative and ambition, particularly if he recognizes the importance of some embryonic activity and assumes its management before "outsiders" take over. So priests run agricultural cooperatives, loan businesses, football teams and raincoat factories.

One of the most fertile fields has been education. In Torregreca, for instance, until 1960 the government provided the first five grades of schooling. Anything beyond was a Church monopoly. Girls could stay at home, but it was important for boys to study. Few families could afford boarding schools; the alternative was the seminary, which prepared boys for the priesthood and was expensive besides. The director there was an old man, settled in his ways and in his work, which he considered well done as long as he followed the methods of his predecessor. However, his assistant, Don Arrigo, was an energetic young man who was too restless to enjoy a static administration. As a child he had been nicknamed "Piglet" because of his snout-like nose and his funny habit of rooting around in garbage just to make sure there was nothing worth saving. He applied the same thoroughness to his career, listening to gossip and keeping tabs on dozens of small enterprises. The first hint of a middle school for Torregreca took him to the provincial director of schools in Matera. He trusted he was not intruding, but since it seemed there was to be a middle school, he had come to offer his help . . . he had a certain experience in such things. He suggested temporary quarters, commented tactfully that there were several teachers it might be impolitic to overlook and left a list. He had only come to offer his time and experience to the provincial authorities. They should call on him if ever . . .

A middle school serving Torregreca and four other townships needed a director: Don Arrigo's appointment was entirely logical. Parents fought to keep their children from failing. The most illiterate peasants knew their sons had no future without a middle school certificate, and they were just as stubborn about their rights as the fathers of children with below average intelligence. Each was determined to keep his place; Don Arrigo had the final say. Three years later the Ministry accepted Don Arrigo's argument that a high school was needed to absorb the middle school graduates. Don Arrigo's appointment as director was again entirely logical. Torregreca's importance was growing and so was Don Arrigo's. He had eased quietly onto the

plateau of immunity that unwritten Southern law allows distinguished personages. Whatever he does will be sanctified by
official right and no matter how questionable his methods may
be, no one would dare investigate or even complain. Don Arrigo's empire will grow and with it the number of people who
must be in his good graces. To date he has added two summer
camps, a technical training school, a car, a driver and a secretary.

He is only one type. There are others with missions less
worldly than his, as for instance Don Pasquale, who was meticulous about his parish duties but used his free time in a one-
man crusade against Communism. He had had printed thousands of red, white and green leaflets, exhorting: CHRISTIANS
STAY WITH CHRIST! DOWN WITH COMMUNISM! and then had
them passed around by a squad of ragged little boys he had
trained in the art of crowd-slithering. He unleashed them at
political rallies which he watched at a discreet distance to
avoid any taint of political activity. His real masterpiece was a
leaflet in black, 36-point type on magenta paper:
HOW MUCH DO YOU KNOW ABOUT COMMUNIST ATROCITIES? Underneath was a list in smaller print: *The Substitution of Das
Kapital for the Bible; Insulting the Honored Memory of Alcide
de Gasperi; The Persecution of Priests in Mexico, Spain and
Russia.*

No one is apt to rouse the Torresi to much action, but with
the persistence of a Fuller Brush salesman Don Pasquale goes
from door to door, handing in his leaflet and trying to start a
discussion with the householder. He tramps the foulest alleys of
the Rabata and clambers up every ragged staircase. Often the
doors are slammed in his face because he has the aggressive
look of a priest collecting for a festa, but he never complains.
He just smiles and says, "As you wish, but I'll be back another
day." It would be hard to measure the effect of his crusade, but
he can be proud, at least, of being part of the local vernacular.

How often one hears, "Sure, they'll lower the taxes the day Don Pasquale runs out of leaflets."

Then there were those who devoted themselves to the elimination of "irregular relationships." The same sort of blind passion that drives American sociologists to insist no family can be truly happy without a bathtub, drove these priests to break up large nests of children because the mothers and fathers were "living in sin." Only once did I get involved in such a situation. The Mother Superior and a priest came to talk to me. They apologized for the disgusting story, begged my forbearance, hesitated, conferred with each other, and then blurted out that it was a matter of a man and a woman "living in sin." By then I expected something much more titillating. It was scandalous immorality and a bad example for the neighborhood. Until recently the priest's aim had been to separate the couple, but the death of the woman's husband had changed the entire picture. Now, he explained, the couple could marry if I obtained a copy of the husband's death certificate. He had died in Schenectady. I could hardly say no to such a harmless request. The priest gave me exact information which I sent off to the authorities. Their patience and courtesy were a reminder of just how helpful American bureaucrats can be, for the man had Americanized his name, changed his address as well as his profession and had died three years before the date I had given. The certificate arrived just the same, and I called on the priest to tell him that I would like to give it to the woman myself. He sent her along that afternoon. My Cleopatra turned out to be a toothless hag of seventy-two who was too frail to walk without the support of her lover's arm. He was a youthful eighty with rheumy eyes, white stubble and a speech impediment. For thirty years they had "lived in sin" and were not pleased at the idea of getting married. It was a question of dower right. There were infinitesimal slivers of land which her children and his children, two legally separate broods, would fight over if they married.

They had not come to accept the certificate, but to plead with me, even bribe me if necessary, to tear it up. A dozen eggs and an endless chain of homemade sausage had been brought along to ease my conscience. I must understand that this marriage would bring two families to disaster. If I insisted on the ceremony I might be responsible for murder. I tried to explain I was not personally involved, that I had simply written for the certificate, but they misunderstood. Thinking I wanted a higher price, they promised at least six eggs a week . . . forever. I had to be firm. I shoved the certificate in the lady's hand, kissed her on both cheeks, and forced the sausage and eggs on the lover as I shook his hand. Then I pushed them gently out the door. Three weeks later a note from the priest invited me to the wedding . . . "In recognition for all you did to retrieve this couple from sin, I feel the Church can make an exception and welcome a non-Christian." Such a gracious invitation, but I declined, promising myself that "irregular relationships" would remain irregular if the legalizing depended on me.

These priests were sincere in their desire to reform their own small world. I never doubted their motives, but like all reformers they deemed Right to be the imitation of their own prejudices, forgetting the standards of those they would reform. At the same time they seemed not to notice pagan usages or dismissed them as theatrical tools that brought the people closer to Christ's mysteries: the wheat sprouts put in Christ's coffin before the funeral procession of Holy Week; the offering to Ceres no one considers out of place in the ceremonies of the Resurrection. Henry Swinburne, who traveled throughout Southern Italy in 1777 comments that the traveler "will recognize the Praeficae of the ancients in the appearance and actions of old women that are hired in Calabria to howl at burials." *
The Synod of Potenza in 1606 had already outlawed such performances, paid or spontaneous, but howling and tearing of

---

* Henry Swinburne, Esq., *Travels in the Two Sicilies,* London, 1790.

hair are still signs of honoring the dead and a practical clergy
has not tried to stop it. In fact the clergy is entirely practical.
They tolerate the pagan for the same reason a mother pops a
rubber nipple without holes in her baby's mouth. They pacify
to clear the way for moral rigidity, no matter how unrealistic.

A peasant boy is not born a bigot; he becomes one in the
seminary where for ten years he must follow the rules and regulations of his ethos, as an army private follows the handbook
on how to make his bed and pin on his insignia. Evil is drilled
into him. Every human is a sinner damned to hell. He is
wicked, foul and can only hope to be less wicked and foul.
Every part of life is redimensioned in the light of evil. Relief is
found in forced morality, which might soften the displeasure of
this vindictive God of ours. Filled with zeal and pat formulas,
the young priest returns to the world and startles everyone by
initiating a campaign to eliminate promiscuity: little girls must
not come in contact with little boys. The priest has forgotten
the years when he slept with his two little sisters and thought
nothing of it except that they had cold feet. Forgotten, too, is
the comfort the smallest felt in the warmth of his parents' bed.
Suddenly boys and girls are sexually oriented monsters to be
kept apart. Knowledge of what they must later consider normal
must not be allowed to pollute them. Town life conspires
against the young priest. He cannot eliminate animals,
crowded houses or the easy, nonsexual give-and-take of growing up. He wears his moral corset proudly and would tighten
the laces for others, but they shrug him off and bolster his fear
that the human is born evil. No one worries much about him.
To peasants his obsession with evil is just part of his profession
as plowing is of theirs. Let him fight it as he likes. If ever he
can be useful, time enough to chant his chorus.

Still, priests fight on for the world shaped in their image of
Right, and the Torresi expected them to cast me as the incarna-
tion of the devil. I was a woman alone, therefore immoral. And

a Protestant. The Torresi prepared for the jousting with the bloodlust of passive spectators. When nothing happened, they thought to tease the champions into the open with a spate of Monday-morning rumors. "They've taken the nursery keys away from the Signora. They're sending her off!" "The carabinieri have orders to take her to Naples!" "Her car's been confiscated." Nothing brought us out on the battlefield. Perhaps the priests felt that with such a curious audience they must wait for offensive action from me. Whatever the reasoning, there was no truth to the rumors. I was treated with great courtesy, at first wary, eventually even friendly. Until the old Bishop died there was never a problem. His successor, a Calabrian of a more medieval turn of mind, was uneasy about a Protestant resident in Torregreca and asked the *Questura* to keep my permit hanging — so that it was not valid, but not rejected either — until he made up his mind. But it was too late. Everyone was used to me and His Excellency could find nothing to object to in my activities except that I did not have a crucifix hanging in each room of the nursery. My argument that the Madonna and Child seemed more appropriate for children was hard to refute. While he thought it over, I discussed my permit with Lieutenant Mazzone. One advantage of a small town anywhere is that nothing remains private for long. Everyone knew the Lieutenant had clashed with the Bishop and it took only a bit of imagination to see that a chance for gentle revenge would be welcome. Within twenty-four hours I had my permit; the Bishop decided on a friendly truce.

Priests always asked me for help: food or clothing or small funds for special projects. I cooperated if I could. If not, I told them the truth, and I believe they accepted my honesty as I accepted their sincerity. I am afraid we laughed at the Torresi rumors and stayed on the best of terms through it all. When I hired a nursery teacher who was the sister of a local priest, I became that strangest of things in a Catholic world — a tame

Protestant, a sort of non-Christian pet of the local priesthood. One gentle priest whom I never actually met even went so far as to write and send me a book about Teresa Neumann. When we met in the streets, he was always very deferential, but would say nothing more than "Good morning to you, Signora." Our discussions of Teresa Neumann were carried on by letter. He was merely being cautious in case the tide should turn and there were some question about his relationship with me.

As the Mother Superior had said, they were men as well as priests, and they were willing to tolerate what was useful. In this alone their attitude toward me was the same as their attitude toward the nuns. Nuns remain for priests one of the constant irritations of ecclesiastical life, the unnatural women who are forever cluttering up the schemes of men. The disenchantment is mutual. When they must work together, they use a resigned patience with each other not unlike the patience of an adult explaining the theory of relativity to a curious five-year-old.

Occasionally after a trying morning with Don Germano, the Mother Superior would complain, "Men and their master plans! Who do they expect to carry them out? Women . . . of course! We know each day is made up of a million details — so is each plan. Overlook one and the whole thing collapses. Just where would men be without women?" That timeless complaint of all women! Clear as her thoughts were, would she ever have said nuns are also women?

I often wondered about this, but never more than on the morning I watched twenty-five novices take their final vows. The Mother Superior, who wanted me to take pictures, had reserved a place for me in the first row. Every bench in the little Convent church was jammed with relatives who had come dressed in their best, tightest clothes, to take part in the girls' renunciation of the world, their death, their rebirth and finally their marriage to Christ. There was no reverent hush.

They had been in their places for hours murmuring tensely, excitedly, as people do when they know the drama of the spectacle will live up to expectations. The chatter rose as the sacristan came out to light the candles. He looked quite unlike himself in a borrowed surplice that trailed loops of coarse lace, but he intended to carry out his part of the ceremony with dignity. "*Zitti,*" he hissed at us and turned back to his candles with such a flourish that his pole slipped through one of the circles of lace. Complete silence. He had our attention. Each thrust of the pole threatened to pull the surplice over his ears, so he finished in awkward haste and disappeared again behind the altar. No one breathed.

In a few seconds the nuns who had come from all the houses of the order began filing in — two by two, two by two, two by two — a mighty flow of black that seemed to envelop us all in a mantle of serenity. Still they came, dignified and flushed with the expectation of shared joy. The novices who followed were a chilling contrast. Their drab black smocks and head scarves had been put aside. Now they wore instead bunchy white gowns, white caps and veils that left their faces uncovered and twitched stiffly about their shoulders. They were the Brides of Christ, but they seemed to be stumbling through a nightmare of fear. One stopped. I thought she was going to turn and run, but she went on toward the altar where the Bishop, his two acolytes, Don Matteo, and another young priest were waiting. The files of older nuns divided off into the pews on either side of the aisle and the novices went to stand before the railing. When the Bishop had been settled on his throne, the Mass began.

The familiar ritual chanted each morning of their lives still held the secret exaltation of reunion. Like all women in love, there was a surge of joy at the rediscovery of the lover, but instead of that private inner singing, two hundred nuns sighed in unashamed tenderness that excluded women less fortunate, made them ache with loss. The voices lofted out beyond this earth to their Lord; we the less fortunate were forgotten.

In trancelike detachment I watched the acolytes move the Bishop's throne from the side to a spot exactly at the middle of the altar. Then chaos sliced through the last wisps of my stupor. At the end of the Mass the relatives surged to the front of the church, pushing and elbowing each other, almost wrestling for better vantage points. The Bishop lifted his eyebrows and fixed them with a disapproving stare. They were quiet, but did not sit down. The nuns, kneeling and immobile, prayed. At a signal from the Bishop the Mother General of the order led the twenty-five novices to stand in two rows in front of him. These were no longer the red-faced peasant girls that I had watched loading hods of coal for the boiler or swill for the pigs. Their feet were still clumsy, their hands red from laundry and scrub water, but their faces were waxy and their bodies almost frail as they shuddered with sobs. In an effort at control, one of them drew in a loud, jerky breath, stopped, her head thrown back and then, beyond the reach of reason, let out a howl of animal terror. It was the stark shriek of the mad; to renounce life and plead for death is madness. The Mother General never twitched a muscle. She might have heard nothing. The Bishop started his exhortation in a voice so gentle it reached us as a rumble without words. One girl dropped to her knees and wailed; another bit her own arm until she yelped. The relatives groaned, then began to sway back and forth in a lullaby of pain. Again the howl lanced through to the rafters; the wails grew louder and still louder, invoking, responding, pleading, denying in a chorus of desperation. The dying and the living grieved together, for themselves, not for each other. The novices were no longer willing to give up life; the relatives had suddenly recognized their own fate in death. Mourning so clouded the air that the vows went unheard. The Bishop rose abruptly and turned to the altar. Limp as puppets the novices prostrated themselves and lay sobbing and hiccoughing while a heavy cloth of black with an enormous cross embroidered in white silk was thrown over them. The bell in the church tower tolled — one slow stroke — then another slow stroke. Across the valley, bells answered from the town, tolling, tolling and tolling again in measured convulsions of despair. Those twenty-five girls died in front of us. We felt their lives snatched from them as they clutched and clawed at the black cloth. Ashes to ashes, the Bishop intoned, and mothers shrieked in a final letting of agony. They raced toward the altar and when they found themselves blocked they turned mindlessly and rushed to the back tearing their hair in frenzy. And the bells tolled on, playing on the strings of human endurance until mind and body twanged with anguish. Then silence too abrupt to be real. The cloth had been lifted and one by one the girls were drawn to their feet by the Mother General and taken to kneel before the Bishop. This was their resurrection, the miraculous dowry of new life which Christ gives to those willing to sacrifice their lives for Him. Each girl, reborn a different person, repeated her vows and heard her new name for the first time. Only then did the Bishop raise his voice so that the nuns and relatives might also hear the long awaited announcement. Each name was greeted with a murmur of pleasure, to be followed almost immediately by a groan when the Mother General snipped off the symbolic lock of hair with shears the size of fire tongs. The Bishop's blessing brought peace again. He gave each girl a neatly folded pile of robes, veils and capes, raised her to her feet and turned her over to the Novice Mistress who took her behind the altar. There her head would be shaved and she would be dressed in her habit, her veil garlanded with orange blossoms and her cape of sheer white wool. When next we saw them they came as brides slowly down the aisle. There had, indeed, been a rebirth in the image of grace. Those raw-boned girls with faces still blotchy from crying were wrapped in a luminous ecstasy that made them oblivious to all save the passion of their celestial lover. In the isolation of their own transport they drifted down the aisle to stand once more before the Bishop.

It was over quickly. A prayer, the Bishop's blessing and the nuns, new and old, filed out to the cloister. During much of the ceremony I had been involved in a silent scrimmage over my seat. When the novices were covered with the black cloth I was knocked from my bench and might have been trampled in the rush to the altar rail had it not been for Don Matteo, who left the Bishop's side to pick me up. He hissed sharply at the four ladies, my neighbors, who had writhed and groaned and torn their hair until they dislodged me. Don Matteo had shamed them. They made room for me and patted my arm solicitously while they argued about which was the guilty party. They left me much more room than I needed, but continued to snarl across me through the rest of the ceremony. Don Matteo had kept an eye on them, and as the service ended he signaled I was to wait for him in the cloister.

"Come along with me," he said without greeting. "We're going to the reception." He broke in on my objection. "No, none of that. You have to go. They're very proud that you're here and you can help me as well. In fact I'll make a bargain with you. I promise you a glass of punch if you'll protect me from the parents who want favors. You know how it is! They give their daughters to the Church and then expect favors in exchange. Come along!" He was leading me through the cloister toward the orphanage dining room.

"Now you're exaggerating. They'll ask the Bishop," I said.

"Oh, no! We do a good job on them. They wouldn't go flat out to the Bishop. If you need saints to intercede with God, don't you think it's logical that priests intercede with Bishops? Eh, Signora," he sighed in mock despair. "At this rate we'll never make a good Catholic of you."

The reception was in full swing with the favors and almonds of a wedding and the confusion of a high school graduation. The brides, still in their long, flowing white capes, giggled and shrieked as they waited to present their relatives to the Bishop. The mothers, exhausted and suddenly too timid to speak, settled down on chairs along the wall and concentrated on their plates piled high with sweets and cookies. One or two looked around slyly and then stuffed an ample supply in their purses. Don Matteo whispered not to notice, that it was their fun at receptions and had been calculated for in the ordering. The fathers huddled together in the middle of the room like sheep. They had nothing to say to each other, but seemed unwilling to desert the refuge of the flock, so they stood staring into their punch cups. Silence was about to suffocate the party when the Mother Superior brought the first of the new nuns up to me.

"Signora, Sister Maria Pia would like to speak to you." The girl blushed and looked intently at the floor.

"Best wishes, Sister Maria Pia, for your new life. May it bring you the joy and peace of God's blessings." It sounded pompous, but she brightened and rushed into her little speech.

"It was an honor to have you here for my *professione* and I want you to have this, as a reminder of today . . . and . . . and Signora, promise you'll come to see me wherever they send me. Please. It would make such a difference if I thought someday you'd come." She had given me a small china dish filled with sugared almonds and wrapped in white tulle. A card attached to it said:

Bride of Christ

Mother, guide me, protect me so that one day I should present myself before your Jesus not with empty hands.

Sister Maria Pia
On the day of her perpetual vows.

Torregreca, 15 September 1960

After her rush of words she ran off, too embarrassed to wait for my answer. Immediately another nun popped up in her place. One after the other they came to make the same little speech, and thinking that I would always be a reminder of that day, I was touched by the repetition of, "It would make such a difference if I thought someday you'd come." It did not take many months for me to understand the practical and at the same time lonely workings of those minds. Letters arrived from un-known Mother Superiors saying Sister such and such had sug-gested I might be able to help them. Nuns who came to Torre-greca for retreats made formal appointments to see me and then presented notes from my young novices as recommenda-tions. In my travels I found them running cold, bare nurseries in mountaintop villages, nursing the paralyzed or struggling to keep thirty mentally defective children alive in the loft of an old people's home. They threw their arms around me and danced with joy and it was always for the same reason. It made no difference whether I could help them or not — I would lis-ten to their problems. The day they took their final vows they became nuns, but they also became women with the cares and worries and frustrations of women; that is what they wanted to talk about. *Their* Don Germanos; the town council that would not supply enough wood; the Sister Lucias who were nasty and behind their backs vindictive. Or a particular child — did I know of an institution that would take him? They wanted news of Torregreca, of their friends, and of the Bishop who was ill. They are no more or less devout than other nuns, but they are very much women too. They needed to talk and com-plain and dream to someone outside the narrow, almost morbid atmosphere of a convent. I think the effort to reestablish oneness with God and find release in Him was often more than their troubled minds could achieve, but many a woman in acute distress has looked at her lover and seen a stranger. I shall never know if they consider themselves women as well as nuns. I only know that I do.

X

THE PROJECT REALIZED

FINALLY one cold drizzly spring day officials came from Bari
for the assignment of the houses in the *villaggio* . . . not that
the houses were ready. Noble intentions had bogged down in a
slough of bureaucratic procedure. Sewers had been laid; in
fact, the pipes ran in uncovered ditches down the middle of the
road. The houses had been connected to the aqueduct line running from the nursery to San Fortunato, for whatever good a
daily three hours of running water might do, but there was no
electricity, and the stalemate between the *Comune* and the util-
ity nabobs was solidifying into a provincial War of the Roses.
Certainly before the three-month interregnum of summer holidays there would be no compromise and at best the work of
setting light poles and lines would not begin until fall. And in
the fall there were elections. The decision to hand over the keys
to the houses had undoubtedly come from a number of smoke-
filled rooms. Psychologically it was probably right; better to
have the houses occupied than delay further and give the Communists another tailor-made local issue. There were several
miscalculations involved.

First, Italian peasants in general are not really so interested
in water pouring out of taps as they are in light. They live in
terror of the dark, imagining all manner of catastrophes that
might be overwhelmed in a lighted room, but are certain hell
by candlelight. To ask them to live without a burning electric
bulb is tantamount to the revival of medieval torture. Second,
there is a cult in the South which even tourists notice in the
plaques, ashtrays and postcards for sale: the misfortunes fate

heaps on man are pitiable, but he who lets himself be duped, *preso per fesso,* is open to ridicule.

The politicians, in an effort to detract from their own fail-ures, announced that *only* the violent protests of the future ten-ants, who wanted to move in under any conditions, had influ-enced their decision to release the houses. Peasants are not naive about local politics. Elections were coming, protests nor-mally achieve nothing but an unpleasant interview with the police, and now this excuse was offered on a platter. Each man who was asked to accept political fictions in place of a *villaggio* finished on schedule felt he had been taken for a *fesso,* and he resented it.

Perhaps the least important of their miscalculations, but still puzzling to me, is that the men in those smoke-filled rooms did not understand the political shifting that would inevitably take place with this first step — a real house — toward prosperity. The pattern is always the same. No matter what the man's for-mer politics have been, he turns farther Left almost as though this first taste of the comforts enjoyed by others has made him doubly bitter, revengeful. Slowly, as he prospers, adds furni-ture, a pig, a plow or a donkey to his possessions, the idea of communal sharing becomes less appealing. He wants the right to keep what he owns, what he has paid for, and Communism loses a vote. Slowly he shifts toward the Center. Many of the tenants thought they had to vote for the Church party if they wanted to get their houses, but once they were inside them they would swing Left. So it would have seemed politically ex-pedient to assign the houses in perfect condition, without wor-rying about the impending campaign.

Whatever the reasons of miscalculations, on the appointed day we collected at the *villaggio*: three out-of-town officials, their driver, thirty-one men and one woman (the new tenants) — and myself. The thirty-one men and one woman stood to-gether well away from the rest of us, watching in silence as we set up a table by the steps of one of the houses and arranged rocks to hold down the piles of papers. There was no real reason for me to be there, but I had felt it would be a day of animosity and side-choosing. I did not want to be appointed by default to the wrong side. The three officials, all Northerners, had been surprised when I joined them.

"It's cold, you know. You don't have to come."

"Oh, that won't bother me. I have to check my lists again to make sure I have all the children . . . for the nursery, you know." That was a lie. I had verified each birth date at the registry office, but they nodded wisely at me. How did I like Torregreca? had led to How did they like Bari (which they did not), and eventually to the fact that their wives had refused to follow them South. The life was too hard, the climate bad, the schools below standard. Good jobs were hard to find, so these decent young men accepted the tedium of their work and exile, and dreamed of transfers back to the world. We had chatted over a cup of coffee about people and places, nothing very brilliant, but as we left the bar one of them said, "It's nice to talk to a woman again who isn't complaining." Sad comment, I thought, but I realized I had been in Torregreca too long: like the Torresi, I was suspicious of men who wore suits.

The men settled down at their table; I sat on the steps at one side and slightly in back of them with my notebook open. The driver, a short, oily ruffian with bloodshot eyes and a three-day beard, stationed himself in front of the table. He was going to be the announcer. "Ambrico, Giovanni," he called. A white-haired man with a young, ruddy face stepped forward and came slowly over to the table. He was asked for various papers, which he had. The driver translated everything he said: Ambrico's face was purple with rage. The general opinion that social workers are nosey may be right; I went over to the young official who had been friendliest and whispered that they would save a lot of ill feeling if they called off the announcer-interpreter whose Italian was no better than Ambrico's if as good. There was a three-way conference: the driver was motioned over, whispered at, then he shrugged and sulked away to the car. The men turned back to Ambrico. They gave him a pen to sign the contract and then a set of keys tagged #1. He was passed on to me. Ambrico lived near me, so I knew him . . . fairly well. More important, for he was still enraged, he knew me.

"Don't have to ask you about your children, do I?" I said and smiled tentatively. "When are you going to move?"

"Haven't got time 'til I get the vineyard hocd, but the way I feel now they can . . ." He stopped. "*Scusate*, you didn't have anything to do with the whole *imbroglio*. Did you want me for something? I gotta work." He meant it. He had a compulsion about work. As soon as he finished the job he had set himself, he tore into another. More often than not, it was well after dark when he came home, and in a town where unemployment was *frutto di stagione* (fruit of the season) he was never without work.

"Just one thing. Why didn't you read the contract before you signed it? I know you can read."

"Sure, so what. So if I read it and found something I didn't like . . . then what? If I want a new house, I gotta sign that contract. What I think doesn't make a shit's worth of difference to anybody. Now remember — you asked — I'm not mad at you." He turned on his heels and left without speaking to anyone.

"Auricchio," called one of the men. "Auricchio, Mario." Only then did I understand their plan of assigning the houses alphabetically, and since these were double houses, each isolated from its neighbors by a garden plot that had to be shared, peaceful coexistence could not be hoped for unless the families were on relatively good terms. A's are not necessarily friendly with A's or B's with B's. They were not necessarily enemies either, but in the case of the *villaggio* at Torregreca the alphabet was disastrous. The automatic neighbors loathed each other and always had. I asked my three official friends if there were no alternative to the strict alphabet; perhaps A's with Z's, B's with V's and so on — anything to soften the regimental coldness of the system. No, there was no way. The master plan had already been filed in Rome with the names assigned to houses alphabetically, as directed. I did understand. One must never ruffle Rome or confuse those newt-headed masters.

· The sky was black with clouds that might have belched out of a thousand factories. Great banks rolled one on top of the other to hang over us while on the ground an icy wind needled at my ears and played with my skirt. Far away across the valley thunder growled and then cleared its throat. The driver rushed over with a umbrella he wanted to hold over the men at the table. Once more he was in the circle of power, but the peasant men sneered at him. Slowly two of them left the group and came over to me with their umbrellas.

"*Permettete*?" asked one.

"Real *cafone*, that one," said the other, pointing at the driver. It was not raining, but that was hardly the point. If they wanted to protect me, my day's work was done; we had chosen sides. Through the rest of the formalities I had two umbrella bearers who never left me. One by one the men came to the table, produced their papers and signed the contract. Not one paused to read it. Then they checked in with me. One sullen, wooden-faced man in tattered clothes refused to go away until I explained exactly why I had something against *his* children. He had eight under sixteen, but none the right age for the nursery. We went around in circles.

"I can only take children between four and six; older than that they go to school. Yours do, don't they?"

"Yes, but I've got one not quite two, another not quite three and the third is almost four. Take him."

"I can't. In a way it's partly your fault, you know. If everyone

didn't have so many children, we could take three-year-olds
. . . as it is, there's barely room for the four-to-sixes. He'll
come next year."

"That's what I said. What you got against my kids? Every
other family has kids in the nursery, some two, but you won't
take mine. What's the matter? You don't like my politics?"

"I don't know anything about your politics . . . and I don't
want to either. It's simply a matter of age."

"If this nursery is supposed to be for the children in the *villaggio* I have a right to a place too, just like everyone else. No
matter what age my children are." He shook his fist at me. "I've
got my rights."

"Aw, for the love of Christ, shut up, Michele. Your turn'll
come," one of the umbrella men interrupted.

"Christ — Christ — " he spat out. "It's too late for Christ
here. You can't cheat me. I'll — "

"You'll what? I don't have anyone either. What about my
right to a place? Look at me, I'm too old. Am I supposed to
make her take my grandchildren? Shut up, Michele, you've got
your head on backwards." This time the interruption came
from a craggy old woman with a beaked nose and hair pulled
back in a bun. I did not know her, but judging from her clothes
she was of the old stamp, still loyal to the local costume, or as
loyal as the fripperies sold in the market would let her be. She
wore a full black shirt down to the tops of her muddy boots
and a white blouse covered by a large rust wool scarf folded
into a triangle and thrown over her shoulders so that it covered
her back down to the waist. The points of the long sides were
tucked into a brown velvet sausage roll that held her together
and served as a money belt and carryall. She turned to me.
"Men never know when to fight, do they? God made them all
fools." She poked Michele. "Come on now, get moving, you
. . ." They started off, but then she stopped and came back a
step or two toward me. "Who are you, anyway?"

I was so unprepared that I laughed and before I could tell her she went on, "Never mind . . . doesn't make any difference. I've got better things to do." And off she went — straight to the table. "Which one of you is the boss?" They looked at each other; no one wanted to claim the honor. "All right, I'll say it to all three of you." She let fly in Tarnese with the foulest epithets I ever heard. There was a lot of confusion and shouting until it was established that she was describing her own husband, not the officials. She had applied for the house and it had been given to her, but now they had called her husband to sign the contract. She would have them understand that they were separated, and she would neither live with the bastard nor let him have what was hers. The only other woman in the crowd, who had come because her husband was too drunk to walk, flew to the defense and the battle was on. It was never settled to anyone's satisfaction, but the old woman and her brawny husband have been so busy fighting each other they have no time for feuding with the neighbors. To this day the first one home locks himself in and ignores the arrival of the other, who rages on the outside. When the neighbors can stand it no longer they threaten to break the door down, which gets the fugitive inside, but does not call a halt to the fight.

Somehow we got through the rest of the list without complications except for one brief bout I had with a young man who carried a small boy wearing a dirty T-shirt and nothing else. He too wanted a place for his child; he had three under three, the eldest was the one he carried.

"Take him, he's bright, won't cause any trouble. He walks and feeds himself," He turned to the boy and joggled him up and down. "Don't you, Bruno? And he's dry . . . has been for more than a year." The father smiled at his son and joggled him some more. "Never cause you any trouble that way . . ." He stopped. Little Bruno was giggling to himself as he sprayed down father's shirtfront and trousers. That was the end of our discussion.

In the next few days children with stacks of pots taller than they were wandered along the road and eventually at dusk showed up at their new homes. Donkeys loaded with bedsteads, women carrying chests on their heads, men with pushcarts piled with oddments and grandmothers driving pigs and chickens all accomplished the moving. Everywhere I went I met tables marching along on their own. Under each was a woman bent over on herself so that the weight rested on her back and kept the center of gravity low enough to avoid sudden top-heavy lunges that would throw table and bearer to the ground. They talked of nothing but the high cost of candles and their fear of the dark, of the lack of garbage collection and mail delivery (people who never receive mail are always offended if there is no delivery). They were worried because there was no school nearby and no oven. The new houses were not a reason for joy, a victory, a step toward something better. They had whetted the appetite of their disgruntled tenants and became the symbols for them of yet another time that they had had to wrest their due from the authorities only to find their reward partial. I opened the nursery as quickly as I could.

Anyone who has children knows the clamor of the first days in a school or nursery. We had it all. The children who howled in terror, those who wanted to sit in a corner by themselves, others who found and clung to a doll in silence and the very few who stalked away from their mothers toward an enticing toy and never looked back. Many sat bewildered looking from the howlers to the players in an effort to decide which group they should join. We had them all; ragged and hungry and incredibly bright. If their manual skills and coordination were limited, so was their use of the spoken word. Speaking was saved for essentials — going to the toilet and food, at the sight of which they turned into vacuum cleaners. The afternoon nap on individual cots was never a struggle. They were sodden and sleepy with food, and the novelty of sleeping alone for the first time in their lives never wore off. They hit their beds like stones and had to be pried out two hours later. The teacher, a pretty Abruzzese girl, thought she would never understand what they said, but after the first week found she could untangle some of their tongue twisters and they, with the elastic ability of children, were rapidly learning Italian. The first strangeness was over for those *inside* the nursery, but not for those outside.

After the first day a rumor had flown through the town; the children were given *meat* for lunch. They had reported it . . . at length . . . when they went home, but no one could believe it. Each day at noon faces appeared at the windows to watch in wonder while the children, not in the least distracted, went about the serious business of filling their tummies with as much food as they could before it ran out. Chichella in her new role of institutional cook made sure there was more than enough. She was the confidante of all the children who cried, or fought, or felt shy, and she appointed herself my spokesman with the mothers as well. How often I caught her whispering out the kitchen window, "And if you don't clean him up, the Signora's going to send him home . . . and you know she'll do it too. That one does what she says."

She comforted the children and chided the mothers with equal ease; the nursery was hers because it was mine; and after eight years she still feels the same way. Every teacher and assistant who has worked there has had to subdue Chichella's sense of protective ownership. Few of them have ever had the last word. She has not been an easy person for them to deal with. Right is right and in her case right is "the way the Signora did it". . . even now.

I had called a meeting of the mothers before the nursery opened and had discussed what we hoped to give the children, and what the mothers would be expected to give the nursery.

For our part there would be hot milk in the morning, a full lunch — *pasta*, meat, cooked vegetable or salad and fresh fruit — and bread and milk before the children went home. Each morning they would change into play clothes and shoes supplied by us. They would be given vitamins and any special medicines the doctor suggested. They would *not* learn to read and write; they would not be divided by sex; they would *not* do anything in long snake lines; they would *not* be forced to sit all day repeating songs and poems; and they would *not* always look gloriously unruffled and clean. They were not little flowers. I promised food and rest, games that would increase their coordination and their ability to get along with children their own age. The families were not asked to pay anything; *however*, there were a few things I expected of them. The children did not have to come elegantly dressed, but I would not take them, nor would I allow a teacher to take them, if they were dirty. They would be sent home. Second, each child's play clothes, his bib, towel and his cot sheet would be sent home to be washed. Third, every Saturday afternoon two mothers would come and give the nursery a thorough cleaning. As they could figure out for themselves, each mother would have to come three times a year, which was not a large sacrifice. No one said a word; I was surprised. Luca, the Mayor, Don Matteo, the doctor, everyone had warned against my asking the mothers to clean. It made no difference what we normally did in other places — the mothers of Torregreca would rebel. They simply would not send their children. I argued that they would come, that they were too smart not to. They had nothing but time, and nowhere else in the town could they get such food for their children . . . and without paying. The children would come and the mothers would do the cleaning — and not because we wanted to save the money of another salary. If the mothers came three times a year, we had three chances to teach them proper cleaning, three chances to woo them from the habit of sloshing dirty water around. It sounds an old saw, but it really does take less time to clean the right way — particularly if every bucket of water has to be hauled from a fountain — and unless the houses, toilets, plates and everything else were cleaner, there was no way to fight worms, impetigo, fleas and lice. There were no objections from the mothers. They divided up into two-women teams and picked their turns. The first Saturday one did not show up. Monday morning her child was turned back from the nursery (I walked home with him and gave the mother hell). The child would not be taken back unless she came the following Saturday. She sent the child every morning; every morning we sent him home. Saturday she came to clean. The try-on had not worked. She washed and starched curtains, or scrubbed toys with strong soapsuds along with the rest, and the problem vanished. It pops up once each year and is dealt with in the same way.

Hundreds of stories could be told of those children, sweet, funny, pathetic ones. They are the stories of all children. The first birthday party when the little boy sat looking at his candles in blushing joy while all the others howled their birthdays to make sure they would not be forgotten. The tears of the first little boy who came dirty and was walked back home. The little girl who woke up screaming from a bad dream and clung to me, saying, "He hit her again. He hit her." I did not ask who or what, but held her and murmured to her until she fell asleep again. The bandage on a skinned knee that was the envy of the others. The girls who retied their bows in front of the mirror in the bathroom before going home and the boys who scowled at themselves as they raked their hair with watery combs and slicked down their sideburns the way their fathers did before going out. The drawings of trains they had never seen, but that they imagined to be a series of carts strung together and attached to a belching dragon-tractor. Boats were another fascinating mystery. Every animal with four legs and two ears was a donkey, a dog, a sheep or a goat and they visualized cities as bigger Torregrecas with animal garages. The boys loved to play house; the girls wanted clay and paint . . . so many, many things they did over the years. A different person might remember different incidents, but there is one I can never forget.

The *villaggio* grew faster than the nursery which today has three sections for ninety-six children. One year we had to choose thirty-two children from some sixty families. The teacher and I visited every family, explaining that we would take the children who, for whatever reasons, seemed to need the nursery most. By then we knew our customers well and there was little chance of fooling us, but no one tried. One child I felt we had to take was Giovanna, a tall scrawny girl of five with fine delicate features and eyes as blue as the Mediterranean. She was next youngest of four children of the *villaggio* whore. In a sense her mother was a professional. She had never been willing to take a job, though priests and nuns were forever finding them for her. "I don't need to work, he'll feed me." *He* was whoever was living with her at the moment and more often than not he did feed her, but he was not interested in the children of other men. They wandered through the streets, abandoned, meek, dirty little things whose only sin in life was stealing food. The first morning Giovanna came to the nursery she was mute, but her eyes sparkled with curiosity and joy. She wanted to do everything, see everything, touch everything. When anyone came near her, she cringed away and hid her head, but she peeked from under her arm with those twinkling eyes. Never a word. We let her alone, tried to include her as normally as possible. I went to talk to her mother about cleaning her up. Her hair was long and matted, her clothes stank, but it was the mother's fault, not Giovanna's. Before I got in the house she was screaming at me.

"You can't send her home . . . you got to keep her now. Isn't my fault she wets her bed. You took her, you keep her." She was a screamer who yowled until the other person gave up in despair and went away. It was a well-planned system, but I tricked her into listening by keeping my voice so low she became curious. She stopped. I had my say and left. Giovanna was cleaned up some days, filthy others, but she played now and even talked a bit. For two or three days at a stretch she would not wet her bed, then she would. No one scolded her. I had worked long and hard on the teachers to make them understand the emotional causes. They were patient and sweet with her, but Giovanna developed a passion for me. If I came into the nursery a hand would sneak into mine and those eyes seemed to beg me to understand. I let her trail around with me. I talked to her, teased her, occasionally got a word out of her, but most of the time her conversation was tongue-clickings and jerks of the head. "No!" that meant. A month went by. She was cleaner, but her hair was a gummy, lice-ridden tangle. I knew that if I sent her home because she was dirty, her mother would turn her out in the road and forget about her. The others could be shamed, but not Giovanna's mother. She had threatened me with an axe when I told her either to cut and wash Giovanna's hair or I would. We had come to a draw, but not a permanent one.

One morning I took Giovanna in the kitchen with me and sat down to talk to her. She leaned against my knees peering into my eyes with such intensity I was afraid she did not understand what I was saying. Chichella came over to squat beside her.

"Did you hear what the Signora said? She's going to make you beautiful. Want to be beautiful, Giovà? Answer, or she'll go away. Who knows? Maybe you don't want to be beautiful . . ."

She nodded so violently her eyes bobbled and then threw her arms around Chichella's neck. They whispered happily; then Chichella stood up.

"Come on, then, if you're going to be beautiful like the Signora, we've got to get started." She winked at me and we three went off to the bathroom for our sesssion with DDT, scissors and soap. Giovanna radiated joy like the heat from an electric fire. She did not complain about the DDT that stung her scalp and got in her eyes. Combing the snarls was fun. Chichella and I made questioning faces behind her back. Something was very wrong . . . and then maybe we both realized at the same time . . . that little girl had never had so much attention, so much love spent on her in her life. We could have cut off her legs as long as we did something for and to her. When it was over and she was deloused, cut, washed, combed and more or less dry she said her first word.

"When do we wash it again?"

"But, *cara mia*, it's up to you to keep it clean now. You come show me a week from now if you've kept it this clean." She was smiling at herself in the mirror.

"I will, I will," and she threw her arms around my neck.

I have found her washing her hair at the fountain with yellow laundry soap and I have admired the scalloped cuts she gives herself; her hair has never been dirty or lousy again. It was a sapphire-eyed peacock who went back into the room with the other children that day; she knew she was special and especially loved, and I think that sense of being loved has stayed with her. She can see Chichella or me miles away. She waves and calls and runs to us with all the silent joy of that dirty little five-year-old.

The end of the story is that love is not enough. Her older brother raped her. The nuns at San Fortunato took her in, have kept her and have been as kind as they know how to be, but they chill my blood when they speak of her in her presence as

"Our little Giovanna who was molested by her brother." She is twelve now, bright in school, beautiful with a strong, solemn beauty, and a few months ago I heard that an older couple wanted to take her into their home, which meant she would be their servant, but safe and perhaps loved. When the nuns told me about it, she was with me holding my hand timidly as she did so many years ago. This might be her chance, I thought, but just last week I heard she had been sent back to the Convent because she still wets her bed and the older couple lost patience with her. I know no answer except love and expert care, but Torregreca can offer neither to Giovanna, I am afraid.

People have asked me what one nursery, or for that matter ten such, accomplished. Little, perhaps. Better-adjusted, more curious children who were ready for school — that hardly seems enough. Health, yes. But less concrete things happened. The mothers reported that now no one in the family could go to the table without washing his hands. Tyranny of the five-year-old. *He* had to do it, so did everyone else. That helps with worms and so many other germy parasites. Clean clothes and occasional baths are habit-forming; fleas and lice do not like them. If nothing else, wood and potatoes cannot be stored in a tub that is used for baths. Curtains and everything else that is admired or found useful are copied. I know that the hundreds of teachers who have spent time in our nurseries — for courses or even short visits — have changed their ideas of what a nursery can and should be. They have seen that any local market can supply a wealth of inexpensive equipment, but that change in their nurseries depends entirely on their willingness to work . . . and they have worked and changed. Those thousands of children and their mothers have lost some of their traditional diffidence. A few have accepted that they can hope for fair treatment. The children are not content only to learn by rote; they want to know why. Is that enough? I cannot judge, but if even the most tentative first wiggle toward true change has been made, we have accomplished much. I and the first nursery mothers still remember best our most galling failure. That it is *our* defeat and not just mine seems much to me.

More houses, built by various government agencies, were finished in the *villaggio*. The nursery was being enlarged, but careful building is slow and the climate our constant enemy. My days were like court sessions. I had to settle the arguments of those alphabetical neighbors who, when they had no real quarrel, goaded each other for spite. I could not show my face at the nursery or the *villaggio* without being surrounded by a horde of screaming people who were not mad at me, but at each other. No peace can come from that kind of chaos, so I told them all if they had problems to invite me to their houses. I would listen, I could promise nothing more. At first they thought they would all crowd in one room and go on yelling, but I pushed them out. One house, one family, one discussion. It took time, but they felt they got a fair hearing and that was important, no matter what the outcome. In one case one of the two tenants had thrown a barbed-wire barricade across the sidewalk that went around the double house. The complaint was not against the blockade, but against the barbed wire. The small children of the family at one end had hurt themselves on it. The children were ruining the garden planted by the other neighbor. While both families watched me, afraid to do anything, I dismantled the barbed wire and told them to get to work building a bamboo lattice that could divide the gardens and could have either a gate or an extension across the sidewalk. They did it, sharing the costs and the work, but never speaking. One man's goat dined on another man's garden; a little boy stoned a neighbor boy. A woman emptied laundry water on a little girl's head . . . it was endless. I became a Lady Solomon. They accepted my arbitration because I seemed so sure of my solutions and impartial in my listening. They never knew I had favorites — and who would not — nor

how I trembled waiting for my judgment to be found impracti-
cal. They plagued me to arrange for camps for their children,
hospital care, pension payments, institutional places, in short,
for anything that might be going for nothing. Too often, particularly in Italy, social workers concentrate on filling out forms,
but I refused to do it. I do not believe people will ever be self-
reliant if everything is done for them. In the *villaggio* there was
a surplus of free time; the problem was what to do with it. I
told people where they should go for the right forms, how to
apply for whatever they wanted, what the waiting period
would probably be and what their chances were, but I would
not do it for them.

It was a bad period for everyone. There was no work, the
land produced less each year; the average income was under
$400 a year. Then suddenly a new world opened up! Milan,
Turin, Switzerland and Germany. There was work there for
unskilled laborers, even contracts which guaranteed a legal
wage and health insurance payments. At first a few went, then
more, always the best, leaving the timid behind to scratch in the
dirt. They came back in six months, discouraged by the climate
and the food, but with money in their pockets. The feckless sold
their handkerchiefs of land and stood in the Piazza waiting to
be called up by the employment office which was responsible
for filling the contract quotas. We did not lose many in the
villaggio then, only one or two, because they were men without
experience and too discouraged to have a sense of adventure.
One, who was a shepherd and at least sixty, was persistent in
his desire to go. Every aspect of his life seemed to have polar-
ized around me, so he courted me for a job in Germany. There
was no reasoning with him. He used all his wiles on me. He
played the bagpipes, a goatskin arrangement which strangely
enough is as native to the mountains of Italy as it is to Scotland.
Each morning before Christmas he came to play traditional,
half-Eastern wailing melodies, kneeling in front of the chil-

dren's crèche. The whine and wheeze singsong shrilled on and
on in Western snake-charming music. The charmer and the
charmed fell into a trance, but the charmer would play on until
I appeared. The mornings that I was out of town were disastrous. He would only stop playing if he had a chance to put his
case to me. Saturday afternoons he came with his pipes and a
puppet he had whittled and dressed as an armored warrior. It
ran free on a long string one end of which he attached to a
chair, the other to his knee. He played his pipes and jiggled his
knee making the warrior dance up and down the string, back
and forth, in intricate steps. At Lent, he made us the traditional
cupa-cupa from an aluminum kettle with a cloth drawn taut
across the top and a hollow reed inserted through and fixed on
the inside of the "membrane." By rubbing his wet hand up and
down on the reed he made the noisy accompaniment of a
whole group of peasant songs. The sound was about as musical
as a constipated bear, but it carried, attracting passersby who
came in to join the informal community sing. On good days
Chichella would even dance the tarantella which, along with
some lusty verses to the traditional songs, was her speciality.
All this attention from the shepherd was an effort to convince
me that I should help him. He could not believe I had no German connections; he could do anything, he did not have to be a
shepherd, just give him a chance. Time did what words could
not. He gave up and stopped coming to play for us. His wife,
much younger than he, thin and dirty and demented, came
after me with a butcher knife, screaming, "You could have, if
you'd wanted to. You could have!" When I had taken the knife
away from her and soothed her, she sat staring despondently at
the floor. Now that some kind of reason had taken hold of her
thoughts, she was terrified I would not keep her little boy at the
nursery. Of course we did.

More and more I was staying away from the nursery. I had
to travel a lot and felt it was time the teacher took over the

daily problems, although I knew that for some reason she had been unable to create any standing for herself with the mothers. They were courteous, but they seldom actually did what she suggested and it must have galled her to hear them answer, "I'll wait until the Signora comes back." When I was in Torregreca I never missed the afternoon closing of the nursery and the chance to talk to the mothers, the chance to find out what was going on without prying. That is what led to our defeat.

The weeks and months had made clear what was lacking at the *villaggio:* an oven. The women walked a mile and a half to the first oven in town and a mile and a half back, carrying a board on their heads that was three feet long and loaded with five large round loaves of bread. Each weighed up to five kilos (eleven pounds). Homemade bread was cheaper, heavier and more filling. They could not afford to buy it, but they hardly had the strength to carry it so far. Their slow, smooth stride that keeps the board balanced is one of the skills they learn as children. The hips pivot, the shoulders are immobile and the knees slightly bent. It looks so easy, but it is not. There is some curving of the spine, maybe an extra set of muscle-springs that we do not have. A young Lucanian woman, straight and lithe before she has children and the abdominal prolapse that automatically follows, can be a beautiful, dignified sight gliding along with her head held high, her load balanced. My women were young, but misshapen and burdened with children who had to go with them wherever they went. The larger the family, the more bread was needed. They sagged at the thought.

"Can't you do something about an oven?" they asked.

"What?"

First they wanted to build individual ovens next to their stalls at the foot of each garden. The housing agency, for reasons unknown even to me, refused permission and threatened to tear down any illegal structures.

"We could build one ourselves . . . for the *villaggio.*"

It started just that simply. The women, with two exceptions — the Communist agitator and the old girl who was separated from her husband — were for it. The communal surveyor, doubling as town architect, drew up plans for the most basic but adequate oven and then calculated the materials we would need beyond the expensive, specially processed stone that served as the oven floor. The Mayor saw to it that a piece of land in the center of the *villaggio* was deeded to me. London headquarters was delighted to supply $500 for building supplies. Now it was up to the men. Their wives had been talking to them. As nearly as we could figure, we would need a paid stonemason and two days' work from every man in the development. The women organized the first meeting at the nursery. I had hoped they would also run it. There was one woman, a giant with black hair and blue eyes whose sense of humor, organization and bullying were such that she could maneuver the women into doing whatever she wanted. She was not afraid of work herself. She had twin girls in the nursery, our curse and our joy, and did double work for them. Her energy supplied the kind of momentum that would convince any woman. Her face got red, her eyes snapped and she let out a great bellow of arguments to refute objections. I had pictured her as spokesman for the women, but I had not known she would be mute in front of the men. The meeting fell to me.

I presented the idea, the blueprint and specifications, the man-hours we thought we would need, and then asked for comments. I peered into the gloom where people were dark brooding shadows. Silence. The men had come in their work clothes, their caps in their hands, some with hoes. There was a gritty shifting of feet, a baby cried, and the women wiggled in their chairs, but no one said anything.

"I guess that's the answer," I said, after what seemed an hour. "I know what the women think. They first mentioned it to me. They have talked to you about it, I know that too, but if there's no more interest than this, let's drop it. It's for you, not for me."

"After we do the work, the oven's yours," said a man's voice I could not identify. "The land's yours, isn't it?"

"No, the land is deeded to me as administrator for my organization, just as the nursery land is. The oven will belong to you all — in a cooperative — once we build it. I have the money for the materials . . . it's a gift . . . but the rest is up to you and the running of the oven will be up to you, too. Is there a baker here? You'll have to work out schedules, and sign up to bake your bread on certain days so she'll be guaranteed a living and everyone will have a turn. There are all these things to consider. I am not going to run it. You would have to plan to . . ."

The Communist agitator, which is a fancy name for an Indian-faced young peasant woman, broke in with, "Well, I can leave. I don't need the oven, so I don't have to work." She stood up. That started it. Some did not have teeth, so they did not eat bread . . . much. Others did not think it would be worth it unless there was a better baker. The *Comune* has to *give* it to us, shouted another. We could get hurt working, then who'd help us? and so on into the cold foggy night. Most of the time I could quiet the others enough to let one man speak. After each, controversy broke out which I interrupted with the answer to the last speaker's objections. Some of the comments were valid, some the evasive excuses of men who still thought modern conveniences should be supplied to them simply because they wanted them. There comes a point in any meeting when nothing is being accomplished and nothing will be. That is the moment to adjourn and I did, but that meeting was followed by half a dozen other mass discussions, and with endless talks with four or five men at a time. Separately, they could agree; together, friends and enemies, they could not.

Discussion and decision and rediscussion are part of that much-vaunted concept — the democratic process. It can be a squirrel cage or a slow unraveling of confusion that eventually leads to the entrance of the maze — but I found out its limitations early. There had been a work camp in Torregreca and the young leader had asked me to sit in on their meetings. He was a bright young man, well liked by everyone and a devotee of democratic procedure. Everything that had the slightest connection with the camp had to be discussed and then a vote taken to establish the group opinion. I found it tedious, particularly when they were cogitating problems totally outside their sphere of influence such as whether the Aqueduct Authority was falling down on the job, and whether it was outdated for women to dance with women and men with men as some still did in peasant families in Torregreca. When, however, we had to vote for or against the purchase of toilet paper for the camp, I felt it had gone too far and said so.

"What alternative would you suggest?" he asked.

"The question is, do *you* have an alternative to toilet paper?" We knew that newspaper would not go down the pipes, so that was excluded. Without thinking he said, "Certainly, lots," and then blushed.

We all laughed and I told them the story of a friend of mine in the Abruzzi mountains, a social worker who had been sent to a wild mountain village to hold a parents' meeting. The director of the provincial summer camp system had said that he could not take any more children from that village unless they promised not to clog the toilets with stones. They had caused irreparable damage the summer before, using them, apparently, as toilet paper. My friend went up, called the meeting and did her best to explain the situation. The faces were blank. She had not gotten through. Finally she said straight out, "You'll have to train your children not to use stones when they go to the toilet. It's not sanitary and it ruins the plumbing." Again there was silence, but a tense, resentful silence. A man stood up and said, "Signorina, you'll understand I speak with all respect . . ."

(Pause while he blushed.) "But you must know that we are civilized people . . . *we* use our shirttails, not stones."

After that, when we approached the Utopian extremes of democratic procedure, the camp leader would laugh and announce that we were civilized people and could skip over that question. In the same way, there were certain questions about the oven that were beyond discussion with the men . . . whether or not that followed the laws of democratic procedure. The makeup of the stone floor for the oven, the number of tufa blocks needed to build the proposed building, the slant of the roof . . . all the technical questions they wanted to use as red herrings and which they knew nothing about, I cut short before they became issues. At one meeting there were visiting professional American community-development workers — and they were scandalized that I should do so. I still feel that lengthy and heated debate for its own sake is not a useful exercise in democratic procedure, particularly with peasants who are hungry and only interested in discussion if it deals with some improvement in their lives. It made no difference basically because for every side issue I chopped off, two grew in its place. And another set of elections was approaching, and the unbuilt oven might come to figure in them as a campaign device to win votes. The whole question might be taken out of the hands of the people to whom it mattered most.

I promised the mothers one final meeting. The Indian-faced Communist, who always purred gently to me, had spread the rumor that if the oven were not built I was morally obligated to divide the money for it evenly between the families of the *villaggio*. There was another who said that if they refused to give two days' work apiece the *Comune had* to build the oven. One man warned me he was going to propose that the $500 be used for a *villaggio* postman's salary. Surely we needed garbage collection more than mail delivery! With all these rumors flying around, the meeting promised to be interesting. It was set for the night before I had to leave on a trip, and I had arranged with the Mayor, the town surveyor and Luca that they would attend. The Mayor would state publicly that the *Comune* did not have funds or plans for an oven; the surveyor was to answer technical questions, if any; and Luca would be there for general support — his straightness was legendary.

That night it started to rain. The wind swooped around the nursery; then the lights went out. Candles flickered and guttered in the draft and still no one came. The first footsteps brought the one man who had volunteered to take on the organizing of the cooperative. He was a small neat man who hired out as a vineyard keeper. His quiet voice and manner and his thoughtfulness made the others listen to him. But they could listen without accepting his opinions. I did not know how strong a leader he might be, although he had called different groups to his house for meetings and had resolved the problems they presented. I was touched to see he had changed to a white shirt and was newly shaven.

"The others may be late . . . they're . . . getting ready." Shaving too, I thought. They came in couples, the men with coats over their heads, the women in dripping shawls. Soon the room was steamy and smelled of manure. They were all there except the Mayor, the surveyor and Luca . . . and that, in case anyone should ever ask, is what usually happens. Public challenge is frightening and public commitment is worse. The three never came. Fortunately I had suspected they might not be coming, and so I did not wait too long before starting the meeting. I said only two things: that I was under no obligation to divide the money among the families and that I would not; and that the *Comune* did not have funds to build an oven, so the problem was squarely up to them. Two hours later all semblance of discussion was over. It was a bitter fight between two-thirds who were ready to sign up and the one-third who thought they could bully someone into giving them the oven. I made my last plea.

"Either we must start building or give up the idea entirely. Now let's look at the question again. You need an oven. This is the only concrete possibility there is at the moment and all it will cost you is two days' work, maybe three if we have bad luck. Is it worth that much to you, or not? It's that simple. When you're through it'll be yours . . . to enjoy and to run . . . but it has to be built first. Either we decide to do it to-night, or we decide *not* to do it tonight. This is the last time I will ever mention the idea to any of you. I don't want to hear any more about your regrets, or your second thoughts or your objections. Do you or don't you want an oven?"

It was all or none, and in the end it was none. It had stopped raining while we argued, so that adjourning the meeting and closing the nursery was not, after all, the end of the discussion. They milled around outside, shouting at each other and then at me. I edged away from them, determined to keep my word. The matter was closed. The last I saw of them that night my tall, black-haired friend and her supporters had taken out after the Communist Indian. They caught her and beat her until she no longer cared if she were alive. It may have been a pointless revenge, but it kept her out of sight for several weeks.

I was a defeated, bitter, hungry woman when I reached town and met Luca, who was shamefaced. He took me to Pa-lazzo Montefalcone and fed me cheese and wine in the kitchen. He was gentle and kind and amusing, but even he knew it was useless. I was numb with the kind of hurt that he understood: his life had been full of futile hopes and ovens that never came to be. As I walked home, Torregreca floated on a cloud of mist and seemed more than ever something from a vicious fairy tale.

When I came back from my trip ten days later, my sense of

proportion had overcome disappointment, and had forced me to accept that century-old habits of mind cannot be changed in one year or in two. Chichella was lurking around waiting to help me unpack, but also waiting for a chance to tell me what had happened at the *villaggio* after I left. I was curt, and she switched ground: "You'd better go to the Piazza tonight. You'll hear something interesting." I waited for more, but Chichella would not commit herself further; and I went, too curious to miss the occasion.

The Piazza was unfamiliar with its campaign posters and red, white and green bunting. The balcony above a barber shop had a ten-foot red backdrop with a sickle and the letters P.C.I. (*Partito Comunista Italiano*). Across the way, above a bar, another balcony was draped in banners with white shields and huge red crosses. The party of Christ. Two sets of loudspeakers were blaring different popular songs which were interrupted periodically by eager young men who thumped and crackled testing the microphones. More people than usual, many more women, milled idly around the Piazza. The entire *villaggio* was there.

Lieutenant Mazzone bowed and then came over to me. "Welcome back! Come to see the fun, have you?"

"Not exactly. What's going to happen? I was told I would find it 'interesting.'"

"Very wise . . . no comment," he answered obliquely. "You've understood a lot . . ."

Don Matteo interrupted him. "Just in time, I see. I thought you'd come back for the show. Now that you're here, I want to lodge a protest." The Lieutenant tactfully moved off a few feet. "Why would you have a Protestant minister come to make political speeches at the *villaggio,* when you know the Bishop has forbidden the clergy to make any public comment about the elections this year? What happened to your own sense of Protestant justice and fair play?" Don Matteo was not gentle

and amused this time. He was truly angry. And I was truly
bewildered. I denied having any knowledge of any Protestant
minister in Torregreca. Don Matteo hesitated. He did not think
I was a liar, but . . . Lieutenant Mazzone leaned over. "You
haven't heard the latest. We broke up his meeting last night.
He was busy denouncing the Signora as un-Christian . . . so
that clears up one issue. He's a little twerp they brought in
from Naples. Oh, he's a 'pastor' all right, but you can be sure
she doesn't have anything to do with him. She wouldn't." He
smiled at me.

Frankly I did not understand what was going on, so I said
nothing. Don Matteo and Lieutenant Mazzone were silent. We
stood huddled together, bowing like mechanical dolls to the
surprising number of people who made a point of bowing to us.
More cracklings from a microphone, spotlights were turned on
the Communist banner and a record of the *"Internazionale"*
vied with the Italian National Anthem. One of the local Communist candidates introduced the speaker whose name I did
not get. He was not Torrese. The crowd collected under the
barber's balcony. Bad microphones can make anyone a dema-
gogue. This one ranted until it seemed he would blow out the
wires; at the end of each phrase his voice rose, the next began at
the higher peg and so on producing a one-man show of public
hysteria. Then suddenly his voice dropped and he started
again. This time I listened.

"And now we have the final show of immorality in this
Church government, these Christian fakers, these thieves who
would hide behind the skirts of priests. They have been so
duped that they have allowed a Protestant . . . a foreigner
. . . to rob the people of this town of money that was theirs
by right. Remember this, good people of Torregreca, this
woman has been repudiated by her own church. She is an ad-
venturess, who has fooled the *fessi* of the *Democrazia Cristiana*
and disappeared with *your* money . . . You needn't worry.

She'll never be seen again . . . but she can serve as a lesson to us all." Pause, while he leered around meaningfully. "She and your dear Mayor have both disappeared . . . with your money . . . does that mean nothing to you? Now, after all these years of patience, of tolerance, of hoping, won't you take action against such thieves?"

One by one the crowd, starting with those at the back, had turned toward me. I smiled. They smiled, cocked eyebrows at me and then turned back, only to turn again to check that I had not disappeared. The lieutenant stood very straight on one side of me; Don Matteo seemed to be watching the clouds on the other.

The Mayor came to stand in front of me, completing the farce. "I speak next," he murmured, "but I beg your forgiveness for such idiocy. They don't know what they're doing."

"Oh, come now, politically it's very good for you . . . since we're both obviously here. Where did you go that made everyone so suspicious?"

"On my wedding trip," he said, and then even *he* laughed.

How the Communist's speech ended I never quite knew. He must have sensed something was wrong. His crowd was too restless and was not following his harangue, but my attention was absorbed by the notables of Torregreca who came to pay me their compliments and offer their apologies. Opinions change in a year and a half, I thought, but they can change again tomorrow. The lights flashed onto the white shield and red cross, and the Mayor came out to announce he had had a delightful wedding trip. The crowd laughed. For twenty minutes he extolled my virtues, my goodness, kindness, benevolence, understanding, intelligence, concern and faith until I remarked to Don Matteo that soon I would think I was dead.

"Some day, when she has left us . . . and you will wait too long, I know you . . . you will mourn her, saying 'Once there was a woman . . .'"

Even after a handy Demo-Christian victory, the Prefecture in Matera panicked at the possibility of trouble in the *villaggio*. Whatever the Torresi might have learned about cooperative effort was voided by the construction of the oven at government expense. The work was improperly done. The oven has been rebuilt three times, the last time properly. A gaggle of lawsuits is still being settled. To the women it is still "our defeat"; to the townspeople, "The Signora's Oven."

EPILOGUE

THE mists and clouds of morning still burn off to be replaced by the mists and clouds of evening, and there underneath is Torregreca but little changed in the years that have passed. I now read in the authoritative newspapers of the world that Southern Italy has been transformed. There is heavy industry, methane gas, work for all. Strange that when I am there I feel none of this Utopian well-being. We have water three hours a day now, peasant boys must go through middle school where they wrestle with French . . . not that they have learned Italian or a trade. There is a high school. Something called meat is for sale at prices higher than those of Rome or New York. The tower is lighted every night at vast expense 'to attract tourists.' Chichella has 'new' second-hand furniture that is very shiny and rather fragile, but at least made of real wood this time. She cooks for the nursery, cleans for the utilities office, washes for a neighbor . . . and is old at forty. Her brothers and all their friends have come back from Turin and Germany. They came six months ago. There is no more work there; there is none in Torregreca, but I learn from *The Economist* that the Southern Italian is better off than ever before. No one seems to have noticed the world has marched off and left them again. Recession has trimmed plans for Southern Industry. Some genius has proposed a huge vocational school . . . a proposal our organization made twelve years ago and would have backed with money, but we were informed 'the moment is not ripe.' It may never be.

Luca tells me that these years of emigration and work have

been years of '*disgregazione di una società*,' the breaking up of a society, which had to happen so that the society could re-form in a modern structure. It has broken up and lost its cohesion. Now this new society must re-form . . . on what basis . . . hunger. That is not new in Southern Italy.

I had a plan once, idealistic perhaps, but I noticed recently that one of the world's largest oil companies had proposed the same experiment in another town . . . with no more success than I had. Italian law provides for *every* conceivable human need — true cradle-to-the-grave care. Agencies proliferate, and their directors while away the years fighting over jurisdiction and prerogatives. If all these services could be coordinated, made to function, change would be immediate and of such force it could not be stopped. Luca and I once figured out that, to do it, fifteen Torresi incumbents would have to be removed from their appointments: an obstetrician, ten years over retirement age, who had no permit or training for surgical operations (he was in fact a male midwife); the superintendent of schools, overage, who saw the schools as a placement center for incompetent relatives; the public health officer, incompetent, overage and unwilling to do his work; the clerk of the Communal Assistance Committee who could not keep the office open because he was always busy singing in the Cathedral; the distinguished old gentleman who represented the infant welfare bureau at official functions — and did not know there was anything else to the job. And so on.

Luca looked at the list and shook his head. "No, Ann, you can't do that. You could remove these men easily enough, but it would upset too much . . . too many people. No, no, it's not time yet." And Luca honestly believed that the *disgregazione* of the peasant society was necessary, but apparently not that of the middle class.

It is a number of years now that I have not lived in Torregreca, though until recently I ran the nursery and spent ten days a month there. I built other nurseries, worked in other places, but always a part of me remains in Torregreca. I know now it always will. Every woman has one love affair that remains unfinished . . . it is over, a closed book . . . but still unfinished in that the mind plays with what might have been if passion and enchantment had been tempered by loving reason. I shall never be free of Torregreca; I have no desire to be. I go there now as to a retreat from frenetic cities and people without direction. I relax in the challenge of staying alive, for in the Torregrecas survival *is* life, all of it. Nothing from the world reaches the Torresi; the Torresi offer nothing to the world. In their vacuum they must feed on themselves. Luca still murmurs, "*Sotto, sotto si muovono le acque*" — way down deep the waters are stirring — with that faith that has been his life's torture. Yes, maybe the waters are stirring, uncounted fathoms down.

When I go back I realize how many years have passed: I am becoming a myth. There are still the long nights when my eyes stream and my throat closes from the smoke of the brazier at my feet and people tell me of their secrets and their longings. Now they also tell me of things I said or did . . . things which only *I* know I never said, I never did. I can imagine them with the wind rattling the windows and driving the smoke back down the stovepipe saying "Once there was a woman . . ." But they have forgotten that woman, or they never knew her. The strands of mist finger the mortar of those houses, caress it, feed on it, weakening the structure as surely as hope that comes to nothing weakens the human will. But I, like the old Bishop, have been fortunate in my loves — my Lucanians, my Torregreca — and am content that Chichella is the keeper of the myth.

FOR THE BEST IN PAPERBACKS, LOOK FOR THE

In every corner of the world, on every subject under the sun, Penguin represents quality and variety—the very best in publishing today.

For complete information about books available from Penguin—including Pelicans, Puffins, Peregrines, and Penguin Classics—and how to order them, write to us at the appropriate address below. Please note that for copyright reasons the selection of books varies from country to country.

In the United Kingdom: For a complete list of books available from Penguin in the U.K., please write to *Dept E.P., Penguin Books Ltd, Harmondsworth, Middlesex, UB7 0DA.*

In the United States: For a complete list of books available from Penguin in the U.S., please write to *Dept BA, Penguin*, Box 120, Bergenfield, New Jersey 07621-0120.

In Canada: For a complete list of books available from Penguin in Canada, please write to *Penguin Books Ltd, 2801 John Street, Markham, Ontario L3R 1B4.*

In Australia: For a complete list of books available from Penguin in Australia, please write to the *Marketing Department, Penguin Books Ltd, P.O. Box 257, Ringwood, Victoria 3134.*

In New Zealand: For a complete list of books available from Penguin in New Zealand, please write to the *Marketing Department, Penguin Books (NZ) Ltd, Private Bag, Takapuna, Auckland 9.*

In India: For a complete list of books available from Penguin, please write to *Penguin Overseas Ltd, 706 Eros Apartments, 56 Nehru Place, New Delhi, 110019.*

In Holland: For a complete list of books available from Penguin in Holland, please write to *Penguin Books Nederland B.V., Postbus 195, NL-1380AD Weesp, Netherlands.*

In Germany: For a complete list of books available from Penguin, please write to *Penguin Books Ltd, Friedrichstrasse 10-12, D-6000 Frankfurt Main I, Federal Republic of Germany.*

In Spain: For a complete list of books available from Penguin in Spain, please write to *Longman, Penguin España, Calle San Nicolas 15, E-28013 Madrid, Spain.*

In Japan: For a complete list of books available from Penguin in Japan, please write to *Longman Penguin Japan Co Ltd, Yamaguchi Building, 2-12-9 Kanda Jimbocho, Chiyoda-Ku, Tokyo 101, Japan.*